T0214760

Lecture Notes
in Business Information Processing   **393**

Series Editors

Wil van der Aalst ⓘ
   RWTH Aachen University, Aachen, Germany
John Mylopoulos ⓘ
   University of Trento, Trento, Italy
Michael Rosemann ⓘ
   Queensland University of Technology, Brisbane, QLD, Australia
Michael J. Shaw
   University of Illinois, Urbana-Champaign, IL, USA
Clemens Szyperski
   Microsoft Research, Redmond, WA, USA

Aleksandre Asatiani · José María García ·
Nina Helander · Andrés Jiménez-Ramírez ·
Agnes Koschmider · Jan Mendling ·
Giovanni Meroni · Hajo A. Reijers (Eds.)

Business Process Management

Blockchain and Robotic Process Automation Forum

BPM 2020 Blockchain and RPA Forum
Seville, Spain, September 13–18, 2020
Proceedings

 Springer

Editors
Aleksandre Asatiani ⓘ
University of Gothenburg
Gothenburg, Sweden

Nina Helander ⓘ
Tampere University
Tampere, Finland

Agnes Koschmider ⓘ
Kiel University
Kiel, Germany

Giovanni Meroni ⓘ
Politecnico di Milano
Milan, Italy

José María García ⓘ
Universidad de Sevilla
Sevilla, Spain

Andrés Jiménez-Ramírez ⓘ
Universidad de Sevilla
Sevilla, Spain

Jan Mendling ⓘ
WU Vienna
Vienna, Austria

Hajo A. Reijers ⓘ
Utrecht University
Utrecht, The Netherlands

ISSN 1865-1348   ISSN 1865-1356 (electronic)
Lecture Notes in Business Information Processing
ISBN 978-3-030-58778-9   ISBN 978-3-030-58779-6 (eBook)
https://doi.org/10.1007/978-3-030-58779-6

This Springer imprint is published by the registered company Springer Nature Switzerland AG
The registered company address is: Gewerbestrasse 11, 6330 Cham, Switzerland

Preface

This volume contains the proceedings of the Blockchain Forum and the Robotic Process Automation (RPA) Forum, which took place during the week of September 13–18, 2020. Both of the forums were organized as part of the 18th International Conference on Business Process Management (BPM 2020). Due to the COVID-19 pandemic, the main conference itself and most of its associated events were held virtually. The authors of the blockchain papers that appear in these proceedings presented their work to a virtual audience and engaged in online discussions with peers, practitioners, students, and others. The RPA Forum was organized in a hybrid form: Presenters had the opportunity to join online or *in situ*, in Seville, Spain. As part of the RPA Forum, additional industrial demonstrations and a panel were organized. Moe Wynn of Queensland University of Technology, Australia, gave the keynote talk at the RPA Forum.

The Blockchain Forum and the RPA Forum have in common that they are centered around an emerging and exciting technology. Blockchain is a sophisticated distributed ledger technology, while RPA software allows for mimicking human, repetitive actions. Each of these have the potential to fundamentally change how business processes are being orchestrated and executed in practice. The BPM community has embraced these technologies as objects of analysis, design, development, and evaluation. The forums were also created to allow for a discussion with researchers from other fields who share their interest in these technologies, whether this is from an economic, sociological, business, mathematical, or other viewpoint. The Blockchain Forum took place for the second time, after its first successful appearance at BPM 2019 in Vienna. The RPA Forum made its debut this year at BPM 2020.

In the spring of 2020, when the deadlines for paper submissions to the forums expired, it was not clear how – if at all – these events would take place. At that time, parts of the world were already suffering from the spread of COVID-19. Despite the uncertainty, both events received a fair amount of submissions by author teams from a wide range of institutes and countries. The Blockchain Forum received 10 papers of which the top 5 were accepted as full papers; the RPA Forum even received 18 submissions, which led to the acceptance of the top 9 as full papers. Given the 50% acceptance for each of the events, this rate applies to these proceedings as a whole. In addition, one submission to the RPA Forum was accepted as a short paper because of its promising nature and timely contribution. For both forums, each submission was reviewed by at least three members of the respective Program Committees.

We hope that the reader of these proceedings will enjoy the versatility of the included papers, as well as the creativity that the authors put into their work. Many of the papers present fresh perspectives, which we expect to shape how the involved technologies will evolve over time and how they will be applied in practice. We would like to thank the authors for submitting and presenting their work. We are also grateful to our colleagues who served as reviewers in the screening process and provided the

authors with meaningful and constructive feedback. We want to explicitly acknowledge the effort of Appian and MCCM Innovations for their contribution to the RPA
Forum: they provided an industrial perspective on RPA by demonstrating how the
technology is applied in practice. Finally, we are indebted to all the people from the
BPM 2020 team, who supported us and created the setting for both events. Without
their help, these forums would not have taken place.

July 2020

Aleksandre Asatiani
José María García
Nina Helander
Andrés Jiménez-Ramírez
Agnes Koschmider
Jan Mendling
Giovanni Meroni
Hajo A. Reijers

Organization

The 18th International Conference on Business Process Management (BPM 2020) was organized by the Research Group of Applied Software Engineering (ISA Group) at the University of Seville, Spain, with the collaboration of SCORE Lab and the Instituto de Investigación en Ingeniería Informática (I3US). It took place online due to the restrictions imposed because of the COVID-19 pandemic. Originally, it was going to take place in Seville, Spain. The Blockchain Forum and the Robotic Process Automation (RPA) Forum were co-located with the main conference, which took place during September 13–18, 2020.

Executive Chair

BPM General Chairs

Manuel Resinas	University of Seville, Spain
Antonio Ruiz-Cortés	University of Seville, Spain

Blockchain Forum

Program Committee Chairs

José María García	University of Seville, Spain
Agnes Koschmider	Kiel University, Germany
Jan Mendling	Vienna University of Economics and Business, Austria
Giovanni Meroni	Polytechnic University of Milan, Italy

Program Committee

Marco Comuzzi	Ulsan National Institute of Science and Technology, South Korea
Florian Daniel	Polytechnic University of Milan, Italy
Claudio Di Ciccio	Sapienza University of Rome, Italy
Alevtina Dubovitskaya	Lucerne University of Applied Sciences and Arts, Switzerland
Luciano García-Bañuelos	Tecnológico de Monterrey, Mexico
Inma Hernández	University of Seville, Spain
Marko Hölbl	University of Maribor, Slovenia
Sabrina Kirrane	Vienna University of Economics and Business, Austria
Julius Köpke	Alpen-Adria-Universität Klagenfurt, Austria
Qinghua Lu	CSIRO, Australia
Raimundas Matulevicius	University of Tartu, Estonia
Alexander Norta	Tallinn University of Technology, Estonia
Sooyong Park	Sogang University, South Korea
Juan Pavón	Universidad Complutense de Madrid, Spain

Stefanie Rinderle-Ma	University of Vienna, Austria
Matti Rossi	Aalto University, Finland
Stefan Schulte	Vienna University of Technology, Austria
Volker Skwarek	Hamburg University of Applied Sciences, Germany
Mark Staples	CSIRO, Australia
Ali Sunyaev	University of Cologne, Germany
Horst Treiblmaier	MODUL University Vienna, Austria
Shermin Voshmgir	Vienna University of Economics and Business, Austria
Ingo Weber	TU Berlin, Germany
Kaiwen Zhang	École de technologie supérieure de Montréal, Canada

RPA Forum

Program Committee Chairs

Aleksandre Asatiani	University of Gothenburg, Sweden
Nina Helander	Tampere University, Finland
Andrés Jiménez-Ramírez	University of Seville, Spain
Hajo A. Reijers	Utrecht University, The Netherlands

Program Committee

Sorin Anagnoste	Bucharest University of Economic Studies, Romania
Hyerim Bae	Pusan National University, South Korea
Christian Czarnecki	Hamm-Lippstadt University of Applied Sciences, Germany
F. José Domínguez Mayo	University of Seville, Spain
Amador Durán Toro	University of Seville, Spain
María J. Escalona Cuaresma	University of Seville, Spain
Michael Fellmann	University of Rostock, Germany
Peter Fettke	German Research Center for Artificial Intelligence (DFKI) and Saarland University, Germany
José González Enríquez	University of Seville, Spain
Florian Imgrund	Digital&, Germany
Hannu Jaakkola	Tampere University, Finland
Christian Janiesch	Technical University of Dresden, Germany
Jari Jussila	Häme University of Applied Sciences, Finland
Mathias Kirchmer	BPM-D, USA
Agnes Koschmider	Kiel University, Germany
Tommi Mikkonen	University of Helsinki, Finland
Esko Penttinen	Aalto University, Finland
Artem Polyvyanyy	The University of Melbourne, Australia
Milla Ratia	Tampere University, Finland
Manfred Reichert	Ulm University, Germany
Minseok Song	Pohang University of Science and Technology, South Korea
Rehan Syed	Queensland University of Technology, Australia

Carmelo del Valle Sevillano   University of Seville, Spain
Inge van de Weerd   Utrecht University, The Netherlands
Judith Wewerka   BMW, Germany

Contents

Blockchain Forum

Silver Bullet for All Trust Issues? Blockchain-Based Trust Patterns for Collaborative Business Processes

Marcel Müller[1]([✉]), Nadine Ostern[2], and Michael Rosemann[3]

[1] Technische Universität Berlin, Berlin, Germany
marcel.mueller@tu-berlin.de
[2] Frankfurt School of Finance and Management, Frankfurt, Germany
n.ostern@fs.de
[3] Centre for Future Enterprise, Queensland University of Technology, Brisbane, Australia
m.rosemann@qut.edu.au

Abstract. In recent years, the advancing digitization and internationalization of business processes led to increasing inter-organizational collaboration. In such collaborative processes, different organizations work together towards a single objective. Usually, subprocesses carried out by one collaborator are beyond the domain of influence of all other collaborators. This leads to uncertainty regarding the execution of the collaborative business process. If collaborators still want to engage in the process, trust is needed. Several studies identified blockchain and distributed ledger technologies as a promising tool to enhance trust in business processes. Therefore, this paper proposes and analyzes a taxonomy of blockchain-based trust design patterns from a process-centric perspective. Process engineers can utilize the taxonomy as an overview of how the blockchain technology can enhance trust in collaborative processes.

Keywords: Business process management · Blockchain · Trust

1 Introduction

In recent years, the progressing digitization and internationalization in a variety of domains, such as e-commerce [1] or supply chain management [2], caused an increasing shift towards more collaboration in business processes. A characteristic of collaborative business processes is that they consist of different subprocesses executed by various organizations. By their nature, subprocesses carried out by one organization are usually beyond the domain of influence of all other collaborators. But in the context of a process, the outcome of subprocesses might be of importance to other collaborators. Hence, from the viewpoint of all other collaborators and process stakeholders, this creates uncertainty in the process. Where uncertainty is present, there is a need for trust. Thus, collaborative business processes are, by their nature, trust-intensive.

© Springer Nature Switzerland AG 2020
A. Asatiani et al. (Eds.): BPM Blockchain and RPA Forum 2020, LNBIP 393, pp. 3–18, 2020.
https://doi.org/10.1007/978-3-030-58779-6_1

Blockchain and Distributed Ledger Technologies have been identified as a tool to foster trust in collaborative business processes [3,4]. But in detail, there are different interpretations of how a blockchain can improve trust-intensive business processes. In financial services, blockchain is often described as a "trustless" system [5], referring to the fact that no trusted third party or intermediary is required to exchange financial assets. In the industry and IoT context, blockchain is described as a substitute for trusted intermediaries, establishing trust rather than being described as trustless [6]. The phrasing of blockchain as a tool to build or increase trust in collaborative business processes [7] has also seen extensive usage across existing literature.

It is essential to understand how the blockchain technology relates to trust, to analyze how it can improve trust-intensive collaborative business processes. However, there is a gap in the existing literature on these concepts. A conceptual view of how blockchain can be used to mitigate uncertainty (unexpected behavior of process elements) is essential. Further, blockchain's impact on reducing the vulnerability (process variations) of a larger fragment of collaborative business processes needs to be analyzed. Finally, it is necessary to study how the blockchain technology can increase confidence (perceived trustworthiness) in a process. With such a fine-granular understanding, the blockchain technology's trust-enhancing capabilities can be precisely described and classified. Process engineers need to understand how the blockchain technology can solve the trust issues relevant to the process and further explore the impact of blockchain technology on more application domains.

This paper aims to close this gap by describing blockchain-based trust patterns concerning and trust-enhancing capabilities. Hence, this paper answers the research question *"how can blockchain technology be utilized to mitigate trust concerns in collaborative business processes?"* First, we establish on a conceptual level what trust concerns can be addressed with the blockchain technology in a business process. Then we discuss how the blockchain technology can reduce uncertainties, reduce vulnerabilities, and build confidence in a process. We synthesize these concepts into a taxonomy, which classifies the trust-enhancing capabilities of different usage patterns of the technology. In contrast to the existing corpus of blockchain-based system design patterns, this paper takes a viewpoint centered on trust-aware business process management [8] and establishes a collection of blockchain-based trust patterns. These provide process engineers with a tool kit to mitigate trust concerns in a process.

The remainder of this paper is organized as follows. Section 2 gives an overview of the concepts relating to trust, the blockchain technology in collaborative business processes, and current blockchain design patterns. Based on that, we introduce a taxonomy to classify trust-enhancing capabilities in Sect. 3. Subsequently, we discuss particular blockchain-based trust patterns in Sect. 4 and analyze them using the established taxonomy. Section 5 discusses the key points of the pattern collection and to what extent the blockchain technology can be seen as a silver bullet to trust issues. Finally, Sect. 6 concludes this paper with an outlook on the impact and future work.

2 Background

Trust is an abstract concept that has been studied extensively across different research fields, such as social sciences, economics, or psychology. In this paper, we define trust as the comfort with the uncertainty of a relevant action conducted by a third party following the definition by Gambetta [9]. Hence, trust only becomes relevant in a relationship when there is *uncertainty* present.

In the context of collaborative business processes Rosemann [8] established a schema to describe uncertainties, vulnerabilities, and confidence in business processes. An extension of the concept can be seen in Fig. 1. An *uncertainty root* causes a concrete *uncertainty*. The uncertainty itself is always described *with respect to a trust concern* and is relevant in a *process component*. For instance, in a process with an activity where an employee of an organization packs objects into a parcel, the following uncertainties can be of relevance: The employee (uncertainty root) causes uncertainty regarding integrity (trust concern) of the activity execution (process component). Here, integrity of an activity describes its correct execution. Uncertainties can lead to process *vulnerabilities*. Vulnerabilities describe the impacts, e.g., costs, when a part of the process or the process as a whole does not perform as desired. To make a process more trustworthy it is possible to reduce *uncertainties, reduce vulnerabilities* or *build confidence*. The reduction of uncertainty aims to reduce the probability or even prevent *that* something undesired happens (proactive). Reducing vulnerabilities, on the other hand, aims to mitigate the impacts *when* something undesired happens in the process (reactive). Implementing compensation workflows in case of a failure in the process is one example of reducing vulnerability. Besides reducing uncertainty and vulnerability, it is also possible to externally *build confidence* in the process to enhance its trustworthiness. Building confidence aims to increase the *perception* of trustworthiness without modifying the process itself. One example of this is a reputation system.

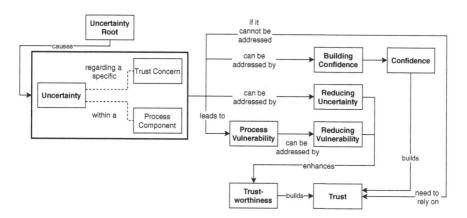

Fig. 1. Relationship of uncertainty, vulnerability and trust in the context of business processes. Extended version based on [8].

Blockchain and distributed ledger technologies have been identified as an approach to increase trust in collaborative business processes [3]. Technically, a blockchain is a tamper-resistant append-only storage of transactions. Blockchain's early inception in the finance domain [10] used transactions mostly for the secure transfer of cryptocurrency. In later generations of blockchains, transactions are utilized to trigger the execution of decentralized programs that inflict state changes of arbitrary information. These programs are called smart contracts. With the distributed ledger of transactions and the smart contracts, every participant in the blockchain network can replay the executed programming logic and validate the state. Several publications have dealt with the identification of blockchain patterns from a perspective of software and systems engineering [11–13]. For example, [11] describes the *Off-Chain Data Storage* design pattern as a way to "ensure the integrity of arbitrarily large datasets which may not fit directly on the blockchain". The focus of the presented description is purely on the technical side of the pattern. The contextualization of the technical pattern with the business process and its trust issues is missing. This paper establishes a methodology to describe blockchain design patterns based on their trust-enhancing capabilities and, hence, closes this gap in current research. For instance, this paper describes the off-chain data storage patterns as a trust pattern to address the *integrity* trust concern of a *data object* associated with a process *activity*. It indicates a purely descriptive way centered on trust in the context of a process model and is independent of the underlying technology.

3   A Taxonomy for Trust Patterns

To describe the trust-enhancing capabilities of a particular technology or technique in a structured way, we propose a taxonomy. The concept has been established following the methodology as described by Nickerson et al. [14] and is specifically tied to the domain of trust-aware business processes and references the business process model of a particular process. The taxonomy consists of five dimensions.

Dimension 1: Trust-Enhancing Method. Reducing uncertainties, reducing process vulnerabilities, or building confidence are three fundamentally different approaches to increase the trustworthiness of a process [8].

Dimension 2: Uncertainty Root. This dimension describes where the fundamental uncertainty originates from, which a trust pattern aims to mitigate. This might be data, an organization in charge of a part of a process, a specific resource of the organization, or an activity itself. It can also be a combination of these sources.

Dimension 3: Trust Concern. Uncertainties are always defined regarding a specific trust concern. For trust concerns, we use integrity, confidentiality, availability, non-repudiation, and performance [15,16]. These trust concerns originate from the security domain and from quality management and have been referenced in other publications [15] as suitable in the domain of trust-aware business processes.

Dimension 4: Process Component. This dimension describes in which elements of the process the trust concern is of relevance. Uncertainty mitigating trust patterns are centered around atomic process elements, while trust patterns reducing vulnerability and building confidence are mostly centered around subprocesses or the process as a whole.

Dimension 5: Limitations. Finally, this dimension describes the limits and tradeoffs of the trust pattern. The most common limitations which blockchain-based trust patterns face are privacy or the trust in interfaces to other systems.

4   Blockchain-Based Trust Patterns

Based on the introduced taxonomy, we discuss blockchain-based trust patterns. Therefore, a literature review [17] of blockchain-based design patterns and blockchain applications has been conducted. Based on a corpus of ca. 40 papers published between 2017 and 2020, available in the Digital Libraries of IEEE, ACM, and Springer, we synthesized common engineering patterns from a trust-centric business process point of view.

To illustrate when which pattern can be utilized, we use a reference business process from the supply chain management domain as a running example. This field has been subject to many uses of the blockchain technology in the past years (e.g., see [18]). The business process model uses the BPMN 2.0 syntax and can be seen in Fig. 2. In the process, a sender wants to send a parcel with dangerous goods, such as firework rockets, to a receiver. Therefore, the sender packs the objects into a parcel and defines service level agreements (SLAs). These agreements state how the parcel needs to be handled by the carrier. For fireworks, the SLAs define that the parcel needs to be kept within an anti-static environment to prevent sparks that can cause explosions. The sender hands over the parcel to the carrier together with the SLAs as instructions. The carrier delivers the parcel to the receiver. If an incident occurs, like the firework parcel exploding, the carrier needs to file a report and stop the process. Otherwise, the carrier hands the parcel over to the receiver, which evaluates the parcel conditions. If the parcel's SLA conditions are not adhered to, for example, if the parcel caught fire, the receiver rejects the parcel and stops the process. Otherwise, the receiver accepts the parcel, notifies the carrier who then creates an invoice. The invoice is sent to the sender, who has to pay it. This marks the end of the process.

The most discriminative dimension of the taxonomy is Dimension 1, which describes if the pattern aims to reduce uncertainty, reduce vulnerability, or build confidence. In this paper, we are mainly focusing on reducing uncertainties and building confidence. Blockchains can be used to directly lower uncertainties in

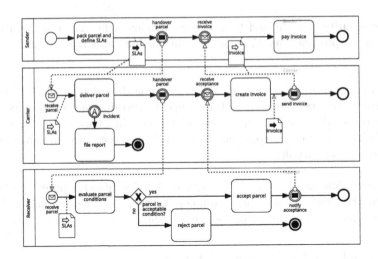

Fig. 2. A business process model illustrating the delivery of dangerous goods

specific business process components. Moreover, reducing uncertainties aims to lower the probability *that* something undesired happens within a process component (proactive). Concerning the running example in Fig. 2, an instance of reducing uncertainty would focus on a specific process element. For the activity "create invoice", reducing uncertainty would aim to lower the probability that something goes wrong during the activity. For example, the calculation of price and taxes can be carried out in a smart contract. This paper discusses four blockchain-based trust patterns to reduce uncertainty in a process.

Reducing process vulnerability, on the other hand, aims to mitigate the impact *when* something undesired happens in the process (reactive). It mostly deals with adding fallbacks or adding compensation activities to the process in case a part of it fails. Therefore, the blockchain technology does not directly help to reduce process vulnerability. Turing-complete smart contracts can be used to implement any programming logic, so they can also implement fallback or compensation workflows in a process. But the vulnerability is not addressed directly. It is addressed by providing certain workflows, and the blockchain as a tool is used to reduce uncertainty in these workflows. In the running example, process vulnerability can be reduced by adding a compensation subprocess after the last handover to reimburse the receiver when an SLA violation occurred. The blockchain technology can implement the compensation workflow and reduce uncertainty in that process. But for the overall process, the blockchain technology contributes indirectly to the mitigation of the vulnerability. This paper does not discuss such cases in detail and focuses on direct approaches. Hence, reducing vulnerability is mentioned here for consistency to the standard process of building trust-aware processes as introduced by Rosemann [8].

While a blockchain can mitigate process uncertainty and indirectly lower process vulnerability directly, it can also enhance the *perceived* confidence in a process. Building confidence aims to increase the *expectations* that the process works like intended by introducing additional *external* sources of trust. The blockchain technology can be used as one technology to build such sources in a trustworthy way. Therefore, we discuss two blockchain-based trust patterns that aim to build confidence. An overview of all patterns concerning the taxonomy can be seen in Table 1.

Table 1. Comparison of blockchain-based trust patterns

Pattern name (section)	Trust-enhancing method	Uncertainty root	Trust concern	Process component	Limitations
Hash storage (Sect. 4.1)	Reduce uncertainty	Data	Integrity	Data object	Data processing outside scope
Transparent event log (Sect. 4.2)	Reduce uncertainty	Organization	Non-repudiation	Event	Initial event submission must be ensured
Blockchain BP engine (Sect. 4.3)	Reduce uncertainty	Resource, activity, organization	Integrity	Gateway, sequence flow, message flow	Time-based logic
Smart contract activities (Sect. 4.4)	Reduce uncertainty	Activity	Integrity, availability	Activity	Oracle, privacy
Blockchain-based reputation system (Sect. 4.5)	Build confidence	Organization	Integrity	Any	Reputation system attacks
Decentralization (Sect. 4.6)	Build confidence	Organization	Integrity	Any	Incentives

4.1 Blockchain as a Tamper-Proof Hashed Data Storage

Method	Uncertainty root	Trust concern	Process component
Reduce uncertainty	Data	Integrity	Data objects

In collaborative processes where different organizations use shared data, the integrity of this common piece of data is a crucial trust concern. When data can be altered and manipulated, this might lead to anomalies and malicious behavior. For collaborators, it is hard to verify the integrity of the data and trace its provenance. Data integrity is an uncertainty where collaborators have to rely on the organization providing data. The blockchain technology can mitigate this uncertainty by storing data hashes to ensure data integrity. From a trust-aware BPM view, the uncertainty concerning the integrity trust concern originates in the data. In a process model, this can be related to data objects connected to activities or control flow.

In the tamper-proof hashed data storage pattern, the collaborator who acts as the data origin hashes the file. The hash is submitted through a transaction to the blockchain. A message with the hash is sent to data consumers. At any point in time, data consumers can verify the file's integrity by comparing the hash of the received file with the hash on the blockchain. If the hashes do not match up, data has been changed. Based on this principle, many different applications have utilized the blockchain as a tamper-proof hashed data storage, for instance, to track data provenance in cloud computing [19] or IoT-based collaborations [20]. The verification of data integrity needs to be executed within the activity that consumes the data. Therefore, all interfaces to the blockchain need to be available to the activity.

With the hashed data storage pattern, the organization that is consuming the data within an activity can verify data integrity. However, how the organization processes the data within the activity cannot be influenced by this pattern.

In the running example, as shown in Fig. 2, the sender creates SLAs as a guideline for the carrier and as a condition to adhere to get paid. For the carrier, these SLAs must not change during delivery. Otherwise, the sender could change to SLAs while the carrier is already delivering the parcel to circumvent paying for the service, even though the carrier adhered to all initial SLAs. This can be mitigated by forcing the sender to hash the SLA document, writing the hash on the blockchain, and distributing the hash to the carrier. The carrier can then refer to the on-chain hash in case the sender wants to manipulate the SLAs.

4.2   Blockchain as a Transparent Process Event Log

Method	Uncertainty root	Trust concern	Process component
Reduce uncertainty	Organization	Non-repudiation	Events

Non-repudiation of event occurrences is a trust concern in collaborative business processes. During the inter-organizational collaboration, incidents like failures during an activity execution might imply following different workflows. One instance of this is the error event. Therefore, it is essential that organizations cannot deny the occurrence of an event afterward to avoid compensation claims from other stakeholders. In terms of trust-aware business processes, the organization causes a trust concern regarding the non-repudiation of event occurrences. The blockchain technology can be used to ensure non-repudiation.

Using the blockchain as a decentralized event log means to save the occurrence of events and data related to them immutably on a shared distributed ledger, as described in [21]. Technically, this can be implemented similar to the blockchain hashed data storage trust pattern. The data related to the event occurrence gets hashed and submitted with a transaction to the ledger. The raw text is distributed to other relevant stakeholders (off-chain). They can ensure the integrity of the event by comparing the on-chain hash with the hash of the data received off-chain. Hashing the data provides data privacy to a certain extent. One example of the decentralized event log trust pattern has been implemented in the logistics domain [18]. The blockchain technology is used for logging violations of SLAs as monitored by IoT devices during the delivery of high-value parcels (escalation events).

The limitations of this pattern are similar to the hashed data store at the organization responsible for the emission of the event. If the organization wants to decide to keep the occurrence of an event concealed and not write it to the blockchain, the trust pattern remains ineffective.

In the running example, as described in Fig. 2, the carrier is obligated to file an incident if the firework parcel exploded during the delivery. In that case, the carrier does not receive any money because the SLA was violated. Hence, the carrier has an incentive to disclaim the event occurrence later to get compensated nonetheless. If the carrier is obligated to log the incident on the blockchain and to log also the condition of the parcel before the handover, the carrier can later not deny the event occurrence. Hence, non-repudiation is achieved.

4.3   Blockchain-Based Business Process Engine

Method	Uncertainty root	Trust concern	Process component
Reduce uncertainty	Resource, activity, organization	Integrity	Gateways, sequence flows, message flows

For the successful execution of an instance of a business process, it is inevitable to ensure the correct control flow between subprocesses and activities of different organizations and within the same organization. To ensure the execution of a business process according to its defining model, business process engines [22] are commonly utilized. Traditionally, such engines are centrally managed. This implies that all other collaborators have to trust that the business process engine managed by one collaborator acts as intended. From a trust-aware BPM view, this means that there is uncertainty regarding the correctness (integrity) of the process flow present. To address these uncertainties, a blockchain-based business processes engine can be utilized.

Blockchain-based business processes engines, as proposed by López-Pintado et al. [23], store business process models in smart contracts on a blockchain. All collaborators have access to the smart contract and can, at any point, verify the model's correctness. A process execution engine is a smart contract itself deployed to the same blockchain. It creates a new instance of the business processes as a new smart contract. The process flow is encoded in the business logic of the contract. Further, the execution engine can also execute automated script tasks or trigger invoking external service calls whenever a service task is needed to be executed off-chain. Automated script task execution is further described in the smart contract activities trust pattern. Further, this pattern can also be seen as a way of software integration between different organizations within the context of one collaborative process [24].

Blockchain-based business process engines cannot execute time-based sequence flows well. Form a design perspective, smart contracts are meant to be triggered through transactions and not have a self-containing time observation functionality.

The process model from the running example in Fig. 2 can be deployed to a blockchain, and a blockchain-based business process engine can create new instances of the delivery process. There are interfaces to the subsystems needed to execute the process activities that cannot be executed on-chain. One example, therefore, is the deliver parcel activity. This is a manual task and hence cannot be executed on the blockchain. The system of the carrier needs to implement an interface to detect when the process engine triggers the execution of the parcel delivery task.

4.4   Smart Contract Activities

Method	Uncertainty root	Trust concern	Process component
Reduce uncertainty	Resource, activity	Integrity, availability	Activity

In an inter-organizational process, different collaborators are responsible for certain activities. The execution of activities carried out by one organization can be seen as a "black box" for other organizations. Without any modifications, collaborators cannot verify the correct execution of the activities of other collaborators. Further, it is also not traceable to them if even the resources to execute the activity at a certain point in time are available. This can be mitigated by the use of the blockchain technology as a highly-available and transparent computing environment.

In this trust pattern, the business logic of an activity is encoded in a smart contract and deployed on the blockchain. The execution of the smart contract is either triggered by the responsible collaborator or by another smart contract, such as a decentralized business process engine. If a blockchain-based process engine triggers the execution of tasks encoded in a different smart contract, this can be seen as a blockchain-based script task [23]. Hence, the blockchain-based process engine focuses on the correct orchestration of the whole process, while smart contract activities focus on the proper execution of one particular activity. As another benefit besides the integrity of the activity execution and its traceability, also availability is improved. As an execution environment, many different peers participate in a blockchain network, which all can execute smart contracts. Depending on the network configuration and the peers, blockchain can be seen as a highly-available computing environment with smart contracts.

The blockchain environment limits the expressiveness of script tasks in smart contracts. Time-based business logic cannot be encoded. Furthermore, data to be consumed by the smart contract can only be provided through input parameters from the triggering organization or store the data on-chain. This can lead to performance and privacy issues. Injecting outside data has been studied as the blockchain's oracle problem before [25].

In the running example, the create invoice task can be automated. The invoice should reflect the SLAs and the way from start to finish. To make the calculation of the price more transparent, the task can be executed as a smart contract script task on-chain.

4.5 Blockchain-Based Reputation Systems

Method	Uncertainty root	Trust concern	Process component
Build confidence	Organization	Any	Any

Reputation systems are a well-established method that has been used from the early ages of e-commerce to symbolize the trustworthiness of online business partners. Hence, they are an approach to build confidence in a process. From a technical perspective, reputation systems store the reputation *claim* that a *source* makes regarding a specific reputation *target* [26]. An example of that is the online auctioning platform eBay [27]. Traditional reputation systems are centralized so that a single authority (e.g., eBay for their marketplace), stores all reputation statements and performs the reputation aggregation for the user. This requires the user to trust the centralized authority not to manipulate the saved reputation data.

The blockchain technology can be leveraged to implement fully decentralized reputation systems. In such decentralized systems, there is no need to trust a centralized party for the integrity of reputation statements and their aggregation since all blockchain participants have access to the data. From a process point of view, reputation systems are an external approach to build confidence. Recently, many different reputation systems have been proposed in various application domains. Examples are in academic reputation, tourism, or in industrial IoT [28].

Blockchain-based reputation systems face many of the same security challenges, such as bad-mouthing or white-washing attacks. [28] provides a comprehensive survey over currently existing blockchain-based reputation systems, their strengths, and their weaknesses.

In the running example business process, a reputation system can be used as an external factor to assess which carrier the sender wants to trust for the sensitive fireworks. The reputation statements can be collected after the payment of the delivery.

4.6 Blockchain to Decentralize Business Processes

Method	Uncertainty root	Trust concern	Process component
Build confidence	Organization	Any	Any

In collaborative business processes, activities executed by one organization are usually outside of the domain of influence of other organizations. If one organization is in charge of particularly many tasks in a process, this can lead to a significant dependency on the organization. Examples for this phenomenon are multi-sided platforms. E-Commerce platforms like Amazon act as a middle man between buyer and seller. During the purchasing processes, such multi-sided platforms are in charge of many activities in the process. For instance, Amazon offers the seller marketing services, delivery, payment processing, and handling of returns. This leads to potentially many uncertainties in the subprocesses such an intermediary is responsible for. The accumulation of a large number of uncertainties at one organization can be mitigated by *decentralization* and the distribution of different subprocesses to different process collaborators.

Blockchain can be used as a tool to connect subprocesses in a decentralized process and as a tool for incentivization of correct behavior. As a software connector [24], the blockchain technology can be used as an interface for message flows between different organizations. Further, crypto-economic mechanisms can be used to incentivize collaborators for correct behavior. The decentralization approach does not reduce uncertainty, but it splits them between different organizations. Depending on the relationships and incentives of them, such constellations might be favorable in some use cases.

In the running example, the carrier is in charge of a large part of the process. Especially in the deliver parcel activity, the carrier causes the uncertainty that an incident is reported correctly is important for the other process stakeholders. One way to decentralize this process is to put a different organization in charge of the parcel monitoring process. For example, IoT sensors can be utilized to monitor the parcel conditions, similar to the approach presented in [18].

5 Discussion

An important consideration for all discussed patterns is the understanding of *transparency* and *privacy* in the context of a specific business process. Blockchain and distributed ledger technologies leverage the principle of consensus over information shared among its peers as the technical basis for its trust-enhancing capabilities. Peers participating in the consensus need to have access to the full history of all transactions to verify their validity. This exposes all information encoded in the transactions to them. Further, it constitutes potential privacy issues and limits the applicability of all discussed blockchain-based trust patterns.

Privacy in blockchain-based applications has recently seen a lot of research, and many different approaches to solve these issues have been proposed. These solutions range from modifications of the network setup (public vs. private, permissionless vs. permissioned) over the use of advanced cryptography (zero-knowledge approaches, trusted execution environments) to the general question of what to store on-chain and what off-chain. However, it is essential to carefully analyze which transparency needs to be maintained to enhance trust in the process while maintaining privacy towards all other entities. This is mostly a complex trade-off, which needs to be analyzed carefully.

The presented collection of trust patterns is based on a limited literature review. No more extensive empirical studies regarding the defined patterns have been conducted. The patterns are not presented in a formal manner. Further, we do not claim completeness of these patterns. These activities are subject to future research.

Table 2. Impact potential of blockchain to mitigate process related uncertainties: HS - Hash Storage, TEL - Transparent Event Log, BPE - Blockchain Business Process Engine, SCA - Smart Contract Activities

	Data	Activity	Event	Gateway	Sequence flow	Message flow
Integrity	HS	SCA	TEL	BPE, SCA	BPE	BPE
Confidentiality						
Availability		SCA	SCA	SCA	SCA	SCA
Non-repudiation		TEL	TEL	TEL	TEL	TEL
Performance						
Resilience						

Based on the established blockchain-based trust patterns, we can analyze the impact of the technology as a trust-enhancing tool. Table 2 shows an abstract indication of the influence of the blockchain technology to certain the six initially discussed uncertainties in a business process. The letters indicate which blockchain-based trust pattern can be used to enhance which trust concern.

The most significant impact on a trust concern offers the blockchain technology on integrity. With the hash-based storage of data objects, data integrity can be verified at any point in time. A smart contract can facilitate the execution of an activity. The transparent event log ensures the integrity of events. The correct execution of business logic for gateways, sequence, and message flows can be enforced by a blockchain-based business process engine or similar working smart contracts. The blockchain technology does not per se improve confidentiality in a business process. Moreover, implementing blockchain-based trust patterns implies privacy challenges that need to be carefully addressed. Blockchain can be seen as a highly available computing tool as a decentralized way to execute programming logic encoded in smart contracts in a peer-to-peer network.

The transparent event log pattern ensures non-repudiation of executable process elements. Towards the quality-related trust concerns, the blockchain technology cannot offer any enhancement. The performance trust concern is, even more, a challenge to address in certain situations. A public blockchain, for instance, often has definite limitations on transaction throughput per second. This can lead to waiting situations for the submission of transactions to the ledger, hence decreasing the overall process's performance. The utilization of a blockchain cannot mitigate process resilience. Additionally, the confidence-building trust patterns which are not depicted in the table can be used as external sources of trust in business processes.

Based on the described patterns, we can say that the blockchain technology is not a metaphorical silver bullet to *all* trust issues of collaborative business processes. The discussed patterns can offer an improvement for the trust concerns of integrity, availability, and non-repudiation related to a process. Further, confidence-building trust patterns based on the blockchain technology have a further impact on the business process itself.

6   Conclusion

This paper provided a taxonomy to classify the trust-enhancing capabilities of the blockchain technology in collaborative business processes. While in this paper, we use the taxonomy to evaluate blockchain-based trust patterns, it can be utilized as a tool to analyze any trust-enhancing technology or technique. Here, we described how the patterns could be utilized to address uncertainties regarding specific trust concerns. Vulnerabilities of processes can be indirectly addressed by decreasing uncertainty in a process. The blockchain technology can also be utilized as a tool to implement external sources of trust and increase confidence in a process.

With the established patterns, process engineers have a structured toolset to evaluate if and how the blockchain technology can be used to address the specific trust issues a particular process has. Future work will focus on more engineering-oriented ways to construct trust-aware business processes with the blockchain technology.

References

1. Laudon, K.C., Traver, C.G., et al.: E-commerce: business, technology, society (2016)
2. Butner, K.: The smarter supply chain of the future. Strategy Leadersh. **38**(1), 22–31 (2010)
3. Mendling, J., et al.: Blockchains for business process management-challenges and opportunities. ACM Trans. Manage. Inf. Syst. (TMIS) **9**(1), 4 (2018)
4. Nakamura, H., Miyamoto, K., Kudo, M.: Inter-organizational business processes managed by blockchain. In: Hacid, H., Cellary, W., Wang, H., Paik, H.-Y., Zhou, R. (eds.) WISE 2018. LNCS, vol. 11233, pp. 3–17. Springer, Cham (2018). https://doi.org/10.1007/978-3-030-02922-7_1

5. Swan, M.: Anticipating the economic benefits of blockchain. Technol. Innov. Manage. Rev. **7**(10), 6–13 (2017)

6. Viriyasitavat, W., Da Xu, L., Bi, Z., et al.: Blockchain-based business process management (BPM) framework for service composition in industry 4.0. J. Intell. Manufact. (2018). https://doi.org/10.1007/s10845-018-1422-y

7. Galvin, D.: IBM and Walmart: blockchain for food safety (2017)

8. Rosemann, M.: Trust-aware process design. In: Hildebrandt, T., van Dongen, B., Roglinger, M., Mendling, J. (eds.) Business Process Management, pp. 305–321. Springer, Cham (2019). https://doi.org/10.1007/978-3-030-26619-6_20

9. Gambetta, D., et al.: Can we trust trust. In: Trust: Making and Breaking Cooperative Relations, vol. 13, pp. 213–237 (2000)

10. Nakamoto, S., et al.: Bitcoin: a peer-to-peer electronic cash system (2008)

11. Xu, X., Pautasso, C., Zhu, L., Lu, Q., Weber, I.: A pattern collection for blockchain-based applications. In: Proceedings of the 23rd European Conference on Pattern Languages of Programs, pp. 1–20 (2018)

12. Wessling, F., Gruhn, V.: Engineering software architectures of blockchain-oriented applications. In: 2018 IEEE International Conference on Software Architecture Companion (ICSA-C), pp. 45–46. IEEE (2018)

13. Autili, M., Gallo, F., Inverardi, P., Pompilio, C., Tivoli, M.: Introducing trust in service-oriented distributed systems through blockchain. In: 2019 IEEE International Symposium on Software Reliability Engineering Workshops (ISSREW), pp. 149–154. IEEE (2019)

14. Nickerson, R.C., Varshney, U., Muntermann, J.: A method for taxonomy development and its application in information systems. Eur. J. Inf. Syst. **22**(3), 336–359 (2013)

15. Wang, H., Wang, C.: Taxonomy of security considerations and software quality. Commun. ACM **46**(6), 75–78 (2003)

16. Menzel, M., Thomas, I., Meinel, C.: Security requirements specification in service-oriented business process management. In: 2009 International Conference on Availability, Reliability and Security, pp. 41–48. IEEE (2009)

17. vom Brocke, J., et al.: Reconstructing the giant: On the importance of rigour in documenting the literature search process (2009)

18. Müller, M., Garzon, S.R., Westerkamp, M., Lux, Z.A.: HIDALS: a hybrid IoT-based decentralized application for logistics and supply chain management. In: 2019 IEEE 10th Annual Information Technology, Electronics and Mobile Communication Conference (IEMCON), pp. 0802–0808. IEEE (2019)

19. Liang, X., Shetty, S., Tosh, D., Kamhoua, C., Kwiat, K., Njilla, L.: ProvChain: a blockchain-based data provenance architecture in cloud environment with enhanced privacy and availability. In: 2017 17th IEEE/ACM International Symposium on Cluster, Cloud and Grid Computing (CCGRID), pp. 468–477. IEEE (2017)

20. Liu, B., Yu, X.L., Chen, S., Xu, X., Zhu, L.: Blockchain based data integrity service framework for IoT data. In: 2017 IEEE International Conference on Web Services (ICWS), pp. 468–475. IEEE (2017)

21. Banerjee, P.K., Kulkarni, P., Patil, H.S.: Distributed logging of application events in a blockchain. US Patent 10,320,566, 11 June 2019

22. Weske, M.: Business process management architectures. Business Process Management, pp. 333–371. Springer, Heidelberg (2012). https://doi.org/10.1007/978-3-642-28616-2_7

23. López-Pintado, O., García-Bañuelos, L., Dumas, M., Weber, I.: Caterpillar: a blockchain-based business process management system. In BPM (Demos) (2017)

24. Xu, X., et al.: The blockchain as a software connector. In: 2016 13th Working IEEE/IFIP Conference on Software Architecture (WICSA), pp. 182–191. IEEE (2016)
25. Antonopoulos, A.M., Wood, G.: Mastering Ethereum: Building Smart Contracts and DApps. O'Reilly Media, Sebastopol (2018)
26. Farmer, R., Glass, B.: Building Web Reputation Systems. O'Reilly Media Inc., Sebastopol (2010)
27. Resnick, P., Zeckhauser, R.: Trust among strangers in internet transactions: empirical analysis of eBay's reputation system. In: The Economics of the Internet and E-commerce, vol. 11, no. 2, pp. 23–25 (2002)
28. Bellini, E., Iraqi, Y., Damiani, E.: Blockchain-based distributed trust and reputation management systems: a survey. IEEE Access 8, 21127–21151 (2020)

Blockchain Oracles: A Framework for Blockchain-Based Applications

Kamran Mammadzada[1], Mubashar Iqbal[1(✉)], Fredrik Milani[1],
and Luciano García-Bañuelos[2], and Raimundas Matulevičius[1]

[1] Institute of Computer Science, University of Tartu, Tartu, Estonia
{kamran.mammadzada,mubashar.iqbal,fredrik.milani,rma}@ut.ee
[2] School of Engineering and Science, Tecnologico de Monterrey, Monterrey, Mexico
luciano.garcia@tec.mx

Abstract. Oracles support the access, validation, and transmission of data from external sources to blockchain systems. They are important components of blockchain-based architectures. However, there exists no guidance on how oracles could be used when designing blockchain-based applications. In this paper, based on the results of a systematic literature review, we propose a framework to explain blockchain oracles and their relationships to blockchain-based applications. More specifically, the blockchain oracle framework addresses the origin of data, oracle properties, encryption method, oracle data source, validation procedures, and the integration of oracles to blockchain-based applications. Potentially, this framework can guide developers when incorporating oracles to blockchain-based applications.

Keywords: Blockchain · Blockchain-based applications · Blockchain oracles · Blockchain oracle framework

1 Introduction

Blockchain has been positioned as a technology with the potential to innovate how companies manage inter-organizational processes [21]. The disruptive potential of blockchain has attracted the attention of many companies to explore various commercial use cases for this technology. At its core, blockchain relies on the concept of a distributed ledger. Data is recorded and secured by means of cryptographic algorithms that ensure the data is tamper-proof and propagated to all nodes [16]. In blockchain, transactions are executed in a distributed manner without relying on trusted third parties. These properties enable cryptocurrencies where transactions are managed without the need of a trusted third party, commonly supported by permissionless blockchain. It also enables collaborative execution of inter-organizational processes [21], such as food tracking that is implemented on permissioned blockchain.

Analysts working with implementing blockchain-based applications, particularly for inter-organizational processes, have to consider the exchange of data

© Springer Nature Switzerland AG 2020
A. Asatiani et al. (Eds.): BPM Blockchain and RPA Forum 2020, LNBIP 393, pp. 19–34, 2020.
https://doi.org/10.1007/978-3-030-58779-6_2

between the blockchain and external systems. However, blockchain itself does not access data from external sources. Therefore, a mechanism that provides data to blockchain is required. This can be achieved by using *oracles*. Conceptually, oracles are trusted entities that enable the collection, validation, and transmission of data from external sources [2]. Thus, oracles are important components for design and implementation of blockchain use cases, in particular for commercial applications. However, the research on oracles so far, has not considered types of oracles and when they can be used. In light of this context, we seek to address the overall research objective of gaining an overview of oracles and how they can be used in blockchain use cases. We conduct a systematic literature review (SLR) and, based on the results, propose a *blockchain oracle framework*. The framework focuses on key aspects of oracles, such as origins of data, methods of integration with blockchain, and the types of data transfer to blockchain.

The rest of the paper is structured as follows. Section 2 provides background information describing the major concepts discussed in the research. Section 3 describes the review protocol used to find the relevant studies. Section 4 presents the results whereas Sect. 5 presents the blockchain oracle framework and discusses threats to validity. Finally, Sect. 6 provides some concluding remarks.

2   Background

Blockchain is a distributed ledger technology where transactions are replicated and stored on a multitude of nodes. Each node holds a full or partial copy of the ledger. New transactions can only be added in an append-only manner. Transactions are collected in blocks that are appended to the ledger. The blocks are linked to the preceding and succeeding block by means of a hash. Transactions that have been appended to the ledger are considered as tamper-proof because changing a transaction of an older block requires changing all of the succeeding blocks. Such a computational effort is very costly. Therefore, blockchain is considered to provide secure, immutable, and tamper-proof transaction records. As all nodes can create blocks in an untrusted decentralised system, the nodes must, by means of a consensus algorithm [26], reach an agreement on which block to append to the blockchain.

The participating nodes agree on the state of the ledger by following the consensus mechanism. The Proof of Work (PoW) [15], Proof of Stake (PoS) [15] and Practical Byzantine Fault Tolerance (PBFT) [26] are some of the used consensus protocols. Blockchain could be classified as permissionless (a.k.a. public) and permissioned [2]. In a public blockchain, the ledger is publicly accessible and open for all to join. A permissioned blockchain enforces network participants to be authorised before joining the network (e.g., Hyperledger Fabric) and ledger accessibility is restricted.

The distributed architecture of blockchain allows for independent entities to directly interact with each other without depending on a central system or authority. Blockchain is commonly categorised as public or permissioned [38]. A public blockchain is fully decentralised and open for all to access and join. Such a solution is, therefore, suitable for digital currencies [34]. A permissioned blockchain, on the other hand, is partially decentralised (managed by several organizations) with restrictions on who can join and access the data. Permissioned solutions are can, therefore, be used for commercial cases where mutually distrustful entities have shared interest. Such solutions have been implemented, for instance, in the insurance domain and in trade settlement between financial institutions [31].

In blockchain, smart contracts enhance the transaction process and automation. A smart contract is a program that is self-verifying, self-executing, tamper-resistant and executes on the blockchain platform. Smart contracts have been defined as programs that digitally facilitate, verify, and enforce contracts made between two or more participants on the blockchain [26]. Smart contracts are event-driven, meaning that they can be activated when a predefined condition is met [26]. However, smart contracts can only use resources available on the network and cannot access or interact with the external data [2]. To address this, blockchain oracles can be introduced to enable an exchange of data available external to the blockchain.

Smart contracts are often required to have relevant information from the outside world to execute the agreement (or to meet certain conditions) [3,4]. Here, blockchain oracles come into play because smart contracts cannot, by themselves, interact with external sources [3]. According to Al-Breiki et al., *"blockchain oracle is an external data agent that observes the real-world events and reports them back to the blockchain to be used by smart contracts"* [3]. Accordingly, oracles are trusted entities that bring external information into the blockchain [1,27] and serve as a bridge between blockchain and the outside world [4]. Furthermore, the role of oracles is not limited to simply querying the information from outside of the blockchain, but can also verify the authenticity and validity of that data. Blockchain oracles can directly interact with smart contracts. Therefore, it is important that oracles provide reliable and valid information to ensure consistency and validity of smart contract execution. Therefore oracles can be essential for blockchain implementations.

3   Review Protocol

The objective of this paper is to propose a framework for oracles and, in particular, when they can be used in blockchain use cases. To this end, a SLR is suitable as the method enables a systematic review of relevant literature. We followed the guidelines proposed by Kitchenham [17]. Accordingly, we specify the research questions, design a search protocol to search, and identify relevant papers. We defined the following six research questions, each covering a different aspect of oracles in blockchain-based applications.

RQ1: *What are the origins of data that oracles provide to blockchain-based applications?*
In order to describe the nature of information oracles provide to blockchain and relationship between oracles and blockchain, it is valuable to explore various origins of data from where through oracles communicate to blockchain.

RQ2: *What are the properties of oracles for use in blockchain-based applications?*
Exploring oracles properties ensures understanding the characteristics that are needed to possess and inject information into the blockchain.

RQ3: *How is data received and sent by oracles encrypted?*
Protecting the data transfer from an external data source to oracle and then oracle to blockchain is critical to the integrity of blockchain-based applications thus discussion of encryption is important to understand methods used to ensure reliable data transfer. The encryption methods represent the cryptography technology that used to secure the communication between entities.

RQ4: *How many sources are used by oracles to collect data from?*
Oracle data source captures the mechanism behind how the decision for passing the data into blockchain is made. It is important to explore how oracle data sources are used by oracles to gather data sent to the blockchain.

RQ5: *How do oracles validate the data they provide to blockchain-based applications?*
Data validation within blockchain oracles is critical since information recorded in blockchain cannot be deleted. In these perspectives, data validation ensures that information collected from external sources to blockchain is legitimate and correct.

RQ6: *How are oracles integrated with blockchain platforms?*
Oracle integration into blockchain platforms contributes to blockchain widespread implementation since oracles help solve the issue of bringing external data into the network. Investigating various oracles integration ways could provide good basis for making necessary decisions when developing blockchain-based applications.

The overall search strategy is to find a body of relevant studies. For this SLR two search strategies were used, as recommended by Okoli et al. [25], Fink et al. [10] and Levy et al. [18], to secure identification of relevant studies. Accordingly, in the first step, called primary search, search strings were used to identify an initial set of papers [10]. Several electronic databases were used for this step. In the second step, a secondary search was performed by means of backward and forward tracing [18,25].

The search strings included the keywords *"blockchain"* in combination with *"oracle"*, *"internet of things"*, or *"IoT"*. We tested the search strings and found that the terms *"internet of things"* and *"IoT"* are extensively included in blockchain solutions and often used, in the context of blockchain solutions, as a quasi-term for an oracle. Thus we decided to include this term in the search string. We applied the search strings on *ACM Digital Library, IEEE Xplore, Scopus, Web of Science, Wiley,* and *Google Scholar.* We included google scholar to identify publications by companies and other non-academic organizations (grey literature) as proposed in [17].

We applied *exclusion (EC)* and *inclusion (IC)* criteria to identify relevant papers. Papers that were duplicates, not in English, shorter than 5 pages, inaccessible (via University subscriptions or Internet search), or published before 2008, were excluded. Papers less than 5 pages were excluded as short papers would not contain enough information for our evaluation. Papers within the domain of blockchain *(IC1)*, covering the integration of oracles with blockchain *(IC2)*, and providing a description of the oracle solution *(IC3)*, were included.

The search resulted in 3015 hits from all sources. Having removed the duplicates, 2356 papers remained and their publishing date is between 2008–2018. After several iterations of filtering, considering the exclusion criteria and the first two inclusion criteria *(IC1 & IC2)*, a total of 70 papers remained. These were subjected to full-text examination *(IC3)*, which resulted in a *total of 23 studies* (Fig. 1) remaining (including backward tracing references). The corpus of papers consisted of *65% academic publications* and *35% grey literature*.

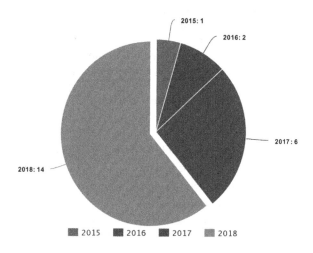

Fig. 1. Papers distribution per year

Following the identification of the final list of papers, relevant data were extracted. To ensure unbiased data extraction strategy, it has been recommended [10] to develop a data extraction form and strategy. The data extraction form was developed after the screening process, allowing for utilising the insights drawn during the screening phase. Three types of data were extracted. The first relates to data about the paper. The second was related to the context of the study and finally, the third type related to the availability of developed solutions. The complete review protocol, list of final papers, and detailed results of the SLR are available here: https://doi.org/10.5281/zenodo.3605157.

4   Results

In this section, we present the results obtained from the SLR in relation to each research question respectively.

4.1   Origin of Data

In determining the best-suited oracle design, the first question to consider is about the origin of the data that the blockchain-based application requires. Our review shows that the data which is sent by oracles, come from two types of origins: from web content and collected using sensors (Table 1).

A large body of the literature describes oracles that provide data, collected by third parties, through web services [15,36]. Web content differs from sensor data in that it is easily available via the browser *(e.g., generic HTTP(s) data)* and does not directly originate from a physical device. Web content covers data such as financial information, sports results, weather updates, operational data, and user inputs that are categorised under generic http(s) data. For instance, Eden-Chain [2], an asset tokenization platform, and Town Crier [12,37], an authenticated data-feed service for smart contracts, aiming to deliver trusted data input through web services. Boolean propositions and scalar measurements are a sub-type of web content and mostly used in prediction markets [1,15,36]. Hence, web content ranges from binary responses to discrete or continuous responses [28,36].

Table 1. Origins of data

Origin of data	Sub-type	Papers
Web content	Generic HTTP(S) data	[2,8,9,12,29,37]
	Boolean or scalar	[1,15,28,33,36]
Sensor data	IoT device readings	[13,26]
	Energy readings	[20]
	Vehicular sensor readings	[16,22]
	Biometric readings	[11]
	Health readings	[35]
	Product readings	[14,24]
	Visual feed	[19]

Oracles providing sensor data to the blockchain are commonly generated by physical devices (e.g., IoT & vehicle sensors [2,12]). In an example from the domain of vehicle data [16,22], traffic-related data and data on road conditions (using embedded sensors) are collected. Similarly, Uddin et al. [35] record health data (e.g., blood pressure, pulse & body temperature) using wearable and implantable medical devices. In [24], a unique RFID chip is used to collect and track clothing-related data (e.g., geolocation & product details). These examples illustrate how sensors are applied as oracles to record and send data to the blockchain.

4.2   Oracle Properties

In this section, we explored oracle and blockchain types that are essential components when designing blockchain-based applications.

Oracle Type: The need for defining oracle types is important for organising the oracles to facilitate developers in navigating through the landscape of potential options. Some [5,6], have divided the blockchain oracles into the following categories:

- Software oracles – oracles that push information available online to blockchain
- Hardware oracles – oracles that push information from physical devices (e.g. sensors, RFID chips, etc.) into the blockchain
- Inbound oracles – oracles that provide smart contracts with data from the external world
- Outbound oracles – oracles that send information to the outside world
- Consensus-based oracles – data passed to blockchain is treated as a result of consensus of multiple oracles

In the blockchain oracle framework, when defining oracle type we consider physical attributes of oracle. For example, the oracle is pushing the information from a physical device *(tangible entity)* or an oracle is a piece of code *(intangible entity)* collecting information from intangible sources (e.g., websites).

Blockchain Type: Blockchain platforms can be categorised as permissionless, permissioned, or hybrid. Our review shows that oracles are used with all types of blockchain platforms; for example, Ethereum (permissionless) [37], Hyperledger Fabric (permissioned) [30] and BlockID (hybrid) [11].

4.3   Encryption Method

The third column of the framework represents the encryption methods (Table 2). This component concerns ensuring data confidentiality when data is transferred from external data sources to the oracles, and from oracles to the blockchain. It is noteworthy that most studies mention encryption methods briefly (e.g., [30]) or does not discuss it at all (e.g., [11,19]).

The most commonly implemented encryption method for data transfer from external sources to oracles is a public key infrastructure (PKI). For PKI, the most common encryption technique is transport layer security (TLS). TLS provides authentication, privacy, and data integrity between communicating entities [32] and is the prevalent form of secure communication on the internet [7]. One paper presented a solution called TLS-N, a novel communication protocol which acts as an oracle and is built on top of TLS [29].

Table 2. Encryption methods when data transmit from external sources to Oracle

Encryption method	Technique	Papers
PKI	TLS	[1,2,9,28,33,37]
	TLS-N	[29]
	Not discussed	[13,19,22,36]
Symmetric cryptography	Not discussed	[35]
Asymmetric cryptography	ECC	[16]
	Not discussed	[11,24]

Apart from receiving data from external sources, oracles also transfer information to the blockchain. The only encryption method proposed from oracles to the blockchain is asymmetric encryption (e.g., [12,35]) (Table 3). Elliptic curve cryptography (ECC) is a form of asymmetric cryptography and is used in Bitcoin and Ethereum. ECC with threshold cryptography (ECC-TC) is a protocol with a cooperative property where data necessary for decryption is shared among participants so that encrypted data can be decrypted only when data of other participants is present as well as yours [2]. This process enables secure decentralised exchange of information.

Table 3. Encryption methods when data transmit from oracle to blockchain

Encryption method	Technique	Papers
Asymmetric cryptography	ECC	[15,16,29,33,37]
	ECC-TC	[2]
	Not explicitly discussed	[12,14,24,35]

4.4   Oracle Data Source

Oracle data source refers to the data sources used by the oracles to gather data sent to the blockchain. If a single data source is used, it is called a single-source oracle; and if multiple data sources are used – multi-source oracle.

In this work, we found studies that employ a single-source oracle where, for instance, smart meters used an IoT enabled smart grid [20] and on-body sensors used to enable tracking of vital information [35]. These examples of sensor data oracles rely on a single source of data. Single-source oracles can also be used for web content, for example, oracles that receive data from single trusted content provider [12,37].

Multi-source oracle receives data from several sources. For instance, a set of roadside units (RSU) collect vehicle data and send the aggregated data to the blockchain. Also, the RSUs interact with each other to verify vehicle identity or request specific data (e.g., reputation score, authorization & data sharing settings, etc.) [16].

4.5   Data Validation

We identify data validation as the method by which oracles ensure that the data provided to the blockchain is correct (Table 4). Some studies propose a consensus-based solution where data is validated by means of majority voting, i.e., on the basis of the wisdom of the crowd [36]. Another consensus-based method relies on weighted voting where each individual vote has a specifically assigned weight [28]. Finally, one study proposes a hybrid of PoW and PoS solution [15].

Table 4. Data validation approaches

Data validation	Mechanism	Papers
Consensus	Majority voting	[1, 8, 9, 36, 37]
	Weighted voting	[28, 33]
	Hybrid of PoW & PoS	[15]
No data validation	Trusted third party	[11, 12, 16, 19, 29, 35, 36]
	Not discussed	[14, 20]
Self-validation	RFID signature validation	[24]

We found that the most common approach is to rely on trusted data providers. As such, the oracles do not have any method for validating the data. Such a strategy operates under the assumption that the data source is trustworthy. For instance, vehicular blockchain networks [22] trust the central governments' authority for issuance of legitimate vehicle plates, while service platforms provide data as trusted web content providers [29]. Some [23] use trusted data exchanges or incorporate certified equipment [30] when deploying IoT devices.

4.6   Oracle Integration Method

Oracle integration is a method by which an oracle is interfaced to a blockchain to provide data (Table 5). We found that smart contracts, software modules, custom solutions, and built-in solutions are approaches used to integrate oracles with blockchain platforms.

The most common integration method is by using a custom smart contract. Several studies [2, 36] use this approach to integrate decentralised web applications (dApps), such as implementing a pair of smart contracts, one on-chain and other off-chain. Another approach relies on custom software modules. Such modules provide additional functionality to achieve integration between the oracle and the blockchain. Software modules are often used when physical devices communicate with a blockchain. The software module serves as an intermediate agent that, according to rules, manipulates the incoming data from oracles before sending it. For instance, in [24], they use RFID readers and a PC with a blockchain node to deliver tracking data.

Table 5. Blockchain oracles integration methods

Integration method	Mechanism	Papers
Custom smart contract interface	On-chain and off-chain smart contract	[2, 9, 36]
	Off-chain smart contracts deployed on-chain	[26]
	Data storage smart contract (DSSC)	[16]
	Information sharing smart contract (ISSC)	[16]
	Chaincode (specialised smart contract)	[30]
	On-chain smart contract accessing Data Cubes	[23]
	Smart contract able to verify TLS-N proofs	[29]
	Server + on-chain smart contract	[37]
	On-chain smart contract + Bridge node	[8]
	TLS Identities linked to content contract	[12]
Custom software module	RFID Reader + PC with blockchain module	[24]
	Software module (ETSE) + Adapter	[20]
	Control system + Blockchain client	[19]
	Patient centric agent	[35]
Custom solution	Blockchain identity bound to government ID	[11]
	OriginStamp	[14]
Built-in		[15, 33]

Some studies propose a custom solution i.e., a unique and separate solution built to cater for the specific needs of the project. Two cases, one involving scanning images for combating counterfeit products [14] and the other, fingerprint scanning for identity management [11], use this method of integration. Finally, some studies [33] developed the oracle inside the blockchain network. In these solutions, the smart contracts self-execute when certain conditions are met.

5   Framework

In this section, we present the framework and the associated components (Table 6) that are derived from the results of the SLR. The goal of this framework is to summarise the results of the SLR in a clear and concise manner that represents the state of the art of blockchain oracles. It serves developers and decision-makers when making decisions in their blockchain-based applications regarding blockchain oracles. The framework covers the possible scenarios of combinations where certain data passed through a specific oracle & blockchain type using a pre-defined oracle data source mechanism and data validation approach could add value to a blockchain network. A visual representation (Fig. 2) of the framework aims to provide visual cues to the reader and communicate the interaction flow.

Table 6. Blockchain oracle framework

Origin of Data	Oracle Type	Blockchain Type	Encryption	Oracle Data Source	Data Validation	Oracle Integration Method	Ref.
Web Content	Intangible	Permissioned	PKI	Single-source Oracle	Trusted Third Party	Custom Smart Contract Interface	[2]
		Permissionless	PKI	Single-source Oracle	Majority Voting	Custom Smart Contract Interface	[37]
					Trusted Third Party	Custom Smart Contract Interface	[12]
				Multi-source Oracle	Hybrid of PoW & PoS	Built-in	[15]
					Majority Voting	Custom Smart Contract Interface	[8,9,36]
						Not explicitly discussed	[1]
					Trusted Third Party	Custom Smart Contract Interface	[29]
					Weighted Voting	Built-in	[33]
						Custom Smart Contract Interface	[28]
Sensor Data	Tangible	Hybrid	Asymmetric	Single-source Oracle	Trusted Third Party	Custom Solution	[11]
		Permissioned	Asymmetric	Multi-source Oracle	Trusted Third Party	Custom Smart Contract Interface	[16]
			Not Covered	Single-source Oracle	No Data Verification	Custom Software Module	[20]
					Trusted Third Party	Custom Smart Contract Interface	[30,26]
			PKI	Multi-source Oracle	Trusted Third Party	Not explicitly discussed	[22]
			Symmetric	Single-source Oracle	Trusted Third Party	Custom Software Module	[35]
		Permissionless	Asymmetric	Single-source Oracle	RFID Signature	Custom Software Module	[24]
			Not Covered	Single-source Oracle	No Data Validation	Custom Solution	[14]
					Trusted Third Party	Custom Smart Contract Interface	[23]
			PKI	Single-source Oracle	Trusted Third Party	Custom Software Module	[19]
		Hybrid	PKI	Single-source Oracle	Trusted Third Party	Not explicitly discussed	[13]

5.1   Example of Oracle Framework

The framework (Table 6 and Fig. 2) is to be read from left to right, following the natural flow of data from external sources to the blockchain. When an oracle is required in a blockchain solution, the first step is to identify the origin of data that needs to sent to the blockchain. This decision paves the way for other choices regarding, for instance, oracle properties (e.g, oracle type). Before navigating further, discussing the scope of the project and stakeholders would aid to identify the blockchain type to use. There are frameworks that assist in this regard. Commonly, if there is a limited number of participants, then a permissioned blockchain would be appropriate. Otherwise, a public permissionless network would perhaps be the better fit. Next, it is important to ensure that data is securely transported to the oracle, thus the developers need to identify an encryption method that best serves their purpose. Although there are few methods, it is important to carefully think about this step. Now that the origin of data and how to secure the data transmission has been determined, it is important to explore the level of trust necessary to handle this information by exploring oracle types and oracles data sources approach. While a single-source approach can be beneficial in projects that are limited in scope or already use a permissioned blockchain, the multi-source approach might be useful for efforts involving multiple actors or to augment a public permissionless blockchain network. Due to the immutable nature of the blockchain, it is critical to set up a data validation mechanism to ensure truthful and correct information is injected into the blockchain. Choosing to trust the third party or relying on a form of consensus mechanism will ensure trusted information is injected. Lastly, an integration approach is identified based on the above parameters.

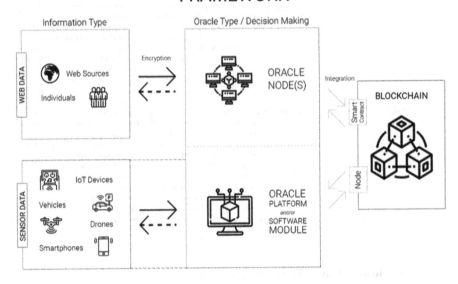

Fig. 2. Blockchain oracle framework (a graphical representation)

5.2 Practical Applicability

Consider an analyst working with developing a blockchain-based solution or a software engineer exploring a potential approach of bringing external data to the blockchain. In this context, the analyst will need to consider the requirements on data being, such as reliability and trust, sent and retrieved from the blockchain. Here, the framework can aid the analyst in understanding what types of oracles are available, their properties, and how they relate to different blockchain solutions, such as permissioned or public ones. An engineer needs to consider, for instance, the origin of data, the level of trust required, and how the data is to be validated. To this end, the framework can assist the engineer in finding a suitable solution by drawing on existing research. For instance (first row of Table 1), in case of web content data (e.g. stock price data) is required to be sent to a permissioned blockchain, PKI being sufficient as encryption, the data can be gathered from a single source provided by a trusted third party e.g., a stock exchange, and the oracle integrated via smart contracts to the blockchain, EdenChain, a programmable economy platform [2], becomes a viable solution to consider. Thus, the framework can aid both analysts who work with conceptual design and engineers focusing on technical implementations in their work to develop blockchain-based solutions.

5.3   Threats to Validity

In this section, we discuss threats to validity as outlined in [39]. Threats to validity that are particularly relevant for SLR are *restricted time span*, the *bias in study selection* and *bias in data extraction*. The threat to validity concerning restricted time span represents the inability of the researcher to anticipate relevant studies outside the time span defined and prepared in the planning phase. Blockchain is a constantly evolving technology with more applications and technologies introduced on a daily basis. Thus, we could not anticipate other relevant studies simply because they were published after the date of our search and, thereby, not included in the primary papers. While it is difficult to account for this, the review protocol includes the dates for all extractions.

Another threat to validity concerns bias in study selection. Such a bias stands for the subjective conjecture which reviewers have in the process of search. This may result in not fully and consistently applying the inclusion and exclusion criteria. This bias could have affected this review due to the knowledge and experience of the authors in the area of blockchain oracles. This is particularly problematic as research on oracles is still in its beginning phases. The terminology is, at times, used inconsistently. For instance, some authors introduced the term *"verifier"* and *"reverse verifier"* as an alternative term for oracles. However, in their more recent work, they use the term oracles. We reduced this threat to validity by testing the search strings. The testing showed that the term IoT was used and we, therefore, included it in our search strings.

Another threat to validity associated with SLR is that of bias in data extraction. As mentioned earlier, the field is still forming and therefore, certain concepts related to oracles are introduced in the papers but not always properly defined and explicitly discussed. In such cases, we had to discuss and, based on our best understanding, extract the data. It is possible that certain data extracted is not fully accurate. We attempted to reduce this threat to validity by discussing all such cases until a common understanding was formed.

6   Concluding Remarks

In this paper, we propose the blockchain oracle framework. This framework could potentially guide developers of blockchain-based applications when incorporating oracles. The framework explains the origins of data provided to the blockchain, oracle properties (how the data is treated during the transactions), encryption method, oracle data source, how it is validated and integrated to the oracle-based applications. As future research, we wish to validate the framework empirically. We also observed that the current literature does not consider the size of the data transferred from oracles. Given that this affects the technical architecture and performance of oracles, this remains as a venue for future study.

References

1. Adler, J., Berryhill, R., Veneris, A., Poulos, Z., Veira, N., Kastania, A.: Astraea: a decentralized blockchain oracle. In: 2018 IEEE International Conference on Internet of Things & IEEE Green Computing and Communications & IEEE Cyber, Physical and Social Computing & IEEE Smart Data, pp. 1145–1152 (2018)
2. Ahn, J.: EdenChain: the programmable economy platform version 1.2 (2018)
3. Al-Breiki, H., Rehman, M.H.U., Salah, K., Svetinovic, D.: Trustworthy blockchain oracles: review, comparison, and open research challenges. IEEE Access **8**, 85675–85685 (2020)
4. Beniiche, A.: A study of blockchain oracles. http://arxiv.org/abs/2004.07140
5. Bisola, A.: Blockchain oracles explained (2018). https://www.mycryptopedia.com/blockchain-oracles-explained
6. Blockchainhub-Berlin: blockchain oracles (2019). https://blockchainhub.net/blockchain-oracles
7. Cloudflare: what is transport layer security (TLS)? (2019). https://www.cloudflare.com/learning/ssl/transport-layer-security-tls
8. De Pedro, A.S., Levi, D., Cuende, L.I.: Witnet: a decentralized oracle network protocol. CoRR (2017). http://arxiv.org/abs/1711.09756
9. Ellis, S., Juels, A., Nazarov, S.: ChainLink: a decentralized oracle network, September 2017. https://link.smartcontract.com/whitepaper
10. Fink, A.: Conducting Research Literature Reviews: From the Internet to Paper, 5th edn. SAGE Publications, Inc., Thousand Oaks (2019)
11. Gao, Z., et al.: Blockchain-based identity management with mobile device. In: 1st Workshop on Cryptocurrencies and Blockchains for Distributed Systems, pp. 66–70 (2018)
12. Guarnizo, J., Szalachowski, P.: PDFS: practical data feed service for smart contracts. In: Sako, K., Schneider, S., Ryan, P.Y.A. (eds.) ESORICS 2019. LNCS, vol. 11735, pp. 767–789. Springer, Cham (2019). https://doi.org/10.1007/978-3-030-29959-0_37
13. Hardjono, T., Smith, N.: Cloud-based commissioning of constrained devices using permissioned blockchains. In: 2nd ACM International Workshop on IoT Privacy, Trust, and Security, pp. 29–36 (2016)
14. Hepp, T., Wortner, P., Schönhals, A., Gipp, B.: Securing physical assets on the blockchain: linking a novel object identification concept with distributed ledgers. In: 1st Workshop on Cryptocurrencies and Blockchains for Distributed Systems, pp. 60–65 (2018)
15. Hess, Z., Malahov, Y., Pettersson, J.: Æternity blockchain (2017). https://blockchain.aeternity.com/\OT1\aeternity-blockchain-whitepaper.pdf
16. Kang, J., et al.: Blockchain for secure and efficient data sharing in vehicular edge computing and networks. IEEE Internet Things J. **6**(3), 4660–4670 (2019)
17. Kitchenham, B., Charters, S.: Guidelines for performing systematic literature reviews in software engineering (2007)
18. Levy, Y., Ellis, T.J.: A systems approach to conduct an effective literature review in support of information systems research. Inform. Sci. Int. J. Emerg. Transdiscip. **9**, 181–212 (2006)

19. Liang, X., Zhao, J., Shetty, S., Li, D.: Towards data assurance and resilience in IoT using blockchain. In: MILCOM 2017–2017 IEEE Military Communications Conference (MILCOM), pp. 261–266 (2017)
20. Lombardi, F., Aniello, L., De Angelis, S., Margheri, A., Sassone, V.: A blockchain-based infrastructure for reliable and cost-effective IoT-aided smart grids. Living Internet Things Cybersecur. IoT **2018**, 1–6 (2018)
21. López-Pintado, O., García-Bañuelos, L., Dumas, M., Weber, I., Ponomarev, A.: Caterpillar: a business process execution engine on the Ethereum blockchain. Softw. Pract. Exp. **7**(49), 1162–1193 (2019)
22. Michelin, R.A., et al.: SpeedyChain: a framework for decoupling data from blockchain for smart cities. In: 15th EAI International Conference on Mobile and Ubiquitous Systems: Computing, Networking and Services, pp. 145–154 (2018)
23. Missier, P., Bajoudah, S., Capossele, A., Gaglione, A., Nati, M.: Mind my value: a decentralized infrastructure for fair and trusted IoT data trading. In: 7th International Conference on the Internet of Things (2017)
24. Mo, B., Su, K., Wei, S., Liu, C., Guo, J.: A solution for internet of things based on blockchain technology. In: 2018 IEEE International Conference on Service Operations and Logistics, and Informatics (SOLI), pp. 112–117 (2018)
25. Okoli, C.: A guide to conducting a standalone systematic literature review. Commun. Assoc. Inf. Syst. **37**, 43 (2015)
26. Pan, J., Wang, J., Hester, A., Alqerm, I., Liu, Y., Zhao, Y.: EdgeChain: an edge-IoT framework and prototype based on blockchain and smart contracts. IEEE Internet Things J. **6**(3), 4719–4732 (2019)
27. Peck, M.E.: Blockchains: how they work and why they'll change the world. IEEE Spectr. **54**(10), 26–35 (2017)
28. Peterson, J., Krug, J., Zoltu, M., Williams, A.K., Alexander, S.: Augur: a decentralized oracle & prediction market (2019). https://augur.net/whitepaper.pdf
29. Ritzdorf, H., Wüst, K., Gervais, A., Felley, G., Čapkun, S.: TLS-N : non-repudiation over TLS enabling ubiquitous content signing for disintermediation. In: Network and Distributed System Security Symposium (NDSS) (2018)
30. Saleh, G., Draskovic, D.: Datapace: decentralized data marketplace based on blockchain (2017). https://datapace.io/datapace_whitepaper.pdf
31. Santo, A., Minowa, I., Hosaka, G., Hayakawa, S., Kondo, M.: Applicability of distributed ledger technology to capital market infrastructure. In: JPX, vol. 15 (2016)
32. ScienceDirect: transport layer security (2019). https://www.sciencedirect.com/topics/computer-science/transport-layer-security
33. Sztorc, P.: Truthcoin: peer-to-peer oracle system and prediction marketplace (2015). https://github.com/psztorc/Truthcoin
34. Tschorsch, F., Scheuermann, B.: Bitcoin and beyond: a technical survey on decentralized digital currencies. IEEE Commun. Surv. Tutorials **18**(3), 2084–2123 (2016)
35. Uddin, M.A., Stranieri, A., Gondal, I., Balasubramanian, V.: Continuous patient monitoring with a patient centric agent: a block architecture. IEEE Access **6**, 32700–32726 (2018)

36. Yayun, F.: Prophet: the prediction platform based on GXChain (2018). https://bitmart.zendesk.com/hc/en-us/articles/360012745833-Prophetset-PPS-
37. Zhang, F., Cecchetti, E., Croman, K., Juels, A., Shi, E.: Town crier: an authenticated data feed for smart contracts. In: 2016 ACM SIGSAC Conference on Computer and Communications Security, pp. 270–282 (2016)
38. Zheng, Z., Xie, S., Dai, H., Chen, X., Wang, H.: An overview of blockchain technology: architecture, consensus, and future trends. In: 2017 IEEE International Congress on Big Data (BigData Congress), pp. 557–564 (2017)
39. Zhou, X., Jin, Y., Zhang, H., Li, S., Huang, X.: A map of threats to validity of systematic literature reviews in software engineering. In: 2016 23rd Asia-Pacific Software Engineering Conference (APSEC), pp. 153–160 (2016)

Foundational Oracle Patterns: Connecting Blockchain to the Off-Chain World

Roman Mühlberger[1(✉)], Stefan Bachhofner[1], Eduardo Castelló Ferrer[2],
Claudio Di Ciccio[3(✉)], Ingo Weber[4], Maximilian Wöhrer[5], and Uwe Zdun[5]

[1] Vienna University of Economics and Business, Vienna, Austria
roman@muehlberger.eu.com
[2] Massachusetts Institute of Technology, Cambridge, USA
[3] Sapienza University of Rome, Rome, Italy
claudio.diciccio@uniroma1.it
[4] Technische Universitaet Berlin, Berlin, Germany
[5] University of Vienna, Vienna, Austria

Abstract. Blockchain has evolved into a platform for decentralized applications, with beneficial properties like high integrity, transparency, and resilience against censorship and tampering. However, blockchains are closed-world systems which do not have access to external state. To overcome this limitation, oracles have been introduced in various forms and for different purposes. However so far common oracle best practices have not been dissected, classified, and studied in their fundamental aspects. In this paper, we address this gap by studying foundational blockchain oracle patterns in two foundational dimensions characterising the oracles: (i) the data flow direction, i.e., inbound and outbound data flow, from the viewpoint of the blockchain; and (ii) the initiator of the data flow, i.e., whether it is push or pull-based communication. We provide a structured description of the four patterns in detail, and discuss an implementation of these patterns based on use cases. On this basis we conduct a quantitative analysis, which results in the insight that the four different patterns are characterized by distinct performance and costs profiles.

Keywords: Blockchain · Design patterns · Software patterns · Oracles

1 Introduction

Conceptually, a blockchain is an append-only store for transactions, which is distributed across many machines and structured into a linked list of blocks [26]. Based on its decentralized nature, structure, and use of cryptographic protocols, blockchain technology provides a modern platform for distributed applications with properties like high integrity, transparency, and resilience against censorship and tampering. This creates, among others, new opportunities and challenges for inter-organizational business processes [16]. These inherent properties make blockchain technology a good fit for use cases where data integrity is of crucial importance, e.g. clinical trials [12,22], food security [3], or financial risk

© Springer Nature Switzerland AG 2020
A. Asatiani et al. (Eds.): BPM Blockchain and RPA Forum 2020, LNBIP 393, pp. 35–51, 2020.
https://doi.org/10.1007/978-3-030-58779-6_3

Table 1. An overview of the four oracle types.

	Pull	Push
Inbound	The **on-chain** component **requests** the off-chain state from an **off-chain** component	The **off-chain** component **sends** the off-chain state to the **on-chain** component
Outbound	The **off-chain** component **retrieves** the on-chain state from an **on-chain** component	The **on-chain** component **sends** the off-chain state to an **off-chain** component

when dealing with business partners [26, Ch. 12]. Consequently, organizations realize efficiency and effectiveness gains with blockchain technology as business processes can have a higher degree of automation, e.g., by running business processes on the blockchain [21] or by automating information exchange between mutually untrusting parties. Many such applications are made possible by a feature of second-generation blockchains, *smart contracts*, which "are programs deployed as data in the blockchain ledger, and executed in transactions on the blockchain" [26]. With smart contracts, blockchains become decentralized, neutral execution platforms for user code.

Regardless of the generation, blockchains are closed-world systems: from inside, one can only access data that is on the blockchain already. Oracles have been proposed to mitigate that limitation. In the context of blockchains, an oracle is a component that can transfer data between the outside world and the blockchain. However, the implementation of oracles provides considerable conceptual challenges as they can be regarded as a centralized point of failure or may introduce security and trust concerns [16]. Consequently, much of the research regarding oracles focuses on how to address these security and trust concerns, e.g., by using multiple independent oracle instances to form a decentralized oracle [25], extending trust properties to off-chain computation [10], or strengthening trust in incoming data [13]. However, foundational aspects of blockchain oracles that allow for their categorization and abstraction have not been subject to close investigation yet.

In this paper, we address this gap by examining two core dimensions of oracles: (i) the *direction*, i.e., whether the data flow is *inbound* or *outbound* from the viewpoint of the blockchain; and (ii) the *initiator* of the data flow, i.e., whether it is *push* or *pull*-based communication. There are four combinations of these options, an overview of which is shown in Table 1. We describe each of these as a pattern, and examine its characteristics. Note that, on this level, the four patterns can be implemented without relying on smart contracts, i.e., even on first-generation blockchains like Bitcoin. Each of the patterns can also be suitably combined with other, higher-level patterns from the literature, like decentralization or provable computation.

To characterise the different patterns, we implemented them in the context of two use cases, and use these implementations for the purpose of obtaining measurements. To this end, the implementations are based on Ethereum, and we sent over 2,500 transactions to the Ethereum test network to obtain concrete data. This allows us to quantitatively study the characteristic differences between the four oracle patterns. In particular, we focus on time (latency) and cost.

The remainder of the paper is structured as follows. Section 2 introduces background literature and related work. The patterns are described and contrasted in Sect. 3. The use cases for the implementation are described in Sect. 4. On the basis of the implementation, we analyze the four patterns with respect to time and costs in Sect. 5.[1] Next, we discuss our results and threats to validity in Sect. 6. Finally, the paper concludes in Sect. 7.

2   Background and State of the Art

In a significant number of times, applications built on blockchain infrastructure require data from real world states and events [4,9]. Examples include financial data, weather-related information, random number generations or arbitrary data from off-chain devices and web services accessible via Application Programming Interfaces (APIs). Blockchain oracles provide a way to interact with the off-chain world [26]. Oracles can be implemented as software (interacting with online sources) or hardware (interacting with the physical world), human (interacting with individuals) or computation-based oracles (performing off-chain calculations), single-source (centralized) or consensus-based oracles (decentralized, using a multitude of sources) [4]. In this paper, we abstract from the way in which oracles are implemented and focus on the foundational patterns they realize. Next, we discuss the basic notions behind blockchains and elaborate on state-of-the-art solutions adopted thus far for the realization of oracles.

Blockchain. At the core of a blockchain lies the transaction, that is, the transfer of value between accounts. Transactions are temporally ordered and stored in a sequential structure named ledger. Every participating full node in the blockchain network keeps a local copy of the ledger. Updates in the network are communicated via blocks, each collating the transactions to be appended to the ledger. To generate and broadcast new blocks, the so-called mining nodes can be required to prove their trustworthiness, e.g., by solving computationally hard problems (Proof of Work). A consensus algorithm allows for the eventual consistency of the distributed ledger. Every block is linked to the previous one via hashing, thus forming a chain – hence the name, blockchain. Smart contracts turn blockchains such as Ethereum [23], Hyperledger Fabric [7] and Algorand [5] into programmable infrastructures. Developers can encode smart contracts with a programming language and compile them to bytecode. Upon deployment, smart contracts are associated with a unique address. They are executed and saved across all connected nodes of the network. The invocations have a computation price expressed in terms of gas. In order to store information, e.g., on the Ethereum blockchain, it can be placed into a transaction payload and possibly added to the contract storage, contract logs, or kept in the transaction

---

[1] The source code can be found at https://github.com/MacOS/blockchain-oracles-data-collection.

payload [24]. After the transaction is included into a block, the information is publicly accessible within the network.

Blockchain Oracles. A plethora of commercial and open-source tools have emerged that implement inbound oracles. *Orisi*[2] is a solution for a distributed set of inbound oracles for Bitcoin, which are executed by independent and trustworthy third parties. The majority of all oracles has to agree on the outcome from external data. To fulfill this purpose, money from senders and receivers is parked into a multiple-signature address, including their signatures as well as the signature address of the majority of the oracles result. In our framework, Orisi is categorized as a pull-based inbound oracle. *Oraclize*, recently rebranded as *Provable Things* (see Footnote 2) is a popular service for inbound oracles that works with multiple smart-contract-enabled blockchain platforms. The service acts like a trusted intermediary between blockchains and a variety of independent data sources. It also provides a mechanism to mitigate *corrupt* oracles [17]. Its Provable Engine executes a set of instructions to react as certain conditions are met, thus making it classifiable both as a push-based and a pull-based inbound oracle. Other services which are natively classifiable as pull-based follow. In the Ethereum-specific *TinyOracle* (see Footnote 2) an intermediary contract acts as a receiver for the actual contract and simultaneously emits an event to the subscribing RPC client. The *lookup* contract stores both query and respondent addresses, while the *sample client* contract calls the oracle service of TinyOracle. *Reality Keys* provides a combination of both automated and human-driven pull-based inbound oracles [17]. *ChainLink* (see Footnote 2) offers a general-purpose framework for building decentralized inbound oracles, providing decentralization on both oracle and data-source levels. A Chainlink node can have multiple external adapters for different data sources. *Witnet* [18] provides a decentralized oracle network protocol based on Ethereum. It also enables miners to earn tokens. An Ethereum bridge is implemented, providing Witnet nodes to run Ethereum nodes with the option to operate with Ether and make contract calls.

Blockchain inbound oracles have also been considered in a number of research works. Xu et al. [24] introduce the concept of *validation oracles*, namely trusted third-party operators (either automatic or human) that act as inbound oracles. The authors distinguish between *internal* ones, periodically transmitting external verified data to the blockchain, and *external* ones, operating as trusted external validators of transactions based on information that is external to the blockchain. According to our scheme, we see that the former is push-based and the latter is pull-based. Adler et al. [2] introduce a decentralized pull-based inbound oracle service. The implementation provides a voting game, which decides the truth or inaccuracy of propositions. Players can be *voters* or *certifiers*. While certifiers play a role in cases with the requirement for high accuracy, voters are utilized for low-risk/low-reward roles. Due to the random selections of propositions, a level of security is provided against manipulation. We remark

---

[2] Orisi: https://orisi.org/. Provable Things: https://provable.xyz. TinyOracle: https://github.com/axic/tinyoracle. ChainLink: https://chain.link/. All links accessed on June 7, 2020.

that the successful implementation of random generators is also part of the realization of oracles. Zhang et al. [27] present *Town Crier*, a push-based inbound oracle that acts like a data-feed system connecting a blockchain with a back-end that scrapes HTTPS websites.

We can observe that, thus far, the vast majority of the efforts has been devoted to the design and implementation of inbound oracles. Indeed, a recent technical report of ISO/TC 307 describes oracles for their sole task of providing off-chain information to the blockchain [14]. In this paper, however, we also investigate and specify the patterns behind the opposite information flow, namely that of outbound oracles, also known as *reverse* oracles [25].

3   Patterns

In this section, we describe in detail basic oracle patterns resulting from the partitioning of the direction (inbound/outbound) and initiation of data flow (pull/push) between on-chain and off-chain components. Figure 1 shows the data flow along the fundamental dimensions outlined above. When applying this partitioning, a basic distinction can be made between inbound oracles and outbound oracles, each of which can be further refined according to data pull and push strategies.

Before discussing each pattern in more detail, we first give a general overview of the patterns and their respective conceptual structural components (also called "pattern participant") in Fig. 2. The blockchain is considered to be part of a larger software system, with software components being located on and off-chain. In such an environment, it is often necessary to be able to communicate across system boundaries in both directions to exchange information. For example, components on the blockchain (such as smart contracts) may require knowledge from software components outside the blockchain, and vice versa. The outside world requires knowledge from the blockchain, too. Regarding the terminology used throughout this paper, note that the term "event" in relation to the blockchain refers to any activity that can take place on the blockchain (e.g., data is persisted, a transaction occurs, a block is added, etc.).

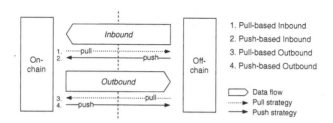

Fig. 1. Conceptual overview of the oracle data flow partitioning.

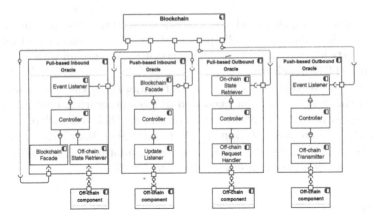

Fig. 2. An overview of the oracle types and conceptual structural components.

3.1 Inbound Oracle

An inbound oracle transmits information from the outside world to the blockchain. As a blockchain cannot directly acquire information from the outside world, it relies on the outside world pushing information into the network. Given this fact, the most obvious approach to obtaining external information on the blockchain is to alert the outside world about the need to push required information into the network. This approach is described in the *pull-based inbound oracle* pattern and is characterized by the fact that the exchange of information is initiated on-chain.

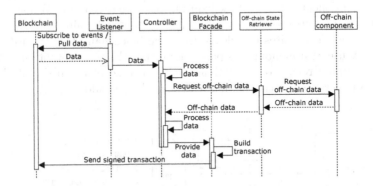

Fig. 3. Sequence diagram showing the component interactions for the *pull-based inbound oracle.*

PATTERN: Pull-based inbound oracle
Problem A blockchain application requires knowledge contained outside of the blockchain, but since blockchains are closed systems, applications cannot directly acquire information from the outside world. **Solution** A *pull-based inbound oracle* allows blockchain applications to request states from off-chain components. When a blockchain application requests an off-chain state, the *pull-based inbound oracle* receives this request, gathers the state from off-chain components, and sends the result back to the blockchain (via a transaction). **Benefits** State requests are initiated in the blockchain. Thus the whole process is transparent. It can be traced whether off-chain data was successfully provided (in time) or not. **Drawbacks** State requests have to be initiated from the blockchain, this induces a passive character. Further, the *pull-based inbound oracle* response time depends on the speed of the blockchain network, which may lead to a bottleneck. Network congestion may result in delayed or missed off-chain state retrieval, as the oracle only starts working after it registers requests from the blockchain.

The conceptual interaction of the pattern participants is shown in Fig. 3: An *Event Listener* subscribes to relevant events on the blockchain, which forwards event data to a *Controller*. The *Controller* gathers required data from an off-chain component via an *Off-chain State Retriever*. The gathered data may be further processed by the *Controller* before it is returned to the blockchain via a *Blockchain Facade*.

Another approach to transferring external knowledge to the blockchain is to monitor changes in the off-chain world that are relevant to the blockchain and to transfer these changes to the network. This approach is described by the *push-based inbound oracle* pattern and is characterized by the fact that the exchange of information is initiated off-chain.

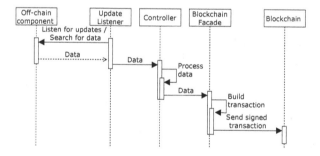

Fig. 4. Sequence diagram showing the component interactions for the *push-based inbound oracle.*

PATTERN: Push-based inbound oracle

Problem A blockchain application must be supplied with knowledge outside the blockchain, but since blockchains are closed systems, this knowledge cannot be directly communicated.

Solution A *push-based inbound oracle* allows off-chain information to be propagated to the blockchain by monitoring off-chain state changes and forwarding them to the blockchain.

Benefits Scattered or irregularly updated data outside the blockchain is proactively pushed to the blockchain application. Therefore, the application does not require capabilities to search and query off-chain data. In addition, data can be checked more easily by the *push-based inbound oracle*, considering the limited functionality of blockchain environments.

Drawbacks The *push-based inbound oracle* is not deployed or triggered on the blockchain, making data provision entirely dependent from (non-distributed) applications running off-chain. To manipulate blockchains with incorrect information, an adversary only needs to compromise the off-chain component(s) from which the oracle receives the data.

The *push-based inbound oracle*, as conceptually illustrated in Fig. 4, listens to relevant off-chain component updates via an *Update Listener* and forwards the data to the *Controller*. The *Controller* may process (e.g., filter, verify, etc.) the data before it is sent to the blockchain via a *Blockchain Facade*.

3.2 Outbound Oracle

An outbound oracle transmits information from the blockchain to the outside world. Due to its underlying properties, a blockchain can store state information in the form of transactions, but it cannot actively communicate that state to the off-chain world. In light of this, the most obvious path to obtaining data from the blockchain is to fetch it. This approach is described by the *pull-based outbound oracle* pattern and is characterized by the fact that the exchange of information is initiated off-chain.

PATTERN: Pull-based outbound oracle

Problem Knowledge contained on the blockchain is needed outside the blockchain, but since blockchains are closed systems, the outside world cannot directly request information.

Solution A *pull-based outbound oracle* allows blockchain data to be queried and filtered to make it available to the outside world. It can be called from (off-chain) components to pull (all) blockchain data and query relevant information.

Benefits The *pull-based outbound oracle* allows to decouple external status requests from the actual status retrieval. Thus, the pattern offers the possibility of uniformly accessing and querying relevant information on the blockchain.

Drawbacks Depending on the size of the blockchain and the knowledge of the location of the requested information, the provision of the data may take some time.

The *pull-based outbound oracle*, as conceptually outlined in Fig. 5, receives off-chain data requests via an *Off-chain Request Handler* and forwards the requests to the *Controller* to process the request before forwarding it to the *State Retriever*, which is responsible for retrieving data from the blockchain. The result is returned to the *Controller*, which may process the data before it is sent to the off-chain requester via the *Off-chain Request Handler*.

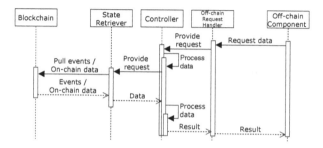

Fig. 5. Sequence diagram showing the component interactions for the *pull-based outbound oracle.*

Another approach to transferring internal information from the blockchain is to observe changes on the blockchain that are relevant to the outside world and to transfer these changes off-chain. This approach is described by the *push-based outbound oracle* and is characterized by the fact that the exchange of information is initiated on-chain.

PATTERN: Push-based outbound oracle

Problem Knowledge contained on the blockchain must be available outside the blockchain, but since blockchains are closed systems, applications cannot directly propagate information to the outside world.

Solution A *push-based outbound oracle* monitors the blockchain for relevant changes to subsequently trigger or perform activities outside the blockchain.

Benefits The *push-based outbound oracle* constantly monitors the blockchain. Thus, it is possible to (partially) automate blockchain related tasks by taking action when a blockchain state is updated.

Drawbacks The *push-based outbound oracle* is required to run continuously in order to monitor all events (on time) on the blockchain. In case the oracle unexpectedly stops, updates (depending on the implementation) may be missed. In addition, depending on the speed of the blockchain network, delays can occur, which can lead to unwanted delays in time-sensitive interactions.

The *push-based outbound oracle*, as shown in Fig. 6, subscribes to relevant events on the blockchain via an *Event Listener* and forwards event data to the *Controller*, which may process the data before it is sent via the *Off-chain Transmitter* to an off-chain component.

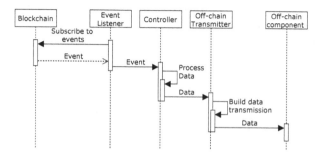

Fig. 6. Sequence diagram showing the component interactions for the *push-based outbound oracle.*

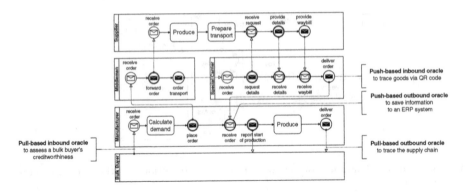

Fig. 7. A supply chain process (in BPMN, from [21]), showing where oracles are employed.

4   Use Cases

Among other successful use cases, the blockchain has been adopted as a backbone for the execution of multi-party business processes [8]. This section describes some use cases in that domain we considered to implement the oracle patterns.

Figure 7 illustrates a simplified model of a supply-chain process inspired by [21]. The initiator of the process is a bulk buyer who places an order. The order is then forwarded to a manufacturer. The manufacturer, in turn, calculates the needed material and delegates a middleman to forward the order to a supplier and to book the transportation by a special carrier. When materials are ready, the carrier takes care of the transport from the supplier site to the manufacturer's. Finally, the manufacturer produces the goods and delivers them to the bulk buyer.

The execution of the process is tightly bound at many stages to data flows from and toward the blockchain system. The transfer of information from the off-chain world to the on-chain environment and vice-versa is carried out by the oracles. We focus in particular on four oracles – one for each pattern. They are highlighted with textual comments in Fig. 7 and detailed next. Our implementations of those oracles are based on the Ethereum blockchain, *Web3* library and *Python*. Our additional modules for QR scans are based on *QR-Code-Scanner*.[3] The source code is available, see Footnote 1.

Figure 8 depicts the oracle-based interaction between a bulk buyer and the manufacturer. The bulk buyer places an order over a web application (1). The order is forwarded to the manufacturer if the creditworthiness of the buyer is verified. The order details including the order ID and information on the customer and bulk buyer are forwarded via a transaction to a smart contract (2). The smart contract publishes an event containing information on the bulk buyer

---

[3] Web3:   https://github.com/ethereum/web3.py.   Python: https://www.python.org/. QR-Code-Scanner: https://github.com/code-kotis/qr-code-scanner. All links accessed on June 7, 2020.

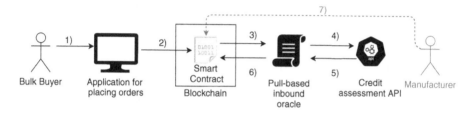

Fig. 8. Oracle-based creditworthiness verification of actors in the supply chain process of Fig. 7.

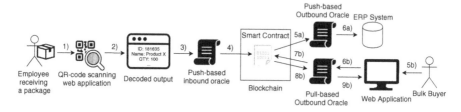

Fig. 9. Oracle-based tracing of goods via QR Code scanning in the supply chain process of Fig. 7.

such as name and Tax ID. The Event Listener of a *pull-based inbound oracle* subscribes to updates on such events. To retrieve information on the buyer's creditworthiness, the oracle calls the API of an external credit assessment service upon request via its Off-chain State Retriever (4). As the oracle processes the response (5) with the Controller, it returns this information as transaction data to the smart contract (6) with its Blockchain Facade. Finally, the manufacturer accesses the order after the verification (7).

Figure 9 illustrates a blockchain-based use-case for the tracing of goods in a supply chain via QR-code scanning. It involves three oracle patterns. The use case starts with an employee registering the delivery of a package. To certify the sending of the package, the employee uses a device with a QR-code scanning application (1). The information from the QR code includes the order ID, the name and the quantity of items (2). Thereafter, the *push-based inbound oracle* receives the data from the scan (3) via its Update Listener. The Controller of the oracle encodes the data into a blockchain transaction, enriching it with the location and current timestamp. Its Blockchain Facade transmits the data to a smart contract (4). The smart contract, in turn, publishes an event that is parsed by the Event Listener of a *push-based outbound oracle* (5a). The Controller of the latter decodes the event data and further passes it along to an ERP system via an Off-chain Transmitter (6a). The bulk buyer traces the production of the items identified by the order ID over the blockchain via a web application (5b). Upon request, the web application calls the Off-chain Request Handler of a *pull-based outbound oracle* (6b). The oracle Controller turns the request into a query for the On-chain State Retriever. As the requested information is found (8b), the application provides the entire data record on the product(s) back (9b). We implemented these use cases to serve as a basis of the analysis described next.

5 Analysis of Performance and Transaction Fees

This section describes our findings from a quantitative analysis on proof-of-concept implementations of the four oracles, based on the use cases presented above.

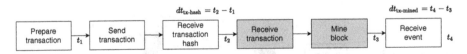

Fig. 10. Schematic process for measuring latency, with off-chain (white) and on-chain (grey) tasks.

Setup. We focus on the time and costs dimensions. Regarding time, specifically latency, we are interested in answering two questions. The first question is whether we observe differences in time among the different implemented patterns. This might indicate that dissecting oracles the way we propose in this paper is not only important from a software engineering perspective, but also with respect to the range of use cases they cater for. The second question is whether the observed timings are caused by our experimental settings. We perform all experiments on Ropsten, a test network for Ethereum. We choose Ropsten as it is accepted in the scientific literature for testing purposes [1,6,15]. The test code and the code used for the quantitative analysis are available, see Footnote 1. The smart contract *arrival.sol* mimics the use case from Fig. 9, which we use to evaluate the *push-based inbound oracle*, the *pull-based outbound oracle* and the *push-based outbound oracle*. It is deployed at address 0x1186aEDAb8f37C08CC00a887dBb119787cfE6AAf. The smart contract *customer.sol* mimics the use case from Fig. 8, which we use to evaluate the *pull-based inbound oracle*. It is deployed at address 0x9c2306eccc5afa6ee0c1eca6deab66cc336c3b3d.

To assess the costs of inbound oracles, we measure the consumed gas. Note that gas costs also captures the computational and storage effort. We convert Ether to Euros by using the mean exchange price for Ether over the evaluation period (144.86 €/Ether), and gas usage converts to Ether using the gas price of the transactions (on average 7.45×10^{-10} Ether/gas).

The outbound oracles read from the blockchain and we thus focus on the time dimension. Note that we keep the retrieval state of the *pull-based outbound oracle* constant to eliminate this as a varying factor. Furthermore, in the implementation of the *pull-based inbound oracle* we do not store any states in the receiving smart contract, because the transaction invokes the client smart

Table 2. Summary statistics of time and costs for oracle invocations (on the Ropsten Ethereum test-net).

	n	mean	std	min	$x_{0.25}$	$x_{0.50}$	$x_{0.75}$	max
Push-based inbound oracle	2437							
$dt_{\text{tx-hash}}$ [seconds]		0.53	0.08	0.46	0.49	0.50	0.54	2.14
Transaction cost [Gas]		44,827	1,265	36,739	45,139	45,235	45,259	45,319
Transaction cost [€]		4.96×10^{-3}	5.78×10^{-3}	2.96×10^{-11}	6.55×10^{-5}	6.53×10^{-3}	6.55×10^{-3}	1.37×10^{-1}
Push-based outbound oracle	438							
$dt_{\text{tx-mined}}$ [seconds]		16.20	15.95	0.53	5.41	10.71	21.44	129.95
Pull-based inbound oracle	126							
$dt_{\text{tx-hash}}$ [seconds]		0.52	0.05	0.46	0.48	0.50	0.52	0.78
Transaction cost [Gas]		22,770	0	22,770	22,770	22,770	22,770	22,770
Transaction cost [€]		8.91×10^{-5}	3.96×10^{-4}	7.91×10^{-7}	7.91×10^{-7}	7.91×10^{-7}	7.91×10^{-7}	1.85×10^{-3}
Pull-based outbound oracle	2611							
$dt_{\text{tx-hash}}$ [seconds]		0.13	0.03	0.11	0.11	0.12	0.12	0.45

contract directly and we exclude its handling of the data in the experiment. In contrast, the *push-based inbound oracle* stores the state and emits an event; this is necessary so that the client smart contract can retrieve the state.

To measure latency (see also Fig. 10) we capture the time between a transaction being sent to the blockchain node (t_1) and the time when we receive the transaction hash (t_2). We indicate the difference as $dt_{\text{tx-hash}}$. For the *push-based outbound oracle*, we measure the period between the timestamp of the block that included the transaction (i.e., the timestamp when the miner started mining that block, t_3), and the time in which we receive the event (t_4). We name the difference as $dt_{\text{tx-mined}}$. When clear from the context, we will refer to both measures as dt. It is debatable whether the mining time should be part of the latency measurement. Note that the time between the submission of a transaction and its inclusion/commitment on the ledger varies drastically between blockchain platforms. Additionally, various other factors need to be taken into account, such as network congestion and, for commit time on Proof-of-Work blockchains, the number of confirmation blocks which is a user-defined parameter – see e.g. [20] for details and measurements. Here, we measured simple inclusion time without additional confirmation blocks, as a placeholder and to highlight this underlying issue.

Results. Figure 11 and Table 2 show the results of our experiments. The *pull-based outbound oracle* is the fastest of the four oracles with a mean dt of 0.13 ± 0.03 s, while the *push-based outbound oracle* is the slowest with a mean dt of 16.20 ± 15.95 s. This difference stems from the fact that the *pull-based outbound oracle* reads historical states from the blockchain, whereas the *push-based outbound oracle* requires a transaction to be included – which is subject to high variance and an average delay of roughly 1.5 inter-block times [26]. This transaction triggers the event that is picked up by the *push-based outbound oracle*.

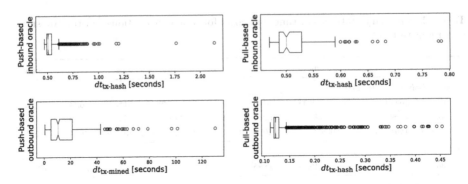

Fig. 11. Performance plots for the four oracle implementations.

We received 75% of the *pull-based outbound oracle* transactions within 0.12 s. For the *push-based outbound oracle*, instead, the third quartile amounts to 21.44 s. From the box plots in Fig. 11, we can observe that the dt measurements of the *pull-based outbound oracle* and the *push-based inbound oracle* have a significant number of outliers and follow a long-tail distribution. This is less pronounced for the other two oracles. Discounting outliers, the dt distribution for the *pull-based inbound oracle* is similar to *push-based inbound oracle*, with mean dts of 0.52 ± 0.05 and 0.53 ± 0.08, respectively, and the same minimum (0.46) and median (0.50) values. They differ slightly in their 25th (0.48 vs. 0.49) and 75th (0.52 vs 0.54) percentiles.

For *push-based inbound oracle* and *pull-based inbound oracle* we measured the transaction costs in Ether, and converted them to Euros with the above-mentioned exchange rate. The results are reported in Table 2. The gas price setting in our setup relied on the current market price – which turned out to be highly variable on Ropsten, and not representative of the Ethereum mainnet. To give an indication of the cost we would have incurred on the mainnet, we retrieved the approximate median gas price from the Google BigQuery public database of Ethereum for the period in question, which was 8.5 Gwei (averaged over 3.15 million transactions). If we multiply this with our mean gas consumption and the exchange rate, we get a median transaction cost of 0.028 € for *push-based inbound oracle* and 0.056 € for *pull-based inbound oracle*.

6   Discussion and Threats to Validity

In the following, we discuss advantages and disadvantages, our experience from the implementation process, the results analysis above, and finally the limitations and threats to validity of this work. An advantage of the foundational viewpoint taken in this paper is the clear separation and composition of concerns we can achieve. For example, our implementation, following the patterns in this paper, enables us to implement logic for distinct abstraction levels. As such, it is possible to implement behaviour for all oracles. More crucially, adding or changing information sources to the oracle only requires us to revise the sole oracle without the need to change the on-chain implementation logic.

Regarding the results of the analysis, we find that latency and cost are both not particularly high. For instance, when comparing the latency with results from [20], where the median commit time of transactions was around 200 s, it is fair to say that the sub-second latency measured in almost all cases (where no transaction inclusion time is part of the latency) is relatively low. This, however, may be different if other blockchain platforms or consensus algorithms are used.

As for cost, we found that a single interaction of either inbound oracle did not incur high fees. For the fairest possible comparison, gas consumption should be used as a metric as it does not depend on current market prices. Comparing the results on this basis, in [11] (a cost-optimized version of [21]) transactions have a typical gas consumption of 24,000 to 27,000 gas. This is in line with the *pull-based inbound oracle*'s gas consumption; for the *push-based inbound oracle*'s gas usage the additional storage cost accounts for the higher gas cost. Specific implementations of this pattern can be optimized in this regard, in particular by storing data on-chain only when necessary. This may be particularly important when many oracle invocations are expected in a given setting, and cost and time delays would add up.

The work we present in this paper has a number of limitations and threats to validity. The patterns are mined using a qualitative mining process (as it is usual). Thus, possible misinterpretations or biases of individual researchers or the whole author team cannot be fully excluded and might have influenced our results. Generalizability can only be claimed for the studied technologies (see Sect. 2), but we aimed to define foundational patterns to mitigate this threat as far as possible. Therefore, despite our implementation resorts on Ethereum, our findings are applicable to other blockhain platforms. Nevertheless, we do not claim any form of completeness. Our analyses are preliminary and can only provide a rough indication of time performance and costs; for claiming generalizability beyond the scope of the studied cases, more research would be needed. Furthermore, the use of a testnet like Ropsten may reduce the representativeness of the analysis results for practical applications. We mitigated these effects by not relying on time and cost measurements from the testnet in our discussion, and by basing relevant cost analyses on data from the Ethereum mainnet instead. In future work, we will also study different strategies on data structures and message rates to further mitigate the impact that information exchanges have on the overall execution costs.

7 Conclusion

In this paper, we have investigated how blockchain oracles can be characterized for the communication between the on-chain and off-chain realms. We abstract individual technical solutions adopted in existing implementations into four foundational oracle patterns. In addition, we have studied their relations, benefits, liabilities, and consequences. Finally, we have quantitatively analysed the four patterns in terms of time performance (latency) and cost impacts. We find that neither cost nor latency are particularly high for a single invocation of any of the patterns, except that latency can be dominated by transaction inclusion time. Also, in our experiments the patterns were in most cases subject to different distributions in terms of cost and latency; the results show these characteristic differences.

In future research, we will deepen our analysis with further studies conducted on multiple blockchain platforms, further study how exchanged data rate and quantity has an impact on execution costs, and apply the patterns to more use cases spanning over different fields including autonomous robotic swarm systems [19]. Furthermore, we want to study the use of patterns for information exchange between blockchains. The combination of oracle patterns would also be the subject of our future studies.

Acknowledgements. The authors want to thank the Research Institute for Computational Methods at WU Vienna for supplying computational resources. E. Castelló Ferrer acknowledges support from the Marie Skłodowska-Curie actions (EU project BROS–DLV-751615). The work of C. Di Ciccio was partly supported by MIUR under grant "Dipartimenti di eccellenza 2018-2022" of the Department of Computer Science at Sapienza University of Rome.

References

1. Abou El Houda, Z., Hafid, A., Khoukhi, L.: Co-IoT: a collaborative DDoS mitigation scheme in IoT environment based on blockchain using SDN. In: IEEE GLOBECOM, pp. 1–6 (2019)
2. Adler, J., Berryhill, R., Veneris, A.G., Poulos, Z., Veira, N., Kastania, A.: Astraea: a decentralized blockchain oracle. In: iThings/GreenCom/CPSCom/SmartData, pp. 1145–1152. IEEE (2018)
3. Ahmed, S., ten Broek, N.: Blockchain could boost food security. Nature **550**(7674), 43 (2017)
4. Beniiche, A.: A study of blockchain oracles. arXiv preprint arXiv:2004.07140 (2020)
5. Chen, J., Micali, S.: Algorand: a secure and efficient distributed ledger. Theor. Comput. Sci. **777**, 155–183 (2019)
6. Delgado-Mohatar, O., Sierra-Cámara, J.M., Anguiano, E.: Blockchain-based semi-autonomous ransomware. Futur. Gener. Comput. Syst. **112**, 589–603 (2020)
7. Dhillon, V., Metcalf, D., Hooper, M.: The hyperledger project. In: Dhillon, V., Metcalf, D., Hooper, M. (eds.) Blockchain Enabled Applications, pp. 139–149. Apress, Berkeley (2017). https://doi.org/10.1007/978-1-4842-3081-7_10
8. Di Ciccio, C., Cecconi, A., Dumas, M., García-Bañuelos, L., et al.: Blockchain support for collaborative business processes. Informatik Spektrum **42**, 182–190 (2019)
9. Di Ciccio, C., Meroni, G., Plebani, P.: Business process monitoring on blockchains: potentials and challenges. In: Nurcan, S., Reinhartz-Berger, I., Soffer, P., Zdravkovic, J. (eds.) BPMDS/EMMSAD -2020. LNBIP, vol. 387, pp. 36–51. Springer, Cham (2020). https://doi.org/10.1007/978-3-030-49418-6_3

10. Eberhardt, J., Tai, S.: On or off the blockchain? Insights on off-chaining computation and data. In: De Paoli, F., Schulte, S., Broch Johnsen, E. (eds.) ESOCC 2017. LNCS, vol. 10465, pp. 3–15. Springer, Cham (2017). https://doi.org/10.1007/978-3-319-67262-5_1
11. García-Bañuelos, L., Ponomarev, A., Dumas, M., Weber, I.: Optimized execution of business processes on blockchain. In: Carmona, J., Engels, G., Kumar, A. (eds.) BPM 2017. LNCS, vol. 10445, pp. 130–146. Springer, Cham (2017). https://doi.org/10.1007/978-3-319-65000-5_8
12. Glicksberg, B.S., et al.: Blockchain-authenticated sharing of genomic and clinical outcomes data of patients with cancer: a prospective cohort study. J. Med. Internet Res. **22**(3), e16810 (2020)
13. Heiss, J., Eberhardt, J., Tai, S.: From oracles to trustworthy data on-chaining systems. In: 2019 IEEE International Conference on Blockchain (2019)
14. ISO/TC 307: ISO/TR 2345 blockchain and distributed ledger technologies - overview of and interactions between smart contracts in blockchain and distributed ledger technology systems. Technical report, ISO (2019)
15. Krejci, S., Sigwart, M., Schulte, S.: Blockchain- and IPFS-based data distribution for the Internet of Things. In: Brogi, A., Zimmermann, W., Kritikos, K. (eds.) ESOCC 2020. LNCS, vol. 12054, pp. 177–191. Springer, Cham (2020). https://doi.org/10.1007/978-3-030-44769-4_14
16. Mendling, J., Weber, I., van der Aalst, W.M.P., et al.: Blockchains for business process management - challenges and opportunities. ACM Trans. Manag. Inf. Syst. **9**(1), 4:1–4:16 (2018)
17. Neidhardt, N., Köhler, C., Nüttgens, M.: Cloud service billing and service level agreement monitoring based on blockchain. In: EMISA. CEUR Workshop Proceedings, vol. 2097, pp. 65–69 (2018)
18. de Pedro Crespo, A.S., Levi, D., García, L.I.C.: Witnet: a decentralized oracle network protocol. CoRR abs/1711.09756 (2017)
19. Strobel, V., Castelló Ferrer, E., Dorigo, M.: Blockchain technology secures robot swarms: a comparison of consensus protocols and their resilience to byzantine robots. Front. Robot. AI **7**, 54 (2020)
20. Weber, I., Gramoli, V., Staples, M., Ponomarev, A., Holz, R., Tran, A., Rimba, P.: On availability for blockchain-based systems. In: IEEE International Symposium on Reliable Distributed Systems (SRDS) (2017)
21. Weber, I., Xu, X., Riveret, R., Governatori, G., Ponomarev, A., Mendling, J.: Untrusted business process monitoring and execution using blockchain. In: La Rosa, M., Loos, P., Pastor, O. (eds.) BPM 2016. LNCS, vol. 9850, pp. 329–347. Springer, Cham (2016). https://doi.org/10.1007/978-3-319-45348-4_19
22. Wong, D.R., Bhattacharya, S., Butte, A.J.: Prototype of running clinical trials in an untrustworthy environment using blockchain. Nat. Commun. **10**(1), 1–8 (2019)
23. Wood, G.: Ethereum: a secure decentralised generalised transaction ledger (2014)
24. Xu, X., et al.: The blockchain as a software connector. In: WICSA, pp. 182–191. IEEE Computer Society (2016)
25. Xu, X., Pautasso, C., Zhu, L., Lu, Q., Weber, I.: A pattern collection for blockchain-based applications. In: EuroPLoP, pp. 3:1–3:20. ACM (2018)
26. Xu, X., Weber, I., Staples, M.: Architecture for Blockchain Applications. Springer, Cham (2019). https://doi.org/10.1007/978-3-030-03035-3
27. Zhang, F., Cecchetti, E., Croman, K., Juels, A., Shi, E.: Town crier: an authenticated data feed for smart contracts. In: ACM Conference on Computer and Communications Security, pp. 270–282 (2016)

The Role of Modeling in Blockchain Process Design

Ruben Post, Stijn Kas, and Koen Smit[✉]

Faculty of ICT, HU University of Applied Sciences Utrecht, Utrecht, The Netherlands
{ruben.post,stijn.kas,koen.smit}@hu.nl

Abstract. Blockchain could introduce a new approach by which organizations view and govern their information and technology projects. Processes involving blockchain are oftentimes transaction-based, decentralized, and require coordinated communization before implementation. This approach may introduce new challenges to conventional modeling techniques. In this study, the role of modeling during the design phase of blockchain processes is explored. This role is described through a theory derived from 30 semi-structured interviews, two case studies, and two focus groups. The results are applied to inter-organizational business process modeling. The role of modeling, the effects on this role caused by the introduction of blockchain, and the shortcomings of current modeling techniques are described. Additionally, the study provides several opportunities for future research.

Keywords: Modeling · Blockchain · Process design

1 Introduction

Blockchain could introduce a new approach by which organizations view and govern their information and technology projects. This approach may introduce new challenges to contemporary modeling techniques. Processes involving blockchain are oftentimes transaction-based, decentralized, and require coordinated communization before implementing [1]. For instance, once a smart contract or consensus algorithm is written, deployed, and enforced its code is final and cannot be changed unless depicted otherwise in the governance [2]. Besides the technological solution, the inter-organizational setting, business processes, and policy & social environment are affected as well: blockchain introduces a transparent, consensus-based, and highly standardized environment where data and processes need to be unified and streamlined. This is in contrast to the current introvert information technology paradigm where most organizations reside in, as these differences force organizations to interact and communicate more with their competition/competing colleagues [3, 4].

Practice suggests that the design phase, with a particular focus on modeling, needs to be adjusted to facilitate the changes blockchain introduces to them [5]. For example, organizations might face unforeseen challenges when attempting to integrate processes incorporating blockchain (hereafter referred to as "blockchain processes") in their current process architecture due to a lack of interoperability or the inability to incorporate

A. Asatiani et al. (Eds.): BPM Blockchain and RPA Forum 2020, LNBIP 393, pp. 52–66, 2020.
https://doi.org/10.1007/978-3-030-58779-6_4

them in the current enterprise architecture, as its distributed nature might not be facilitated by contemporary architecture modeling techniques [6]. Besides this, blockchain processes could enable new ways in which organizations collaborate, communicate, and share information because it makes trust less impactful in ecosystems where it was previously lacking, like peer-to-peer money transfers [7]. This could introduce challenges usually not associated with process (re)design or challenges which organizations have not yet faced. For instance, if process control is handed over to participants outside of an organization, data accuracy cannot be validated, obligations cannot be enforced and it is harder to check if conditions are met [8]. Moreover, inter-organizational relationships, collaborations, and communication might be affected by a technological solution, altering the way they are perceived and governed [9, 10].

Current literature on the modeling of blockchain process also suggests a need to facilitate the changes blockchain introduces [5, 6, 11]. The design or engineering phase is often the most important aspect of process (re)design, as this phase requires extensive communication between partners, coordination between data, and process unification [1]. Research triggers found in literature and practice show the need for research regarding the role of modeling in blockchain processes. These research triggers led to the following research question: *"What is the role of modeling during blockchain process design?"*

The next section discusses the current state of the research field. After this, the methodology, together with the data collection and analysis, is described. Next, the results of the research are presented and elaborated. The last section presents the conclusions and discusses the utilized methodology and results of the research, followed by possible directions for future research.

2 Background and Related Work

The current knowledge domain of blockchain modeling is nascent, but not non-existent. Previous internal research included a literature analysis [12]. This research views the literature analysis as current and valid because it was conducted shortly before this study started. However, because the literature analysis encompassed a low amount of literature (five relevant contributions identified in total), they will be discussed separately, and relations or opposite views will be described.

The analysis showed that Porru and Michele [5] suggest that, when dealing with Blockchain-Oriented Software engineering (BOS), many challenges must be responded to. Among these challenges is the need for testing the software of blockchain applications, especially because there are multiple programming languages used during this development. Additionally, smart contracts should be created through software tools to streamline development in specialist languages (e.g. solidity, a language designed for writing smart contracts in Ethereum).

Developing further on the work of Porru and Michele [5], Rocha and Ducasse [11] attempt to create this specialist language to model BOS. Rocha and Ducasse [11] add that modeling is an important part of designing software, therefore developers may struggle to plan their BOS. They attempt to start the discussion on specialized blockchain modeling notations by applying three complementary modeling approaches to a BOS example. Rocha and Ducasse [11] conclude that every approach had its strengths and weaknesses, and that a specialized notation for BOS is needed to properly design it. These weaknesses were shown when attempting to cope with aspects specific to blockchain, e.g. decentralization and consensus.

Mendling [13] focusses less on the entirety of BOS, but rather on how Business Process Modeling and Notation (BPMN) can facilitate blockchain processes. Mendling [13] provides seven challenges for blockchain-based process support, two of which imply the role of modeling. The first challenge described the need for an understanding of how business processes can be best innovated using the potentials of blockchain. The second challenge describes new governance models with an overall impact on business strategy. The first challenge is further elaborated upon in Mendling et al. [6], where they reiterate the challenge of understanding how business processes can be best innovated using the potential of blockchain but adds that insights from operations management and organizational science could be informative. Mendling et al. [6] do not suggest the need for a specialized language for BOS, in contrast to Porru and Michele [5]. This suggestion is supported by García-Bañuelos, Ponomarev, Dumas, and Weber [14], who demonstrate a method to compile a BPMN process model into a Solidity smart contract without running into insurmountable obstacles.

3 Research Design

The data for this study is collected over a three-and-a-half-month period, between February 2019 and late-May 2019, through 30 semi-structured interviews, two case studies, and two focus groups. The semi-structured interviews, case studies, and part of the focus groups were used as data collection. For sampling, a combination of convenience sampling and snowballing was utilized.

3.1 Interviews

The first method of this study consists of 30 semi-structured interviews. The goal of the interviews was to let the participants expand on their perspective on modeling during their experience with blockchain processes design. This goal was warranted with a criterion: they should have previous experience with utilizing modeling techniques when conceptualizing blockchain processes. The number of interviews that were conducted is 30, which is adequate for qualitative research [15]. During the interviews, an interview protocol with three sections was used. Section one discussed the participants' background and current occupation. Section two discussed one or multiple blockchain projects the participant was involved with. Section three discussed the role of modeling during those cases. After each subsequent interview, the interview protocol was reviewed and adjusted. Changes made to the interview protocol were meant to improve the data derived from the subsequent interviews. It was not necessary for each participant to answer the same questions, as the goal of the interviews was to extract the participants perspective on modeling during their experience with blockchain process design. In total, 1655 min (27,5 h) of data has been recorded over 30 interviews, averaging 55 min per interview.

Starting from interview 11, the researchers consolidated the interviews and made preliminary conclusions to the research questions. These preliminary conclusions were validated at the end of all interviews following interview 11. After each time the preliminary conclusions were validated, they were reevaluated by the researchers. This helped validate the results and, in some cases, trigger subjects during the interview that were not yet discussed, increasing the richness of the information the participant could convey during the interview.

3.2 Case Studies

If a specific interview had more depth to it than could be covered during the interview, the researchers asked the participant to lend their project for case study analysis. Two criteria were established for a project to be considered for a case study: 1) the existence of documentation for both the processes and technical architecture of the application and 2) a working application. The first criterion allowed the researchers to review the documentation referenced and discussed during the interview. The second criterion meant the project had experience translating the documentation into a working application, completing the design phase, which ensured and grounded their experience of modeling in this phase.

In total, two case studies were conducted. The selection of projects was based on the group of individuals, organizations, information technology, or community that best represents the phenomenon studied [16]. During the case study process, a holistic multiple-case design was used, according to Yin's [17] Multiple-Case Study Procedure. A multiple case study design was chosen because the units of analysis were essentially unrelated and thus should not be combined into an embedded case study design [18]. The multiple-case study procedure consisted of three phases: 1) Define and Design, 2) Prepare, Collect, and Analyze, and 3) Analyze and Conclude. During phase one, the theory was developed, the cases selected, and the data collection protocol designed. The second phase consisted of the execution of the case studies themselves. The third phase consisted of the following actions: 1) drawing cross-case conclusions, 2) modifying theory, 3) developing policy implications, and 4) writing cross-case report. As described by Yin [17] and supported by Eilbert and Lafronze [19] and David [20], a Multiple-Case Study with two or more cases is much preferred to a single-case study by providing 1) analytical benefits and 2) the possibility of comparing contrasting situations, leading to further new insights leading to 3) theoretical replication and further generalizability.

3.3 Focus Groups

The results of the interviews and case studies were discussed and validated with two focus groups. Before a focus group was conducted, several aspects were addressed: 1) the goal of the focus group, 2) the selection of participants, 3) the number of participants, 4) the selection of the facilitator, 5) the information recording facilities, and 6) the protocol of the focus group [21].

For this study, the goal of the focus group series is to validate the conclusions of the interviews and case studies and go in-depth into the role of modeling techniques in blockchain processes. The selection of participants should be based on the group of individuals, organizations, information technology, or community that best represent the phenomenon studied [16]. In this study, organizations and individuals that deal with the use of modeling techniques during blockchain process design; examples being project managers or software engineers. The participants were selected based on the same criterion as the participants for the interviews. In total, two focus groups were held. The first focus group had four participants, the second five. Okoli and Pawlowski [22] and Glaser [23] state that the facilitator should be an expert on the topic and familiar with group meeting processes. The selected facilitator has conducted research on the topic before and has experience with interviewing participants on the topic. In addition to the facilitator, the second researcher was always present during the focus groups, thus participating as a 'back-up' facilitator that monitored whether each participant provided equal input, and if necessary, involved specific participants by asking for more in-depth elaboration on the subject. All focus group sessions were audio and video recorded. Each focus group session followed the same protocol, each starting with an introduction and explanation of the purpose and procedures of the session. After the introduction, ideas were generated, shared, discussed, and refined by the participants. This allowed the participants to respond to a statement that represented a specific preliminary conclusion effect. After every focus group session, the researchers analyzed and consolidated the results. Each focus group took about three and a half hours to complete.

4 Data Analysis

After the interviews were conducted, the main findings were summarized by the researchers. All interviews and focus groups were transcribed and analyzed in detail using the qualitative data analysis tool NVivo 12.0 [24]. As established in the introduction, blockchain modeling is a nascent research domain [12]. For nascent research domains, thematic content analysis coding for evidence of constructs is an appropriate method [25]. Thematic content analysis is a descriptive presentation of qualitative data. For thematic content analysis, grounded theory is often used [26]. However, grounded theory insists that theoretical sampling is part of the methodology [16]. Because the method used in this study does not comply with this rule, it will not be considered grounded theory. However, Strauss and Corbin [27] indicate that their guidance for qualitative data analysis can also be useful for research that does not leverage grounded theory. Because of this, Strauss and Corbin's [16] process of 1) open coding, 2) axial coding, and 3) selective coding is used, see Fig. 1, which helps structure the chain of reasoning during the data analysis.

The first cycle was open coding, involving the analysis of sentences and groups of sentences [16]. During the open coding process, the researchers tried to identify what Boyatzis (1998) refers to as "codable observations". Here, the researchers coded the data by identifying sentences in which the role of modeling was discussed. Open coding was followed by the second cycle, axial coding, in which the researchers identified how the participants viewed the role of modeling and why they had this perception [16]. The second cycle started with one interview that was coded separately by both researchers. The coding of this interview was compared and discussed to align the perspective the researchers had on the process. After comparing and discussing a separately coded

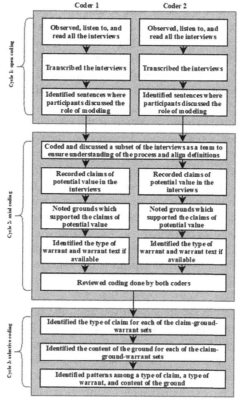

Fig. 1. Coding process

interview, the researchers coded three interviews together to ensure the understanding of the process. This improved reliability of the process [28]. After the process alignment, Toulmin's [29] framework was utilized to code the interviews, which consists of three elements: claim-ground-warrant.

When a participant discussed their perspective on the role of modeling during blockchain process design, it was coded as a claim. Each claim had a ground, in which the participant elaborated on the claim. Warrants were not explicitly coded, as they are not explicitly stated by the participant and, therefore, reflected the researcher's assumption. In the end, only one warrant was identified in the data: "Authority – Asserts the reliability or validity of a presumed expert source and their statements (i.e., grounds) expressed [30]." Whenever a participant expressed their opinion that was accompanied by a ground based on assumptions instead of experience, it was not coded as a claim of a warrant, as the researchers could not identify the warrant. After both researchers concluded the coding of their interviews, one interview was randomly picked and coded again to provide a "reality check" [28] for the researchers, making sure the process established at the beginning of this cycle was adhered to until the end of the process. After axial coding, the third cycle, selective coding [16], started. In this cycle, the type of claim and the content of the ground were coded. The types of claims were not pre-determined, but rather coded along the theme the researchers interpreted the claim to be part of. This process required inductive reasoning, which was applied to reason from empirical observations (interviews, case studies, and focus groups) to a theory.

After the interviews, the case studies were analyzed. This started with interviewing at least one of the organizations associated with the case, analyzing the documentation, and cross-referencing this documentation with the interview. The interview in which the case study is identified is also considered as the interview conducted in this case study, as the information about the case derived from the participant was considered saturated by the researchers. By analyzing primary and secondary data concerning the same case, inconsistencies in the data collection where identified. To reduce the chance of inconsistency, the participants were asked to elaborate on the secondary data during the interview. Based on this process, no inconsistencies were identified. The last data to be analyzed were the focus groups. The focus groups consisted of data collection and data validation. The data collection part was analyzed using the same method as the interviews. The data validation part was analyzed by both researchers listening to the reactions and discussion of the participants in the video recording and by analyzing the answers they submitted through Socrative; a tool that was utilized to structure the discussion and topics.

The process of how the results are derived from the data should be seen as an extension of the selective coding process and is based on Runeson and Höst's [18] process of deriving a chain of evidence. The first phase consisted of interpreting the results. It started with categorizing themes based on commonalities observed by the researchers. Because blockchain changes the function of trust, the categorization of the results of this paper should encompass inter-organizational aspects as well. Therefore, we apply the results to inter-organizational business process modeling [31] and discuss how it may affect modeling. The second phase consisted of interpreting relationships between the themes and deriving effects on the role of modeling during the design phase of blockchain processes caused by these relationships. These effects simultaneously formed the conclusions drawn from the data. Finally, the conclusions are translated into a theory and structured alongside the categories identified by the researchers.

5 Results

The results are structured along the two facets of inter-organisational business process modeling: the modeling facet and the process facet.

5.1 Inter-organizational Modeling

Two effects that the introduction of blockchain has on the activities and decisions made during inter-organizational modeling are identified: inter-organizational processes and architecture. **Inter-organizational processes** become more complex and inclusive. Because of the collaborative and inter-organizational nature of blockchain, more stake-holders are introduced that have to participate in an ecosystem. This makes the inter-organizational processes more complex because more stakeholders are involved, more communication channels exist between these stakeholders, more power is to be distributed because of on-chain governance aspects like voting power and different consensus mechanisms, and the network effect is more important because more stakeholders are involved. Besides more complex, they also become more inclusive because stakeholders that would normally not be considered for collaboration are now an integral part of the project. For example, one participant noted: *"Construction workers now have to use the same application as everyone else, meaning they have to be aware of how and why the application is used, up until a certain point. This is something they are not used to, as these applications usually only encompass a few big organizations."* Additionally, processes become compartmentalized, meaning the integral process consists of interchangeable components. This is supported by a, as one participant of the focus groups called it, "information architecture", in which stakeholders standardize definitions. The **inter-organizational architecture** is defined as the 'minimal compliant architecture' of the application. This refers to an application architecture that is compliant up to its weakest link, creating the "minimal compliant architecture". This means that the application architecture is compliant with both general legislation as well as organization-specific legislation, which might apply to external- and internal stakeholders of the ecosystem. During the focus groups, all participants agreed that this effect was magnified by the introduction of the General Data Protection Regulation (GDPR) legislation and had a significant impact on the architecture of blockchain processes. One participant noted: *"Some organizations very strictly adhere to the GDPR legislation, and if you want to collaborate with these organizations you have to adhere to their standard of data privacy."*

The modeling approach should start with stakeholder identification. Identifying these stakeholders is increasingly important when blockchain is introduced, as stakeholders in a blockchain application are often external stakeholders of each other. One participant noted: *"Blockchain is always with the outside, collaborating with multiple parties."* Which give baring to the statement that external stakeholders are what gives value to blockchain applications. Another participant noted: *"If you want to do something with blockchain, you have to do it with multiple [external] parties, otherwise you do not need a blockchain"*. This is in line with previously reviewed literature which noted that inter-organizational collaboration is key to leveraging blockchain [7]. After the stakeholders have been identified, the business model of the ecosystem is defined. One participant noted that conceptualizing the business model attracted the attention of different professions and expertise. The participant noted that: *"If you change a business model it has an impact on business operations. Chief Financial Officers (CFO's) are often one of the first people to join these meetings. They might not participate in the project, but they for sure are in the engineering."* Modeling is also used for communication and creating a common understanding among stakeholders. This communication is especially difficult when it concerns layman stakeholders, as one participant noted: *"Trying to place yourself in the shoes of a layman is the essence of a good model, I think. Only then can you convey complex models to different groups of people."* However, these models should not only be used to communicate towards layman stakeholders but to all stakeholders, as they convey essential information in a way that is understandable for all. Lastly, the information and minimal compliant architecture with regard to the stakeholders and the ecosystem is created. This entire modeling approach is outwards instead of inwards. Inwards modeling means stakeholders view themselves as the starting point of their perspective and differentiates between internal and external processes. With an outwards modeling perspective, the ecosystem is the starting point of the perspective and the processes modeled are those used by the entire ecosystem (usually crossing organizational borders).

The only shortcoming identified is the difficulty of communicating complex subjects to layman stakeholders. One participant noted: *"Self-explaining models would be a great step forward. Something that already works really well is modeling something as simple as possible, just the essence of what you are trying to say really. Also, visualization in a way that is visually attractive: a video or animation of sorts. But that could just as easily be someone who tells a story while being filmed: a man and a woman who are perceived as experts that explain what is going to happen in an easy and understandable manner."* It should be noted that this is not necessarily a shortcoming to the modeling of blockchain processes. However, blockchain does magnify this shortcoming because more layman stakeholders are involved in the design phase.

5.2 Organizational/Business Processes

Three effects that the introduction of blockchain has on the activities and decisions made in the organizational/business processes design are identified: process architecture, transactional focus, and evolving project roles. **Process architecture** concerns the need for information standards. Stakeholders need to provide data to the application in a standardized manner so that other stakeholders know how to interpret the data. This does not mean that they have to adjust their internal processes of collecting, storing, and using the data in accordance with that same standard. For example, a stakeholder might collect data using XML but when the stakeholders provide the data to Application Programming Interface (API) of the application, it gets stored in a JSON format. This way, all the data in the application is stored in a standardized manner, creating an open standard (a standard that is publicly available but has certain demands for usage). If layman stakeholders are not aware of this difference, it could be solved by letting them provide their data through, for example, a web portal. One participant noted: *"As soon as you cross organizational borders, communication will be a lot stiffer. But another thing that is very important is that if there is no standard for data communication, you add another dimension. Sometimes there is a standard which is open to a lot of interpretation. Sometimes, this causes you to define something a little different than [other stakeholders]. In that case, you need to have to harsh discussion to figure it out together. Right now, we often solve this inter-organizational problem by sending messages. If you place one application in the middle you will not be able to do that, then you all have to adhere to one standard."* In the focus groups, the participants noted that, although they agreed with this effect, this open standard is always subject to the governance of an application. For example, if a majority of the ecosystem wants to change something to the application, they could impose a different standard. **Transactional focus** refers to how the application functions. Blockchain applications are inherently made out of state changes instead of linear processes because they store transactions, not data. This means that an application doesn't necessarily follow a linear process (first activity a, then activity b, etc.) but consists of application states which are altered by transactions. This is done by stakeholders in the ecosystem sending transactions to one another. For example, a patient can go to doctor A to get their bloodwork done. Doctor A will provide the application with the results of this bloodwork, creating the first state. This first state consists of the patient's data and the bloodwork results. The patient can then go to doctor B, who diagnosis his bloodwork results and provides the application with the diagnosis, creating the second state. However, doctor B has to know how to interpret the bloodwork results of doctor A. This effect reiterates the need for an application-wide information standard.

Evolving project roles means that certain professions and expertise is used in different phases and/or have different activities. Because the need for projects to be privacy- and compliant by design, the data model has to be as well before going into production. For example, whether a data model contains personal data or not could impact the compliance of a model to legislation such as the GDPR [32]. To get a model privacy- and compliant by design, lawyers are often involved in the project from an early phase. Instead of lawyers saying what is not compliant, they help by figuring out how it can be changed to be compliant. One participant noted: *"At some point, people just learn that is it not ideal to involve legal afterwards. [GDPR] enhanced that need because we have to be more careful with personal data. Because this became more important legal got more tools and methods to control and observe where personal data is stored and where people can access this data."* Additionally, other project roles considered to have increased in importance in blockchain projects, as named by participants, include procurement, marketing, communication, and risk management.

During the design process, the function of an application is visualized or conceptualized. Standardized modeling techniques like BPMN and UML and other techniques like PowerPoint and wireframes are utilized. For example, PowerPoint can be used to digitize decision made in a meeting between stakeholders about what features the application must include. This PowerPoint document will then be translated into wireframes, visualizing how the interface of the application could look. After that, state diagrams (a behavioral diagram in UML [33] can be used to show transactions between stakeholders and BPMN 2.0 [34] can be used to make a visualization of the integral process in the ecosystem. Participants noted that they use modeling techniques in three degrees: 1) no adherence to standardized modeling techniques, 2) their interpretation of standardized modeling techniques allowing them to navigate aspects of blockchain process design they thought were not supported by the techniques, and 3) adhering completely to the standardized modeling technique. On the subject of not adhering to standardized techniques, one focus group participant noted: *"We do not use standardized modeling tools because they want to know things we are not even thinking about in these stages. They require too much detail to be used in this stage."* Another participant, when asked how they differentiated which data is stored on the blockchain and which is not, noted: *"With color, we denoted which data is stored in the blockchain and the changes of a transaction."* On the subject of adhering completely to the standardized modeling technique, one participant noted: *"Blockchain, in the end, is just a database that can alter process flows. You are no longer looking at your individual databases but at a shared database. I do not see how contemporary modeling techniques are not sufficient. We do not need a completely new modeling technique for this, current techniques really are sufficient."* One participant argued that even though contemporary modeling techniques are sufficient for blockchain process design, they could benefit from updates to their standards to better facilitate certain aspects of blockchain. Participants also experienced difficulty modeling which data is stored on the blockchain, facilitating their processes with a transactional-based application, how stakeholders reach consensus, and how the consensus was reached (or was not reached) by the application.

Four effects that the introduction of blockchain has on the technology solution are identified: blockchain type, on-chain governance, transactional focus, and psychical location. **1) Blockchain type** refers to the nature of a blockchain being public or private. If a blockchain is public, it means that everybody can join the ecosystem. In private blockchains, stakeholders have to be validated before they can join the ecosystem. In a public blockchain, transactions are only processed if consensus is reached by the miners. This means that once a blockchain or smart contract goes into production, it gets increasingly difficult to make changes to the application as more stakeholders join the ecosystem. This leads to projects wanting to be sure the application is correct before putting it in production, adhering to the first-time-right principle. This leads to a greater need for testing, which is in line with literature [5]. During development, the application has to be tested more thorough because once it is placed in production it is hard to correct mistakes. Because of this, the design phase gets more attention, making it a more structured project. In the focus group, one participant added that even though the project is more structured than other information system projects, the development can still be iterative. Before the focus groups, it was presumed that this effect was only applicable to public blockchains. However, the participants of the focus groups disagreed and noted that this would also apply to private blockchains because it depended on the governance structure. Even once an application is live in a public blockchain, it can still be altered through various governance mechanisms. **2) On-chain** governance enables incentivized applications and causes applications to be structured in a transactional manner. This affects the technical architecture of an application because it has to support state transitions and a form of cryptocurrency. **3) Transactional focus** means that processes get compartmentalized. this effect means that the technical architecture of the application needs to be based on state changes instead of a linear process. **4) Psychical location** of the data is also an important decision. Because of the privacy- and compliance by design principle, projects need to know where their data is stored because the psychical location of the data dictates to which legislation the project has to adhere.

The role of modeling also involves the technical descriptions of the applications. According to the focus groups, this is done more detailed than in other information system projects. One participant explained that because of the difficulty of changing features after the application has gone in production, they spend more attention on how they described the application. By spending more attention on the description, all stakeholders got a better idea of how the application will function once in production and could identify mistakes beforehand. This made the project more structured. The participants of the focus groups added that even though the project is more structured, the development was still done iteratively. The application was coded based on the functional specifications made while designing the business/organizational processes. Participants noted that programming a blockchain application is similar to other information systems and did not encounter any shortcomings while programming the application. On the subject of the progression of innovation in blockchain application programming, one person noted: *"When we started with blockchain there was no tooling to create the business network, it was manual labour and coding. Now we can just model it. You model which stakeholders are in your network, which assets they exchange, whether they go through some kind of lifecycle etc. You model transactions, and when you have modelled that (it takes a while as you have to really think about it) you just generate the network, all the API's, a dummy User Interface (UI), and you can continue."* This means that low-coding environments for blockchain applications might be available in the near-future, lowering the abstracting level of blockchain development, making modeling a more important aspect of blockchain process projects.

One participant noted an interesting approach to modeling smart contracts during the interview: *"If there is a mistake in the hardware, for example in the chips, you have to throw away all those chips. It is the same in the blockchain. If we upload twenty faulty smart contracts and put them in circulation you cannot just have a small vote and get them off the blockchain because they are online and just continue operating."* The participant continued by detailing how a smart contract is developed, from a policy written on paper to coding specification. The participant started in a room filled with lawyers who had to translate these policies to logic which can be modelled. They used the Decision Model and Notation (DMN) for this [35]. After the policies had been translated into DMN, they translated the DMN models into First Order Logic (FOL) (the symbolization of reasoning in which each sentence, or statement, is broken down into a subject and a predicate [36]), which would then be coded into a smart contract. By using DMN and FOL, the smart contract was logically sound, reducing the threat of a smart contract being hacked once it was put in production. This does not mean that the smart contract is un-hackable because a smart contract consists of both logic and code. The code could still be hacked.

6 Conclusion and Discussion

In this paper, we aimed to find an answer to the following research question: "What is the role of modeling during blockchain process design?" To answer this question, 30 semi-structured interviews, two case studies, and two focus groups were conducted in a study that, to the knowledge of the authors, has not been conducted before in this research domain. The role of modeling stays consistent with the definition of having at least four purposes: 1) supporting communication between developers and users, 2) helping analysts understand a domain, 3) providing input for the design process, and 4) documenting for future reference [37, 38]. However, the data identified 11 effects blockchain has on the role of modeling. The 11 effects identified should be taken into account when conceptualizing blockchain processes. From a theoretical perspective, our results are mapped to aspects of inter-organizational business process modeling [31]. The gained insights provide knowledge to better understand the role of modeling during blockchain process design. From a practical perspective, this research provides insight into how blockchain affects the role of modeling. This insight should be used as foresight into the role of modeling when initiating a blockchain project. Additionally, organizations who concerns themselves with blockchain should learn from the insights presented and start developing best practices, concepts, and methods as this could guide them to better facilitate the effects the introduction of blockchain has.

This research has several limitations. Considering our sampling and sample size, all research participants in the sample had a Dutch nationality, and most of them (apart from one) worked at Dutch organizations. This might make the sample less generalizable to projects at foreign organizations and countries. Additionally, most participants only had experience in relatively small projects, therefore limiting the insights of these participants to smaller projects. Future research should focus on generalizing towards international organizations. Especially because of the inter-organizational nature of blockchain processes. This same argument also holds as a basis for future research into implementation challenges experienced in other countries. Such research could identify research patterns which can form best practices, concepts, or methods to model blockchain processes. With regards to the sample size, while 30 interview participants, two case studies, and two focus groups is a sufficient sample to conduct explorative research on the role of modeling during blockchain process design, future research should also focus on including more participants, preferably in conjunction with the aforementioned future research directions.

References

1. Post, R., Smit, K., Zoet, M.: Identifying factors affecting blockchain technology diffusion. In: Twenty-Fourth American Conference on Information System, pp. 1–10 (2018)
2. Peters, G.W., Panayi, E.: Understanding modern banking ledgers through blockchain technologies: future of transaction processing and smart contracts on the internet of money. In: Tasca, P., Aste, T., Pelizzon, L., Perony, N. (eds.) Banking Beyond Banks and Money. NEW, pp. 239–278. Springer, Cham (2016). https://doi.org/10.1007/978-3-319-42448-4_13
3. Jones, G.R., George, J.M.: The experience and evolution of trust: implications for cooperation and teamwork. Acad. Manag. J. **23**(3), 531–546 (1998)
4. Pardo, T.A., Cresswell, A.M., Dawes, S.S., Burke, G.B.: Modeling the social-technical processes of interorganizational information integration, p. 8 (2004)
5. Porru, S., Marchesi, M.: Blockchain-oriented software engineering: challenges and new directions, pp. 169–171. IEEE (2017)
6. Mendling, J., et al.: Blockchains for business process management - challenges and opportunities. ACM Trans. Manage. Inf. Syst. (TMIS) **9**, 1–16 (2017)
7. Beck, R., Müller-Bloch, C.: Blockchain as radical innovation: a framework for engaging with distributed ledgers as incumbent organization (2017)
8. Nakamura, H., Miyamoto, K., Kudo, M.: Inter-organizational business processes managed by blockchain. In: Hacid, H., Cellary, W., Wang, H., Paik, H.-Y., Zhou, R. (eds.) WISE 2018. LNCS, vol. 11233, pp. 3–17. Springer, Cham (2018). https://doi.org/10.1007/978-3-030-029 22-7_1
9. Gil-Garcia, J.R., Schneider, C.A., Pardo, T.A., Cresswell, A.M.: Interorganizational information integration in the criminal justice enterprise: preliminary lessons from state and county initiatives, vol. 00, no. 2002, pp. 118c–118c (2005)
10. Pardo, T.A., Tayi, G.K.: Interorganizational information integration: a key enabler for digital government. Gov. Inf. Q. **24**(4), 691–715 (2007)

11. Rocha, H., Ducasse, S.: Preliminary steps towards modeling blockchain oriented software, pp. 52–57 (2018)
12. Toppenberg, S.: Blockchain modellering in een ecosysteem (2019)
13. Mendling, J.: Towards blockchain support for business processes. In: Shishkov, B. (ed.) BMSD 2018. LNBIP, vol. 319, pp. 243–248. Springer, Cham (2018). https://doi.org/10.1007/978-3-319-94214-8_15
14. García-Bañuelos, L., Ponomarev, A., Dumas, M., Weber, I.: Optimized execution of business processes on blockchain. In: Carmona, J., Engels, G., Kumar, A. (eds.) BPM 2017. LNCS, vol. 10445, pp. 130–146. Springer, Cham (2017). https://doi.org/10.1007/978-3-319-65000-5_8
15. Baker, S.E., Edwards, R.: How many interviews are enough? Expert voices and early career reflections on sampling and cases in qualitative research. In: National Centre for Research Methods Review Paper (2012)
16. Strauss, A., Corbin, J.: Basics of Qualitative Research: Grounded Theory Procedures and Techniques. Sage Publications Inc, Thousand Oaks (1990)
17. Yin, R.: Case study research - design and methods. In: Applied Social Research Methods Series (1983)
18. Runeson, P., Höst, M.: Guidelines for conducting and reporting case study research in software engineering. Empir. Softw. Eng. **14**(2), 131–164 (2009). https://doi.org/10.1007/s10664-008-9102-8
19. Eilbert, K.W., Lafronza, V.: Working together for community health—a model and case studies. Eval. Program Plann. **28**(2), 185–199 (2005)
20. David, H.: Five gifted boys in one classroom: a case-study. Gift. Educ. Int. **20**(2), 229–245 (2005)
21. Morgan, D.L.: Focus groups as qualitative research. Mod. Lang. J. **82**(4), 594 (1997)
22. Okoli, C., Pawlowski, S.D.: The Delphi method as a research tool: an example, design considerations and applications. Inf. Manag. **42**, 15–29 (2004)
23. Glaser, B.: Theoretical Sensitivity: Advances in the Methodology of Grounded Theory. Sociology Press, Mill Valley (1978)
24. QSR International, NVivo 2019. https://www.qsrinternational.com/nvivo/nvivo-products. Accessed 23 May 2019
25. Edmondson, A.C., Mcmanus, S.E.: Methodological fit in management field research. Acad. Manag. Rev. **32**(4), 1246–1264 (2007)
26. Boyatzis, R.: Thematic Analysis and Code Development: Transforming Qualitative Information. Sage Publication, Thousand Oaks (1998)
27. Corbin, J., Strauss, A.: Basics of Qualitative Research: Techniques and Procedures for Developing Grounded Theory, 3rd edn. Sage Publication, Thousand Oaks (2008)
28. Saldaña, J.: The Coding Manual For Qualitative Researchers. Sage, Thousand Oaks (2015)
29. Toulmin, S.E.: The Uses of Argument. Cambridge University, Cambridge (2003). (Updated edition)
30. Brockriede, W., Ehninger, D.: Toulmin on argument: an interpretation and application. Q. J. Speech **46**(1), 44–53 (1960)
31. Bouchbout, K., Alimazighi, Z.: Inter-organizational business processes modelling framework. In: CEUR Workshop Proceedings, vol. 789, pp. 45–54 (2011)
32. European Union, Regulation 2016/679 (GDPR). Off. J. Eur. Commun. **2014**, 1–88 (2016)
33. Object Management Group (OMG), Unified Modeling Language (UML), Version 2.5.1., 2017. https://www.omg.org/spec/UML/2.5.1/PDF. Accessed: 10 May 2019
34. Object management group (OMG), business process model and notation (BPMN) specifications version 2.0, January 2011
35. Object management group, decision model and notation (DMN), version 1.1 (2016)
36. Smullyan, R.R.: First-Order Logic, vol. 43. Springer, Dordrecht (2012). https://doi.org/10.1007/978-1-4020-8265-8

37. Wand, Y., Weber, R.: Research commentary: information systems and conceptual modeling a research agenda. Inf. Syst. Res. **13**(4), 363 (2002)
38. Kung, C.H., Sølvberg, A.: Activity modeling and behavior modeling (1986)

External Data Monitoring Using Oracles in Blockchain-Based Process Execution

Jan Ladleif[1(✉)], Ingo Weber[2], and Mathias Weske[1]

[1] Hasso Plattner Institute, University of Potsdam, Potsdam, Germany
`{jan.ladleif,mathias.weske}@hpi.de`
[2] Chair of Software and Business Engineering, Technische Universitaet Berlin,
Berlin, Germany
`ingo.weber@tu-berlin.de`

Abstract. In blockchain-based process execution, operational aspects of business processes are encoded in smart contracts on blockchains, enabling powerful auditing and compliance capabilities due to the platforms' trust and integrity guarantees. However, smart contracts are subject to the blockchain's conceptual limitations, which particularly restrict the real-time integration of external data. This potentially leads to non-compliant runtime behavior of process instances when data updates are missed and conditional constraints are wrongly evaluated. In this paper, we analyze the semantics of established external data interaction patterns in business processes with regards to their support on blockchain platforms. We extend and propose various oracle-based implementation strategies to alleviate conceptual issues independent of the concrete blockchain used, and discuss their properties and merits.

Keywords: Smart contracts · Data monitoring · Oracle architectures

1 Introduction

Business processes and choreographies produce and maintain diverse sets of data [13]. Account balances, customer details, or invoices are only some examples of data influencing the flow of individual process instances, which often need to react to changes in data immediately to stay compliant and competitive in today's interconnected business environments. In Business Process Management (BPM), it is the responsibility of the process engine to make sure of that—irrespective of whether the data is local to a process instance, part of the process environment at an organization, or managed externally by third parties [13].

Especially monitoring data hosted at third-party entities poses challenges, which has been particularly evident in recent moves towards blockchain-based process execution [10,14]. Here, process specifications containing data descriptors and conditions are transformed into one or more smart contracts encoding the process logic. While smart contracts readily store and engage with internal data, continuous monitoring of external data is restricted by the idiosyncratic properties of common blockchain technologies: Smart contracts operate

A. Asatiani et al. (Eds.): BPM Blockchain and RPA Forum 2020, LNBIP 393, pp. 67–81, 2020.
https://doi.org/10.1007/978-3-030-58779-6_5

in a closed-world environment without access to external services for integrity reasons [17]; and they are inherently passive, being exclusively driven via synchronously executed transactions [5].

Current state-of-the-art frameworks like Caterpillar [9] and Lorikeet [7] principally follow this philosophy and regard the blockchain as the single source of truth, as a consequence lacking continuous external data monitoring capabilities. They also largely omit the capabilities of oracle patterns, which somewhat mitigate the closed-world assumption [16], but raise questions as to the trustworthiness of the provided data [3]. This restricts the range of supported processes, and remains an impediment to the wide-spread acceptance of blockchain-based process execution approaches in practice.

In this paper, we pave the way towards external data monitoring in processes within the confines of current blockchain environments. Our contribution is twofold: First, we formally describe the semantics of general monitoring patterns, and transfer them to the transaction-driven blockchain environment. Second, we give structured insights into the challenges faced when using existing oracle approaches to implement compliant behavior—in particular avoiding that crucial data updates may be missed, and resolving temporal conflicts in deferred choice scenarios. We suggest various novel strategies and architectures to this end.

The paper is structured as follows. First, preliminary knowledge is conveyed in Sect. 2. We then formally introduce the semantics of data monitoring patterns in business processes in Sect. 3. Oracle-based implementations and novel solutions to certain runtime issues are developed in Sect. 4. Our results are evaluated in Sect. 5, and compared to related work in Sect. 6. The paper closes with a discussion in Sect. 7 and a conclusion in Sect. 8.

2   Preliminaries

In this section, we establish basic notions of data interaction patterns in business processes with a focus on external data monitoring. We then describe core concepts of blockchain technology and blockchain-based process execution.

2.1   Data Interaction Patterns

In their seminal work, Russell et al. describe patterns of data visibility and interaction in business processes [13]. They arrive at an eight-level hierarchy of data, starting at task data accessible by single tasks, up to environment data including services and databases outside the process engine's control. In the context of the latter *external* environment data, Russell et al. stress the importance of mechanisms which provide "new items of data as they become available" [13] from outside sources—that is, to continuously monitor the data.

The process shown in Fig. 1 describes the ticketing system of a railway company, which we will use as a running example throughout the paper, modeled using a Business Process Model and Notation (BPMN) collaboration diagram [11]. It contains many references to internal data such as the "request" data

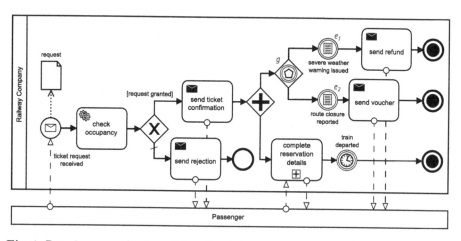

Fig. 1. Running example of a collaboration between a passenger and a railway company during a simple ticketing scenario

object. There are various instances of discrete external data interaction as well. The message flows between the passenger and the railway company, for example, constitute mutual external data exchanges transferring information like the ticket request and reservation details.

The conditional events e_1 and e_2 after the event-based gateway g go a step further and wait for some condition to become true, in this case exceptional circumstances like a severe weather warning or a route closure which result in the train's cancellation. Ensuring these events are captured in the right order requires continuous monitoring of the external services involved [11, Ch. 10.5]. The exact "specification of mechanisms to access such [environment] states" [11, p. 240] is not discussed in the BPMN standard and deliberately left as an implementation detail for concrete process engines. Smart contracts on blockchain platforms, for example, may use oracles for that purpose.

2.2 Blockchain Technology and Oracles

Blockchain technology has moved on from being a purely financial instrument and has emerged as a core application platform [17]. Applications benefit from cryptographic algorithms, consensus protocols, and incentivization schemes resulting in strong integrity, transparency, and immutability guarantees [14]. To this end, executable application code and its associated state—generally called a *smart contract*—are stored directly on the blockchain.

Smart contracts are not constantly running, but exclusively triggered using *transactions*. Code executed in the scope of a transaction is subject to a strict closed-world assumption, i.e., data external to the blockchain which could be tampered with or disappear can not be accessed. Rather, the blockchain needs to be entirely self-contained for later validation. This has severe implications for blockchain-based process execution, in which participants drive the process via transactions to ensure run time compliance and after-the-fact auditing.

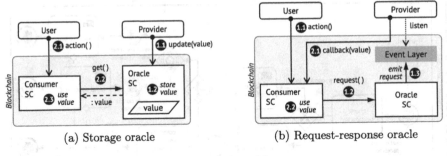

(a) Storage oracle   (b) Request-response oracle

Fig. 2. Basic oracle architectures

Common patterns to bypass the closed-world assumption are *oracles*, which are operated by third-party providers and supply external data to the blockchain [15,16]. While there are various architectures [1], two general principles illustrated in Fig. 2 are usually followed depending on whether data is permanently stored on the blockchain or delivered to it on request.

The former, which we will call *storage oracles* (see Fig. 2a), regularly update data inside a publicly known smart contract (1.1, 1.2). The value of this data can then be read by other smart contracts (2.1–2.3). For example, OrFeed[1] provides current cryptocurrency exchange rates on Ethereum using this mechanism. *Request-response oracles* (see Fig. 2b), on the other hand, operate smart contracts which can be called with specific requests, for example queries to a web service (1.1, 1.2). These requests are emitted using an event layer, which the provider actively listens to (1.3). The query is performed off-chain, and the provider calls back the original contract with the result of the query (2.1, 2.2). Provable[2] is a prominent real-world example of such a general-purpose oracle service.

3   External Data Monitoring Semantics

When processes reach states in which they wait for some external events and conditions, relevant data sources need to be monitored. In this section we formally describe the semantics of such patterns, which we will call *monitoring points*, and discuss their support in a transaction-driven setting like the blockchain.

3.1   Core Semantics of Monitoring Points

In the pattern literature (see Sect. 2), Russell et al. describe variants of *external data interaction* to transfer data between the environment and the process engine [13], e.g., off-chain data to on-chain smart contracts. For example, the conditional events e_1 and e_2 in the ticketing process in Fig. 1 require data from

---

[1] https://orfeed.org/docs/, accessed 2020-05-25.
[2] https://provable.xyz/, accessed 2020-05-25.

outside the process engine, or blockchain for that matter. In different languages and even BPMN itself, there are various other elements used to express such constraints. To argue more generally, we will refer to instances of this behavior as *monitoring points* (for external data) in the following:

Definition 1 (monitoring points). *Let M be the set of monitoring points and $S = \{\mathsf{ACTIVE}, \mathsf{TRIGGERED}, \mathsf{ABORTED}\}$ be the set of monitoring lifecycle states. The function $\mathsf{state} : M \to S$ maps each monitoring point to a lifecycle state.*

In our running example in Fig. 1 two monitoring points occur once the process reaches the event-based gateway g; one for monitoring the weather warning service (e_1), and one for monitoring the route closure service (e_2). For simplicity, we label the monitoring points with the event labels, i.e., $e_1, e_2 \in M$ and $\mathsf{state}(e_1) = \mathsf{state}(e_2) = \mathsf{ACTIVE}$ after reaching g. In the following, we will refer to these examples frequently.

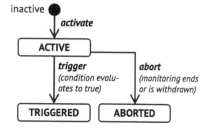

Fig. 3. Monitoring point lifecycle

Figure 3 shows the possible transitions between lifecycle states. Once they are ACTIVE, monitoring points can either be *triggered* once their associated condition evaluates to true, or they are eventually *aborted*. An abort may occur if the monitoring ends without the condition arising, e.g., when the process is stopped, or a different monitoring point is triggered first [11]. The latter may happen in *deferred choice* scenarios, in which process decisions are "based on environmental input" and create a "race between different branches" [12]. We will refer to such competitors as siblings:

Definition 2 (siblings). *Let $\mathsf{siblings} : M \to 2^M$ be a function mapping each monitoring point to its set of siblings, i.e., monitoring points within the same deferred choice pattern.*

The monitoring points e_1 and e_2, for example, are mutual siblings since they follow an event-based gateway g, that is, $e_1 \in \mathsf{siblings}(e_2)$ and vice-versa.

3.2 Extension to Transaction-Driven Environments

The core semantics of monitoring points assume permanent tracking to trigger them promptly once the associated condition evaluates to true. This, however, does not align with transaction-driven semantics, where lifecycle transitions must be explicitly invoked as part of synchronously executed transactions [5].

Consider the timeline in Fig. 4, which shows a sample scenario of the ticketing system (see Fig. 1) with real-world off-chain data indicated along the time line at the top. Assuming they were activated at some earlier time, both e_1 and e_2 are expected to reach a final state when the severe weather warning is issued, triggering e_1 and thus aborting e_2.

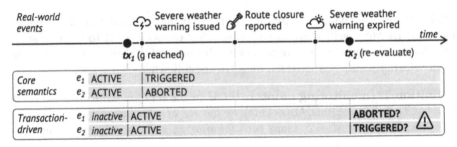

Fig. 4. Timeline of transactions invoking a process smart contract alongside real-world external data on the example of the ticketing process

For the transaction-driven setting, assume tx_1 and tx_2 invoke possible lifecycle transitions and convey the current state of external data. When the gateway is reached in tx_1, none of the events trigger and they remain in ACTIVE until tx_2 initiates a re-evaluation. This leads to a *temporal conflict*: At this point, not only has the severe weather warning expired, but an additional route closure was reported. Taking an isolated data snapshot at the point of time of tx_2 being issued wrongly implies that e_2 should be triggered instead of e_1.

This example shows that it is necessary to not only check a condition at the atomic point in time when a transaction is executed, but take into account the whole timeline since monitoring started, i.e., a monitoring point was activated:

Definition 3 (activation time). *Let $\mathbb{T}$ be a totally ordered time domain containing timestamps. For each monitoring point $m \in M$, let $t_m \in \mathbb{T}$ be the timestamp at which monitoring started.*

For the sake of simplicity, we assume monitoring starts when the lifecycle state ACTIVE is reached. Further, we define a timed evaluation function that is aware of historical states of data:

Definition 4 (timed evaluation). *For a monitoring point $m \in M$, we define the timed evaluation function* evaluate $: M \times \mathbb{T} \to \mathbb{T} \cup \{\top\}$ *with*

$$evaluate(m,t) := \begin{cases} min(t') & for\ t \leq t' \in \mathbb{T}\ and\ m\ evaluated\ to\ true\ at\ t' \\ \top & if\ no\ such\ t'\ exists \end{cases}$$

that returns the earliest timestamp after t at which the condition associated to m evaluated to true, or $\top$ with $t'' < \top \forall t'' \in \mathbb{T}$ if that has never been the case.

Intuitively, $\top$ can be interpreted as a fixed point arbitrarily far in the future and always larger than other timestamps, i.e., the "greatest element".

We now suggest the algorithm in Listing 1 to transfer the core monitoring semantics into the transaction-driven setting under the assumption that a timed evaluation function is available. The algorithm models a function **step** that advances the lifecycle state of a monitoring point $m \in M$, if possible. We focus on lifecycle transitions and omit implementation specifics like token propagation. This function is called in transactions on all relevant monitoring points.

The algorithm first determines whether the monitoring point is in state ACTIVE (line 1), since all other states are terminal, after which the associated condition is evaluated (line 2). Regardless of the result, the algorithm checks if any of the siblings evaluated to true earlier (lines 3, 4), "winning" the deferred choice, in which case the state changes to ABORTED (line 5). If that is not the case and m evaluated to true (line 6), the state is set to TRIGGERED (line 7).

Listing 1. Pseudocode algorithm for lifecycle state updates in transaction-driven settings

FUNCTION **step**$(m \in M)$
1   IF **state**$(m) = $ ACTIVE THEN :
2   LET $result \leftarrow$ **evaluate**(m, t_m)
3   IF $\exists m' \in$ **siblings**(m) such that
4   **evaluate**$(m', t_{m'}) < result$ THEN :
5   **state**$(m) \leftarrow$ ABORTED
6   ELSE IF $result \neq \top$ THEN :
7   **state**$(m) \leftarrow$ TRIGGERED

Consider the example timeline in Fig. 4 again. If the algorithm was applied to the "route closure reported" monitoring point e_2 in tx_2, it would detect that $e_1 \in$ siblings(e_2) evaluated to true *earlier* when a severe weather warning was issued, and would thus set the state of e_2 to ABORTED. Independently, calling step on e_1 would correctly trigger it. It is important to note here that the algorithm does not require a certain invocation order—lifecycle transitions are correctly performed even if calls are delayed or switched.

4   Monitoring Strategies and Architectures Using Oracles

The semantics of monitoring points in transaction-driven environments such as blockchains work under the assumption that a notion of timed evaluation is available, that is, data can be queried over time. In this section, we discuss implementation aspects and develop strategies and architectures to this end.

4.1   Sampling Strategies for Basic Oracles

Basic oracle architectures, specifically history and request-response oracles as described in Sect. 2, provide discrete access to external data. Consumer smart contracts call them within a transaction and receive external data valid at that specific point in time, which already hints at a core issue: There is no way to query historical data and resolve temporal conflicts, the same fundamental problem present in the abstract case in Fig. 4. Thus, they may potentially miss data updates and can not be used to implement fully compliant semantics.

However, basic oracle architectures are available in practice [1], and in the following we propose several strategies to cope with their limitations and approximate the intended semantics using them. Arguably the probability of missing updates can be reduced by increasing the sampling frequency and lowering the amount of time that passes between subsequent oracle calls. For example, weather warnings are often only updated a few times within an hour, so any such frequency would be sufficient. The general goal is to perform the sampling in a way which limits implementation and transaction overhead.

To this end, we introduce three sampling strategies (see Fig. 5) which use different sets of transactions to sample an oracle and evaluate a monitoring point. First, some transactions are part of the immediate *context* of a monitoring point. This includes all transactions which activate it, e.g., because it was reached as a part of the process execution. In the ticketing system (see Fig. 1), this could be the case for e_1 and e_2 with the transaction targeting "send ticket confirmation". Additionally, the context also includes those transactions specifically but manually issued by some

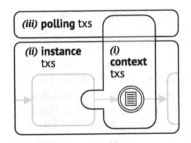

Fig. 5. Sampling strategies related to a monitoring point

participant to re-evaluate a monitoring point.

As a second sampling strategy, the set of context transactions can be augmented with *instance* transactions targeting any element of the process. If a monitoring point happens to be ACTIVE during one of those transactions, its evaluation could simply be performed "on the side" even though they are not directly related. For example, this is the case for the monitoring points e_1 and e_2 and all transactions happening as a part of the parallel "complete reservation details" sub-process (see Fig. 1).

As a third strategy, additional transactions with no other purpose but periodically *polling* and evaluating monitoring points may be introduced. They are similar to manual re-evaluation transactions as discussed before, but are instead issued automatically in regular intervals, either by a designated participant or a dedicated system component. Alternatively, the *incentivized execution* pattern [16] could be used, where third-party agents issue those requests and are rewarded, e.g., by small payments of tokens or cryptocurrency if available.

Figure 6 shows an exemplary timeline view of how the strategies work on the example of the weather warning monitoring point e_1 (see Fig. 1) and a storage

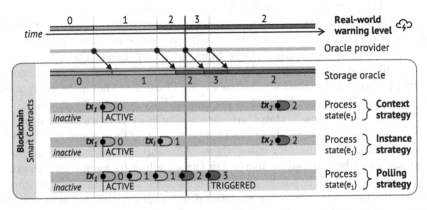

Fig. 6. Sampling strategies on the example of the storage oracle and the weather warning monitoring point e_1

oracle. The request-response oracle would be used similarly, shifting the evaluation of the monitoring point into the callback transaction. Suppose now that the weather warning level is a scalar value between 0 and 3, where 3 designates a severe weather warning. For all strategies, a context transaction tx_1 initially activates e_1 but does not yet trigger it. For the context strategy, only one later transaction tx_2 is issued, but still does not trigger e_1—even though the weather warning actually was at level 3 for a time as indicated by the thick vertical line. For the instance strategy another transaction tx_i, e.g., in the course of the "complete reservation details" sub-process, is issued, albeit before the relevant weather warning. Only the polling strategy actually notices and reacts correctly to the weather warning because the polling frequency was sufficiently high.

4.2   Extended Oracle Architectures

While the sampling strategies decrease the probability of missing updates, gaps may still occur. The core problem is the lack of a continuous view on the external data, which can not be reliably solved by just increasing the sampling frequency of the oracle, in the general case. Instead, we propose novel extensions to the basic oracle architectures described before which approach the problem from two sides: (i) by providing a historical perspective on data that allows consumers to resolve temporal conflicts after-the-fact; and (ii) by immediate communication using a publish-subscribe pattern, avoiding temporal conflicts before they happen.

History Oracles. The idea of *history oracles* is to provide a historical values on top of current data. Consumers can then determine at which point in time a value changed to first fulfill the condition associated with a monitoring point. This would allow straightforward implementations of a timed evaluation function. In principle, both storage and request-response oracles can be extended with these capabilities, requiring the oracle provider to store data on-chain or off-chain, respectively, subject to technological storage limitations. We will call those variants on-chain and off-chain history oracles.

The top half of Fig. 7 shows how the former, an on-chain history oracle, could be used to resolve the temporal conflict of the weather warning monitoring point e_1 (see Fig. 1). As before, tx_1 activates e_1 but does not trigger it yet. In tx_2, however, the situation is now different than for basic storage oracles (see Fig. 6): Using the history, the severe weather warning which was issued and expired in the meantime can be detected. This leads to the correct triggering of e_1.

Publish-Subscribe Oracles. Further, we propose *publish-subscribe oracles*. Instead of only receiving the data once, consumers receive new data immediately as it changes as long as they are subscribed, i.e., an active monitoring point requires the data. Thus, the process can promptly react to changes in data and trigger monitoring points accordingly before any temporal conflicts arise. This is a fundamental difference to history oracles, which may exhibit some delay in triggering a monitoring point depending on when they are called, but do not require proactive subscription. Again, the publish-subscribe oracle can be implemented on top of both storage and request-response oracles, depending on

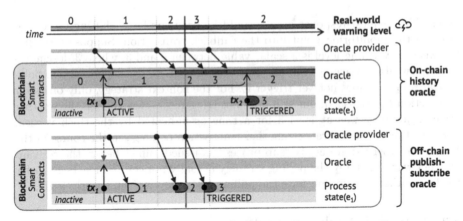

Fig. 7. Usage of novel oracle architectures on the monitoring point e_1

whether the subscription is handled on-chain by the oracle smart contract or off-chain by the oracle provider, respectively.

The lower half of Fig. 7 shows the same weather warning example as before for the off-chain publish-subscribe oracle. As is evident, no updates are missed anymore since the process receives all of them directly. The first two updates do not trigger e_1, but the third finally does. Unsubscribing is not explicitly shown in the figure, but may be performed if no further updates are required.

Condition Interfaces. A further variant of both the history as well as the publish-subscribe oracles concerns the interface. Until now, we assumed that the process smart contract queries the data, and implements the timed evaluation function used in the **step** algorithm (see Listing 1) locally. However, one could also implement the oracles so as to take a condition expression as an input, and only call back the process once that condition evaluates to true, partly externalizing the task of monitoring data to the third-party oracle provider. In the weather example, the condition could filter for warning level 3 only. This may cut down on the number of callback transactions, especially for the off-chain publish-subscribe oracle—in Fig. 7, for example, two of the callback transactions would be saved.

5   Results and Preliminary Evaluation

The sampling strategies and oracle architectures introduced support the implementation of monitoring points to varying degrees. In this section, we will summarize the level of compliance that can be achieved, and give preliminary arguments as to the overheads incurred by the various approaches from both a process and an oracle perspective.

Process-Perspective Overhead. From the perspective of the process smart contract, the overhead of the approaches is gauged using two metrics: (i) the

Table 1. Overview of overhead and compliance metrics of the oracle architectures

Oracle architecture		Process-perspective overhead			Compliance	
		Sampling strategy	Oracle invocations	Additional transactions	Miss probability	Temporal conflicts
Storage oracle		Context	Few	Few	High	May occur
		Instance	More	Few	Medium	May occur
		Polling	Many	Many	Low	May occur
Request-response oracle		Context	Few	Few	High	May occur
		Instance	More	Few	Medium	May occur
		Polling	Many	Many	Low	May occur
History oracle	*On-chain*	—	Few	Few	**Zero**	**Resolved**
	Off-chain	—	Few	Few	**Zero**	**Resolved**
Pub/sub oracle	*On-chain*	—	**One**	**None**	**Zero**	**Avoided**
	Off-chain	—	**One**	**None**	**Zero**	**Avoided**

number of invocations of the oracle smart contract, (ii) and the number of additional transactions issued solely to evaluate the monitoring point, which accounts for reuse of transactions which were scheduled either way to invoke the oracle.

The results are shown in Table 1. For the storage and request-response oracles, the overhead depends on the sampling strategy chosen as each sample requires one invocation. Notably, the instance strategy wraps extra oracle invocations in existing transactions. The history oracle essentially incurs the same overhead as the context strategy. The publish-subscribe oracle architecture only ever needs a single transaction to subscribe to the oracle, which can be performed on activation and thus causes little to no overhead.

Oracle-Perspective Overhead. Storage and request-response oracles are already available in practice and their implementation overhead is well-known; contrary to history and publish-subscribe oracles which lack such reference points.

For the history oracle approach, storage considerations are paramount. In principle, the entire data history must be held, which could induce large storage requirements over time. Especially the on-chain history oracle may become infeasible quickly as on-chain storage can be prohibitively expensive in practice. Typically, one would thus opt for storing large amounts of data in off-chain storage, and use the blockchain to ascertain its authenticity using hashes. Arguably, the off-chain variant is more prone to traffic limitations: If the condition is not externalized to the oracle, the entire data from the time span requested needs to be relayed to the consumer smart contract. While many blockchains allow arbitrary parameter payloads, they too become expensive rapidly.

The publish-subscribe oracle's performance depends on the subscriber count and the frequency of data updates. Each data update schedules one transaction to each subscriber in the off-chain variant, which may become hard to manage. In the on-chain variant, those transactions may be merged by instructing the oracle smart contract to notify consumers via inter-contract calls, which is subject to blockchain-specific limits on transactions complexity.

Cost. The metrics discussed above are an important indicator as to the overall cost of the approaches. To operate at a profit, transaction and storage fees are reflected in the oracle provider's pricing model and passed down to the consumers [1]. For example, the request-response oracle provider Provable prices regular API calls at USD 0.01, up to USD 0.04 if a notary proof is requested.

Presumably, history and publish-subscribe oracle architectures will be more expensive in practice compared to the basic variants since they offer additional functional value and tend to incur higher blockchain network fees on the oracle provider's end. To the best of the knowledge of the authors, though, no provider currently offers such services, hence no market-adjusted pricing data is known and no holistic assessment can be made as yet.

Transaction-Driven Semantics Compliance. The overall goal of the oracle approaches is to comply to the transaction-driven semantics developed in Sect. 3 (see Listing 1) as closely as possible. Table 1 shows whether this is the case. The history and publish-subscribe oracles have been designed specifically to fit these requirements. They eliminate the chance of missing data updates and handle temporal conflicts by resolving them after-the-fact or proactively avoiding them. The storage and request-response oracles, on the other hand, do not resolve temporal conflicts reliably, and the chance of missing data updates is inversely proportional to the number of oracle invocations as discussed in Sect. 4.

6   Related Work

Blockchain-based process execution is a promising topic in BPM research [10]. Many implementation aspects are being worked on, and some virtually production-ready process engines have emerged. Naturally, existing approaches allow modeling and executing conditional constraints, and some have provisions for accessing external data through oracles. However, in most cases this is not a core aspect of the respective publication, and the support for oracles is discussed sparsely; also, most prototypical implementations are not publicly available.

Only few approaches consider native modeling elements for external data interaction, namely via BPMN service tasks in Caterpillar [9]; on-chain asset registries in Lorikeet [7]; and black-box message exchanges [4]. In the first work in this area, Weber et al. already discuss the possibility of connecting to external services via a dedicated trigger component [14]. Even though not explicitly stated, this trigger component may assume the role of a request-response oracle.

The notion of continuous monitoring is rarely found, and if so only works on data and events entirely local to the process: In our own previous work, BPMN conditional events are used to monitor local process data using an instance-wide re-evaluation strategy on data updates similar to the instance strategy proposed in this paper [5]. Caterpillar supports BPMN event sub-processes, which likewise requires instance-wide monitoring of local events [9].

Some approaches, including all of the above, also allow arbitrary scripts to be added to the model which are then executed by the process smart contract [2,8]. These scripts can be used to call oracle smart contracts, potentially enabling the usage of storage and our proposed history oracles. However, oracles implemented using callbacks are harder to access since the callback needs to be properly picked up by the process smart contract. A few approaches provide specific interfaces for their own callback mechanisms, e.g., subscription services [4] or triggers [14], which could potentially be used if the oracle was adapted.

Part of our contribution is the proposal of novel oracle architectures, namely on-chain and off-chain history and publish-subscribe oracles, in the conditional variant or not. These build on top of patterns from literature [15,16] and operating oracle services [1]. We are not aware of related work in oracle literature with a focus similar to ours. Instead, work on existing oracles mostly aims at securing the way of the data from the source to the smart contract, that is, trust [3] and reliability [6] are more important than monitoring and historical data.

In a recent survey, Al-Breiki et al. perform an exhaustive comparison of blockchain oracle platforms focused on trust considerations [1]. They identify three primary design patterns, including the basic request-response and storage (which they call "immediate-read") oracles. A third pattern is named publish-subscribe pattern, but only shares the name with the proposal in this paper. While the idea is still to manage data "that is expected to change" [1], subscribers are notified via an on-chain or off-chain flag that they poll manually. As such, their architecture can not be used to solve temporal conflicts, missing the continuous aspect we strive for in this paper.

In summary, we assess that a dedicated investigation into the issues of external data monitoring from within the blockchain has as yet been missing, both in a wider practical context and in BPM research. This paper thus provides a significant conceptual and technical extension of knowledge in the field.

7   Discussion

We have shown that publish-subscribe and history oracles can account for fully compliant external data monitoring from smart contracts, while all other approaches are lacking in some aspects. In practice, however, the results need to be put into context, as research is still in its infancy when it comes to oracle technology and its wider implications [1]. The intersection with BPM exacerbates these issues, which we can only selectively discuss in the scope of this paper.

First and foremost, any approach represents a tradeoff in trust. Oracles bend the blockchain's integrity philosophy, and need to be trusted to provide correct data in time. Until technologies or patterns are found that eliminate this responsibility—and arguably, research in that area is focused primarily on that [1,3]—, concrete approaches will have to walk the line between supporting more process features and staying true to the blockchain's original vision.

On a more grounded level, we did not consider some common blockchain protocol characteristics. One problem that occurs in practice is that the transaction order on the blockchain ledger may not reflect the real-world order in which the transactions were actually sent, depending on fees and incentives. Further, the interval in which the blockchain produces new blocks and thus adds new information might be insufficient for quickly changing data sources, even when updating the value in every block. Since the extent of these issues dramatically varies, though, we decided to maintain a platform-agnostic perspective.

From a modeling perspective, we assume that each monitoring point depends on exactly one external data source. This may not always be the case if complex conditions, for example comparing prices at different online shops, are evaluated. However, this does not pose major conceptual issues but rather adds another layer of complexity to concrete implementations, which need to aggregate and store data from multiple oracles between transactions. This may be readily achieved using our proposed architectures.

Finally, the semantics presented in Sect. 3 view monitoring points as rather isolated, only interfering with each other if they are siblings in a deferred choice pattern. This may not apply to some business processes, e.g., when timers, messages and signals may be part of the choice. Those concepts exhibit their own difficulties in blockchain-based process execution environments, and the exact semantics when combined with monitoring points will be interesting future work.

8   Conclusion and Future Work

The blockchain's closed-world assumption and inherent passiveness severely complicate facilitating common business process patterns, like external data monitoring within smart contracts. In this paper, we contributed a first assessment of the exact nature of these issues, and developed a compliant transaction-driven semantics working in these circumstances. We further proposed implementation strategies and architectures using oracles to access external data from within the process smart contracts in a way satisfying the semantics. As such, this work contributes towards a holistic support for business processes on blockchain.

Several open points, partly discussed in the previous section, remain and are left for future work. Notably, we did not provide an implementation of our proposals on actual blockchain platforms, instead discussing properties and restrictions on a conceptual, technology-independent level. An empirical evaluation on the basis of an implementation could elicit valuable further insights.

References

1. Al-Breiki, H., Rehman, M.H.U., Salah, K., Svetinovic, D.: Trustworthy blockchain oracles: review, comparison, and open research challenges. IEEE Access **8**, 85675 (2020). https://doi.org/10.1109/ACCESS.2020.2992698
2. García-Bañuelos, L., Ponomarev, A., Dumas, M., Weber, I.: Optimized execution of business processes on blockchain. In: Carmona, J., Engels, G., Kumar, A. (eds.) BPM 2017. LNCS, vol. 10445, pp. 130–146. Springer, Cham (2017). https://doi.org/10.1007/978-3-319-65000-5_8

3. Heiss, J., Eberhardt, J., Tai, S.: From oracles to trustworthy data on-chaining systems. In: IEEE International Conference on Blockchain, pp. 496–503 (2019). https://doi.org/10.1109/Blockchain.2019.00075

4. Klinger, P., Bodendorf, F.: Blockchain-based cross-organizational execution framework for dynamic integration of process collaborations. In: 15th International Conference on Wirtschaftsinformatik (WI), pp. 893–908 (2020). https://doi.org/10.30844/wi_2020_i2-klinger

5. Ladleif, J., Weske, M., Weber, I.: Modeling and enforcing blockchain-based choreographies. In: Hildebrandt, T., van Dongen, B.F., Röglinger, M., Mendling, J. (eds.) BPM 2019. LNCS, vol. 11675, pp. 69–85. Springer, Cham (2019). https://doi.org/10.1007/978-3-030-26619-6_7

6. Lo, S.K., Xu, X., Staples, M., Yao, L.: Reliability analysis for blockchain oracles. Comput. Electr. Eng. **83**, 106582 (2020). https://doi.org/10.1016/j.compeleceng.2020.106582

7. Lu, Q., et al.: Integrated model-driven engineering of blockchain applications for business processes and asset management. CoRR abs/2005.12685 (2020). http://arxiv.org/abs/2005.12685

8. López-Pintado, O., Dumas, M., García-Bañuelos, L., Weber, I.: Interpreted execution of business process models on blockchain. In: IEEE International Enterprise Distributed Object Computing Conference (EDOC), pp. 206–215 (2019). https://doi.org/10.1109/EDOC.2019.00033

9. López-Pintado, O., García-Bañuelos, L., Dumas, M., Weber, I., Ponomarev, A.: Caterpillar: a business process execution engine on the Ethereum blockchain. Softw. Pract. Exp. **49**(7), 1162–1193 (2019). https://doi.org/10.1002/spe.2702

10. Mendling, J., Weber, I., et al.: Blockchains for business process management - challenges and opportunities. ACM Trans. Manag. Inf. Syst. (TMIS) **9**(1), 4:1–4:16 (2018). https://doi.org/10.1145/3183367

11. OMG: Business Process Model and Notation (BPMN), Version 2.0.2 (2013). http://www.omg.org/spec/BPMN/2.0.2/

12. Russell, N., ter Hofstede, A.H., van der Aalst, W.M., Mulyar, N.: Workflow control-flow patterns: a revised view. BPM Center Rep. BPM-06-22 (2006)

13. Russell, N., ter Hofstede, A.H., Edmond, D., van der Aalst, W.M.: Workflow data patterns. Technical report. FIT-TR-2004-01, Queensland University of Technology, Brisbane (2004)

14. Weber, I., Xu, X., Riveret, R., Governatori, G., Ponomarev, A., Mendling, J.: Untrusted business process monitoring and execution using blockchain. In: La Rosa, M., Loos, P., Pastor, O. (eds.) BPM 2016. LNCS, vol. 9850, pp. 329–347. Springer, Cham (2016). https://doi.org/10.1007/978-3-319-45348-4_19

15. Wöhrer, M., Zdun, U.: Design patterns for smart contracts in the ethereum ecosystem. In: IEEE International Conference on Blockchain, pp. 1513–1520 (2018). https://doi.org/10.1109/Cybermatics_2018.2018.00255

16. Xu, X., Pautasso, C., Zhu, L., Lu, Q., Weber, I.: A pattern collection for blockchain-based applications. In: Conference on Pattern Languages of Programs (EuroPLoP). ACM (2018). https://doi.org/10.1145/3282308.3282312

17. Xu, X., et al.: A taxonomy of blockchain-based systems for architecture design. In: IEEE International Conference on Software Architecture (ICSA), pp. 243–252 (2017). https://doi.org/10.1109/ICSA.2017.33

Robotic Process Automation Forum

A Conversational Digital Assistant for Intelligent Process Automation

Yara Rizk, Vatche Isahagian$^{(\boxtimes)}$, Scott Boag, Yasaman Khazaeni,
Merve Unuvar, Vinod Muthusamy, and Rania Khalaf

IBM Research AI, Cambridge, MA, USA
`vatchei@ibm.com`

Abstract. Robotic process automation (RPA) has emerged as the leading approach to automate tasks in business processes. Moving away from back-end automation, RPA automated the mouse-click on user interfaces; this outside-in approach reduced the overhead of updating legacy software. However, its many shortcomings, namely its lack of accessibility to business users, have prevented its widespread adoption in highly regulated industries. In this work, we explore interactive automation in the form of a conversational digital assistant. It allows business users to interact with and customize their automation solutions through natural language. The framework, which creates such assistants, relies on a multi-agent orchestration model and conversational wrappers for autonomous agents including RPAs. We demonstrate the effectiveness of our proposed approach on a loan approval business process and a travel preapproval business process.

Keywords: Business process automation · Interactive automation · Robotic process automation · Conversational assistant · Orchestration

1 Introduction

Business processes are the backbone of business enterprises and organizations [31]. A business process is a collection of tasks or activities that must be executed in a certain sequence to achieve a goal. In the era of digital transformation, robotic process automation (RPA) presents a low cost approach to inject automation in business processes. An RPA is developed for tasks that are frequent, repetitive, and error-prone. RPAs learn to execute such tasks in the user interface from humans through demonstration, behavior logs or business process descriptions. Unlike back-end automation approaches, this approach reduces the overhead of adopting automation by operating on top of legacy software.

However, highly-regulated industries still require human-in-the-loop automation due to compliance regulations, increased risk, and liability. Unfortunately, the end users are not tech-savvy, making it difficult for them to interact with RPAs and other automation solutions in their current format [12]. This lack of accessibility hinders a business user's ability to monitor and customize these

A. Asatiani et al. (Eds.): BPM Blockchain and RPA Forum 2020, LNBIP 393, pp. 85–100, 2020.
https://doi.org/10.1007/978-3-030-58779-6_6

solutions [8]. A human-consumable interactive automation, through natural language, would reduce the barrier of entry to business process automation.

We propose a framework to build conversational digital assistants, merging the two multi-billion dollar markets of RPA [3] and enterprise chatbots[1]. An assistant consists of multiple conversational software bots that automate specific tasks within a business process. It can be used by business users and domain experts who do not possess any programming or software development skills to customize and interact with their business process automation solutions through natural language. The assistant can be adopted in different enterprises depending on the domain of the agents, from banking and finance to retail, customer care and others. This interaction would foster trust because it makes the system more transparent to the users, allowing them to gain valuable insights into the system's operations. This trust increases the probability of the business users adopting more automation solutions [21]. With the increased interest in trusted business processes in this digital transformation era [25], the conversational assistant would serve as a crucial enabler to this paradigm.

Beyond trusted processes, researchers have investigated business process individualization [33]. Pursued by many businesses to differentiate themselves from a large pool of competitors, process individualization has historically been a challenge because it reduces efficiency and increases costs. The digital revolution overcame these challenges by enabling automated modification of individualized processes. Our framework can contribute to this space by further reducing the overhead of creating custom processes and monitoring them through natural language interactions.

The main research question we address in this work is: *what are the necessary characteristics of a software framework that enables interactive automation in business processes through natural language?* To that end, we present a unified conversational multi-agent orchestration assistant, which consists of multiple building blocks. Skills, including RPAs, automate tasks within a business process They can be composed into more powerful automation bots, and wrapped as conversational agents to interact with business users. As the user converses with the assistant, the orchestrator determines which agents should respond to the user. Therefore, the assistant provides business users access to their RPAs through natural language. We present a taxonomy of skills and agents, define an agent contract to enable such an orchestration and present an orchestration workflow that integrates diverse conversational agents.

Next, we briefly discuss related work in two main relevant fields: business process automation and conversational agents. Then, we present our proposed framework, before discussing our qualitative analysis on two use cases: travel preapproval, and loan application processing.

---

[1] https://www.businessinsider.com/chatbot-market-stats-trends.

2   Related Work

2.1   Business Process Automation

RPAs have recently been the main driver of the digital transformation with their light-weight approach to automating repetitive tasks [1]. They have enabled automation in multiple enterprises including accounting [19], auditing [6], human resources [22], banking [28], public administration [10] and energy sectors [15]. Multiple RPA vendors have offered state-of-the-art solutions to clients in various sectors. A survey of these products can be found in [2].

These RPAs have leveraged diverse technological advancements in the fields of artificial intelligence and software development. Gao et al. adopted deep learning optical character recognition (OCR) and classification models in document flow automation within a debt collector business process [8]. RPAs identified relationships between tasks from user behavior in [32] and used first-order logic to deduce automation rules. Crucial to RPA's success is automatically identifying RPA-eligible tasks; [16] relied on supervised machine learning and natural language processing of business process descriptions to identify these tasks.

Business process automation takes a step beyond RPAs to automate decision making in business processes. Marella et al. identified the field of automated planning as an enabler to more sophisticated business process automation [17]. Machine learning is another enabler; deep learning models, long short-term memory recurrent neural networks specifically, have also been trained to model business processes, a crucial component for more advanced automation [4]. Machine learning algorithms like support vector machines, shallow neural networks and random forests have been adopt in process mining applications [29]. An interactive process mining recommender system for business process discovery based on machine learning has also been investigated in the literature [26]. However, end-to-end process automation has not been widely adopted in enterprises due to business users' lack of trust in such technology [13] and limited accessibility and customization capabilities. Since business users lack the technical skills to monitor and customize automation solutions, a natural language interface may be key to the success of the digital transformation.

2.2   Conversational Agents

Enterprises have been interested in natural language processing advancements, given their heavy reliance on this communication modality. Considering the breadth of this field, we will only focus on conversational agents that are most relevant to the scope of our framework. Enterprise chatbots, a multi-billion dollar market dominated by giants like IBM, Google and Amazon, have been researched for decades and experienced significant improvements recently [7]. They have evolved from simple question answering customer support bots to fully autonomous assistants capable of performing tasks on behalf of humans [7]. One shopping bot is capable of custom-pricing products to increase sales [9]. Food delivery services adopted a delivery bot to reduce the effort customers need to order pizza [9]. Another bot crowdsourced answers generated by multiple chatbots, gradually reducing the reliance on the crowd through learned selection models [11]. The model estimated the likelihood of an agent returning the correct answer based on the crowd's votes and previous answer selections. Instead, we adopt a different orchestration model that doesn't solely rely on user feedback but has a more sophisticated scoring and selection model to pick one or more agents.

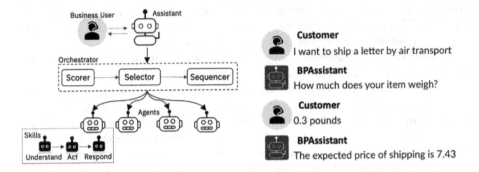

Fig. 1. A conversational digital assistant framework

Researchers have also combined RPAs and chatbots to increase automation. A chatbot for agile software development teams was developed to provide insights into a team's performance by analyzing commits in version control software [18]. From a business process workflow, Kalia et al. derived a dialog tree-based chatbot to converse about the process [14]. Despite the systematic approach to chatbot design, it required significant effort and domain expertise.

3   Proposed Framework

The conversational digital assistant provides business users with two core functionalities beyond RPAs: conversational interaction and collaborative automation. Our proposed framework, illustrated in Fig. 1, achieves these functionalities by relying on an orchestrator capable of coordinating the execution of agents within the system, and agents that can converse with users in natural language while executing tasks in a business process [23]. Agents are composed of skills which can perform natural language understanding and generation in addition to task automation (e.g. RPAs). The orchestrator expects agents to adhere to a specific contract to determine which agents respond to a user's utterance. This modular approach simplifies the task of converting RPA to conversational agents, the system's maintenance and life cycle. It also allows us to add or remove certain domains and functionality from the scope of the assistant with minimal effort.

3.1   Skills

Skills are the assistant's building blocks and consist of atomic functions to *understand* a user's request, *act* to satisfy the user's request, and *respond* to the user.

Understand skills are generally natural language understanding functions that determine the user's intent and identify any entities in the user's utterance that would be needed by the *act* skill to properly execute. Such skills can be created using existing tools that create dialog bots such as IBM's Watson Assistant or Google's Dialogflow which can involve defining entities and intents and providing examples of them.

Act skills are generally RPAs that execute the user's intent to produce an outcome. They can be of two types. World-changing skills can change the state of the world, i.e. have side-effects on their environment; examples include skills that send emails or check credit scores. Non-world changing skills do not have side effects on their environment; examples include skills that read emails or check a bank account status. *Act* skills automate business process tasks and can be placed at decision points within a process to move it forward.

Respond skills produce a human-consumable response from the *act* skill's output. This can be a natural language utterance, a visual representation, or another modality. This skill can be as simple as adopting a template response or as sophisticated as a deep learning text generation model.

3.2 Agents

In our framework, an agent is simply a conversational RPA: the RPA is preceded by an *understand* skill and succeeded by a *respond* skill. Thus, we obtain an interactive RPA that communicates with business users in natural language. This modular approach enables the integration of RPAs that were not inherently interactive, while reducing the overhead of improving agents throughout their lifetime. However, not all RPAs are suitable to be conversational RPAs.

Composing an agent using the *understand-act-respond* pipeline achieves the interactive RPA aspect of the assistant and creates a standardized agent creation method. Enforcing a contract enables their integration within the same assistant. Thus, agents could cooperate on tasks and achieve more powerful functionality. Agents receive the input utterance and current context or state; they return a response, an updated context, a confidence in their response (a numerical value between 0 and 1 that quantifies their comprehension of the input and relevance of their response) and possibly other flags related to the conversation.

Within the conversational digital assistant paradigm, we identified five main types of agents. While many more can be created, we consider the ones that would be most relevant and commonly used in process automation: dialog, information retrieval, task execution, data analytics, and alert agents.

Dialog agents provide more human-like interactions. They are composed of an *understand* skill and a *respond* skill to answer user queries. They do not change the world and they can be implemented using any conversational agent technology; examples include chit-chat, FAQ or "help", etc.

Information retrieval agents query information sources to achieve their goal. They perform advanced reasoning to respond to user queries or information retrieval tasks in a process. They are composed of an *understand* skill, an information retrieval RPA and a *respond* skill. In general, most agents within this category do not contain world-changing skills (exception: credit score checks).

Task execution agents perform tasks within a business process that change the state of the world by moving the business process forward. Examples include submitting applications, filling in information in forms, and making decisions at decision points. Such agents may more intuitively fit within the RPA definition.

Data analytics agents cover a wide scope of functionality from data transformation and modeling to predictions and recommendations. Such agents go beyond information retrieval which provide factual and statistical data but do not go as far as task execution agents that act on the information; they still rely on humans to drive the business process. Examples include visualization and data export agents that manipulate and transform the data to more complex business process forecasting and performance prediction models.

Alerting agents allow users to conversationally customize alerts and notifications triggered by the occurrence of specific events within or related to the process, in essence enabling asynchronous monitoring of the process [24].

3.3 Orchestration

The orchestrator is the core component that allows interactive and cooperating agents in our framework. Its main functionalities include selecting a subset of agents that must respond to a user's request, managing the context and passing it among agents, and acting as the central dialog manager (controls a multi-turn conversation's state and flow).

Selecting the agent(s) to respond to a user's request can be achieved by different orchestrators. Stateless orchestrators, unlike their stateful counterparts, do not possess a central state tracker, i.e. context is maintained in every turn by passing context variables between the orchestrator and the agents. Maintaining context about the dialog also influences agent selection: if the user is in the middle a conversation with an agent, the orchesetrator must ensure a smooth interaction. If users digress from the conversation (i.e. move away before completing the conversation) or provide ambiguous statements, the dialog manager should properly handle such situations. Apriori orchestrators select agents based on the user input and some knowledge about agent capabilities. On the other hand, posterior orchestrators request a preview response from agents that factors into the orchestrator's selection. Such orchestrators could also request a confidence score to better assess an agent's response. Confidence is a quantification of an agent's understanding of the input and relevance of its response to it. Posterior orchestrators require agents to have a preview mode in order not to change the world if they are not selected for execution. They are agnostic to what agents exist in the assistant as long as they abide by the contract; they simply need to know of the agents' existence and how to reach them (API endpoint).

Each orchestration model has specific computational costs, architectural requirements, and contract constraints. These factors influence the assistant's orchestration model. In this work, we adopt a stateless, posterior orchestrator, called 3 S orchestrator, that consists of three main steps: scoring, selecting, and sequencing [30, 34]. Outlined in Algorithm 1, it assumes an agent (a_i) contract that returns a preview response (r_i), a confidence in the response (c_i), and a stickiness value (κ_i) that indicates whether the agent has been interacting with the user in previous turns (i.e. is in the middle of a conversation). A preview mode ensures that world-changing agents do not cause irreversible changes before the orchestrator makes its selection. Furthermore, preview and execute modes can be adopted to optimize the computation/latency of non-world changing agents. The nomenclature that is adopted throughout this work is defined in Table 1.

Table 1. Nomenclature

Symbol	Definition	Symbol	Definition
A	Set of agents	$n = \lvert A \rvert$	Number of agents
$a_i \in A$	Agent i	r_i	Response of agent a_i
$c_i \in [0, 1]$	Agent a_i's confidence	$\kappa_i \in \{0, 1\}$	Agent a_i's stickiness
u	User's utterance	$f_i(.)$	Function per agent a_i
s_i	Agent a_i's score	$g(.)$	Scorer function, computes a score per agent a_i
A_s	Set of selected agents	$h(.)$	Selector function
R	Final response	$k = \lvert A_s \rvert$	Number of selected agents

---

Algorithm 1. 3S Orchestration

1: **procedure** BROADCASTER(u, A)
2:   **for** $a_i \in A = \{a_1, ..., a_n\}$ **do**
3:     $(c_i, \kappa_i, r_i) = f_i(u)$
4: **procedure** ORCHESTRATOR(Responses, Confidences)
5:   Scorer: $s_i = g(c_i, \kappa_i), \forall a_i \in A$
6:   Selector: $A_s = h(\{s_i \forall a_i \in A\})$
7:   Sequencer: $R = order(\{r_i, \forall a_i \in A_s\})$
8:   **return** R

Scorer. When the orchestrator receives a natural language utterance from the user, as shown in Fig. 2, it forwards the input to all agents. Once it receives the agents' preview responses, the scorer processes the agent confidences (and possibly other variables) to obtain normalized values. This is necessary in multi-agent environments where agents are developed by independent software developers or diverse frameworks that compute confidences differently. A scorer can be as simple as an identity function that does not modify the confidences (if inherently

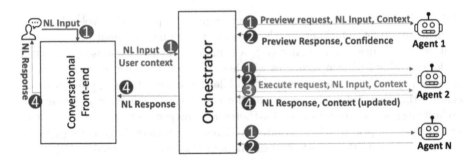

Fig. 2. Graphical representation of a posterior orchestration pipeline

normalized) or as complex as a Bayesian approach that incorporates statistical and probabilistic models to scale the confidences. For example, per our agents' contract, a confidence between 0 and 1 is returned in addition to a flag, called stickiness equal to 0 or 1, that states whether an agent had been selected in the previous turn and is expecting an answer from the user. One scorer we adopted simply takes the maximum of both values, $s_i = max(c_i, \kappa_i)$.

Selector. Next, the selector processes the scores and determines which agent(s) must execute to respond to the user. The selector model can be a simple *Top 1 (or Top K)* selector that picks the agent (or K agents) with the highest score (above a minimum threshold, T, to identify cases outside the scope of the assistant), e.g. $A_s = max\{s_i : a_i \in A \quad s.t. \quad s_i > T\}$ (adopted in our experiments). It could also be a machine learning algorithm that utilizes other features such as previous conversation turns to select the next best agent(s). In a supervised learning domain, labels can represent agents that are the output of classifiers and the input to the classifier would be a feature vector consisting of the agents' scores and/or user utterances. In a reinforcement learning domain, actions can represent agents and the environment produces a reward when the correct agent is selected. With enough data, deep learning models can be trained.

Sequencer. If multiple agents were selected for execution, a sequencer determines the order to execute these agents and show their responses' to the user. This is crucial to the proper execution of collaborating agents since one agent's output is another's input; agents' execution is not independent. Various approaches ranging from relatively simple heuristic rules to more complex planning-based algorithms can be adopted.

4   Empirical Results

4.1   Implementation and Use Cases

The proposed framework is implemented in Python where most skills are accessible through API endpoints. A *top K* orchestrator is exposed as a Rest API, and called by a Slack bot[2]. Conversational skills were implemented in Watson Assistant[3]. *Act* skills were either external microservices or internal Python functions. The assistant, referred to as *BPAssistant*, consists of multiple agents (see Fig. 3) to handle two simplified business processes: loan application and travel preapproval [23]. Some agents are domain agnostic and can operate on multiple business processes without any overhead. Others are domain specific, developed for a very specific task in one of the business process. Finally, a set of agents were created from domain agnostic agents but must be instantiated for a specific domain. Hence, they require some configuration when deployed in a process.

The travel use case considers two persons that can interact with the *BPAssistant*: employees and managers. The travel preapproval process, shown in Fig. 4, was implemented in a business process management software. Employees submit a travel preapproval request to attend a conference (or event) by filling a form. Once submitted, the employee's manager processes the application. If approved by the manager, the application is forwarded to the director who makes the final decision on the travel request.

The simplified loan application process consists of a bank customer submitting a loan application and a bank officer processing this request to determine whether to approve or reject it. The assistant can help a loan officer automate certain parts of the process, in addition to query and analyze the process data.

These use cases are interesting because of their relevance to many enterprises, especially those that are about to start or are in the middle of their digital transformation journey. These processes (or parts of them) may need to suddenly become agile overnight in response to a pandemic (e.g. loan officer remotely approving a loan), or readjusted processes to address a sudden change in company policies (no flights to certain countries). Creating interactive agents from RPAs that automate tasks would enable employers' adoption of such systems. Natural language interactions reduce the necessary learning curve, leading to quick deployment.

Fig. 3. Agents in *BPAssistant*

---

[2] https://api.slack.com/bot-users#bots-overview.
[3] https://www.ibm.com/cloud/watson-assistant.

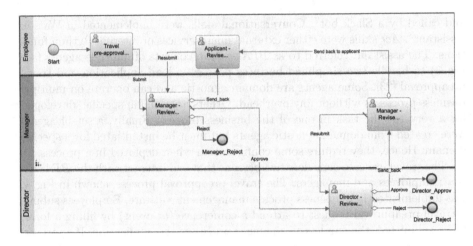

Fig. 4. Travel preapproval process

Conversation driven.   RPA cooperation.

Fig. 5. Conversation with *BPAssistant*: business rules agent.

4.2 Conversations with *BPAssistant*

BPAssistant allows users to accomplish different goals by relaying their intentions in natural language. First, consider a loan officer who wants to process a customer's loan application while consulting the bank's rule engine. The "Business Rules" agent would allow the loan officer to make decisions about tasks in a business process such as approving or rejecting the loan application. Figure 5a shows a sample multi-turn conversation with this agent through the assistant.

The agent was instantiated for the banking domain and implemented in IBM Decision Service[4], where users input the available information and the agent recommends whether to approve or reject the loan based on the business rules.

However, the interaction can be improved by automating information gathering using an RPA (configured as an agent) to extract this information from a document, for example. Figure 5b shows the same example but with cooperation among agents. The "content analyzer" agent, capable of extracting information from PDF documents, retrieves key-value pairs from the loan application file and saves them in the context of the orchestrator. Then, the "business rules" agent obtains this information through the orchestrator to determine whether the loan should be approved or rejected. Outside of the assistant framework, enabling such an RPA cooperation would require the creation of another RPA that transfers the data from the first RPA (content analyzer) to the second RPA (business engine). The orchestrator presents a more generalizable paradigm to achieve this functionality.

The loan officer can also use *BPAssistant* to analyze recent loan applications by querying the data associated with the loan process, as shown in Table 2. The natural language utterances in the table invoke the "Business Process Query" agent capable of converting natural language sentences to formal queries that are executed on a database to retrieve the data [27]. Furthermore, the loan officer can manipulate the data by plotting it and exporting it to a file, using the Visualization and Data Export agents, respectively. Both agents use the data from information retrieval agents, stored in the context of the orchestrator, as input to fulfill the user's request. Figure 6 displays these multi-modal responses, namely the visualization and CSV file generated based on the queried data.

Now, let's say the loan officer needs to attend training or a seminar on new loan processing procedures at the bank's headquarters. The travel costs can be expensed to the bank since it is a work trip[5]. The "Business Process (BP) Execute" agent can move the business process forward by asking the assistant to execute a step in the process on their behalf, such as submitting a travel request by saying "submit a travel request to the headquarters". *BPAssistant* would then submit a request on the employee's behalf and automatically populate the fields of the form by using appropriate *act* skills that can retrieve information.

Furthermore, a bank manager can use the same *BPAssistant* to set up alerts about employees' submitted travel requests using the "Alerts" agent. This agent enables users to create and customize alerts related to a process [24]. Once an notification is received, the manager can review the employee's travel preapproval request and determine whether to approve it or not, as shown in Table 2.

---

[4] https://www.ibm.com/products/operational-decision-manager.

[5] Travel preapproval processes are common in many enterprises including IBM Research. Employees submit preapprovals to attend academic conferences, client meetings, training events, etc.

Table 2. Sample conversation with *BPAssistant*

Conversation	Responding agent
Loan Officer: Who are the top 3 borrowers with average amount more than 10000 *BPAssistant*: These are the average value: 1). 584,917\$ for J. Smith, 2). 575,692\$ for V. Doe, 3). 557,615\$ for Y. Doe	Data query
Loan Officer: List all borrowers with yearly income more than 50000 but credit score less than 150 *BPAssistant*: Total records found are 82. Here is the link: \<url\>	Data query
Loan Officer: Plot the bar chart per yearly income *BPAssistant*: \<image\> (Fig. 6)	Visualization
Loan Officer: Export this data to a CSV file *BPAssistant*: The result for your query is: \<csv\> file (Fig. 6)	Data export
Manager: Hello *BPAssistant*: Hi there	Chit-chat
Manager: How many travel requests does John Smith have? *BPAssistant*: John Smith has 1 application	Travel query
Manager: Approve John Smith's request *BPAssistant*: John Smith's application has been approved	Business process Task execution

4.3   Discussion

Based on our prototypical implementation above, we observed multiple advantages and some limitations of the proposed framework. First, the assistant successfully handled the users' diverse requests by orchestrating agents from multiple domains. Business users interacted with RPAs such as the "alerts" agent or the "business rules" agent through natural language without switching between multiple interfaces. Querying their data did not require business users to possess the knowledge of formulating formal queries executed on their databases; they simply formulated natural language statements using business domain terminology that they frequently use. Performing tasks within their business processes no longer required them to juggle multiple user interfaces either.

The framework eliminated the need to create custom RPAs by the business user; instead, developers created general RPAs that could be customized through natural language by the business user in the assistant. However, this shift came at the cost of creating conversational wrappers for the RPAs. Future iterations

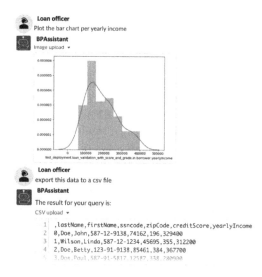

Fig. 6. Multi-modal responses from the *BPAssistant*.

should consider approaches to automate this task to further reduce the coding overhead. Additionally, automated composition techniques, such as the ones explored in [5,20], can further reduce the overhead of authoring these agents by automatically composing sophisticated agents out of more atomic skills.

As more heterogeneous agents are added to the assistant, the orchestration problem becomes more complex, especially when considering posterior orchestration approaches. One method to reduce the cost of previewing agent responses is to implement a hybrid orchestration method that adopts an apriori algorithm to select a subset of agents to ask for a preview. This reduces the computational cost as the system is scaled, while maintaining high selection accuracy.

The stateless orchestrator offered a lightweight solution to enable cooperation among agents, the second contribution of this work. However, as the size of data exchanged between agents increases, a stateful implementation may be more suitable. Shareable data can be stored in memory while the orchestrator keeps track of other state-related information to handle more complex dialog constructs and cooperation opportunities. A stateful orchestrator that combines apriori and posterior models could also alleviate the problem of legacy programs not having a preview mode to invoke in posterior orchestrators. The statefulness of the orchestrator would compensate for the missing preview responses by using other features of the system to make the best selection possible.

Furthermore, the orchestrator's modular principles simplify the problem of system lifecycle. As business processes become obsolete, the agents linked to them can simply be deactivated without incurring costs to update the framework or other agents. The framework also supports agent versions: as updates to agents are rolled out, the affected agents can be independently updated.

We believe this framework generalizes well to many types of RPAs because the goal of RPAs is to reduce the amount of work done by humans. Hence, they require minimal human intervention beyond launching the RPAs which can be implemented as a natural language instruction. Functions that still require a large amount of input from users may not be suitable for conversational interaction and should remain in their original user interface. However, as the number of RPAs increases, users will have too many RPAs to keep track of individually; we believe a unified, conversational interface would simplify the life of users.

In summary, our framework addressed some of the key weaknesses of RPAs, namely providing an interactive, human-in-the-loop automation assistant and cooperative RPAs. Even though the framework can undergo further improvements, it is a solid step forward towards interactive business process automation that can gain business users' trust in process automation solutions and advance service lines like customer care and process automation.

5   Conclusion

Conversational automation solutions will be critical to the digital transformation. To that end, we presented a framework that combines RPAs with conversational agents (or chatbots), both popular paradigms in business enterprises, to create an interactive business process automation solution. The framework relies on multi-agent orchestration where conversational agents are composed from RPA skills. The resulting assistant allows business users to monitor and customize their business process automation solutions through natural language. Future work will incorporate more sophisticated orchestration models and autonomous agents to address existing challenges in the current framework.

Acknowledgement. The authors would like to acknowledge Tathagata Chakraborti, Pierre Feillet, and Stephane Mery for the valuable conversations that contributed to expanding the vision of this work.

References

1. van der Aalst, W.M.P., Bichler, M., Heinzl, A.: Robotic process automation. Bus. Inf. Syst. Eng. **60**(4), 269–272 (2018). https://doi.org/10.1007/s12599-018-0542-4
2. Agostinelli, S., Marrella, A., Mecella, M.: Towards intelligent robotic process automation for BPMers. arXiv preprint arXiv:2001.00804 (2020)
3. Biscotti, F., Mehta, V., Villa, A., Bhullar, B., Tornbohm, C.: Market share analysis: robotic process automation, worldwide, 2019. Technical report (2020)
4. Camargo, M., Dumas, M., González-Rojas, O.: Learning accurate LSTM models of business processes. In: Hildebrandt, T., van Dongen, B.F., Röglinger, M., Mendling, J. (eds.) BPM 2019. LNCS, vol. 11675, pp. 286–302. Springer, Cham (2019). https://doi.org/10.1007/978-3-030-26619-6_19
5. Chakraborti, T., Khazaeni, Y.: D3BA: a tool for optimizing business processes using non-deterministic planning. In: AAAI IPA (2020)

6. Fernandez, D., Aman, A.: Impacts of robotic process automation on global accounting services. Asian J. Acc. Gov. **9**, 123–132 (2018)
7. Galitsky, B.: A content management system for chatbots. Developing Enterprise Chatbots, pp. 253–326. Springer, Cham (2019). https://doi.org/10.1007/978-3-030-04299-8_9
8. Gao, J., van Zelst, S.J., Lu, X., van der Aalst, W.M.P.: Automated robotic process automation: a self-learning approach. In: Panetto, H., Debruyne, C., Hepp, M., Lewis, D., Ardagna, C.A., Meersman, R. (eds.) OTM 2019. LNCS, vol. 11877, pp. 95–112. Springer, Cham (2019). https://doi.org/10.1007/978-3-030-33246-4_6
9. Heo, M., et al.: Chatbot as a new business communication tool: the case of naver talktalk. Bus. Commun. Res. Pract. **1**(1), 41–45 (2018)
10. Houy, C., Hamberg, M., Fettke, P.: Robotic process automation in public administrations. In: Digitalisierung von Staat und Verwaltung (2019)
11. Huang, T.H., Chang, J.C., Bigham, J.P.: Evorus: a crowd-powered conversational assistant built to automate itself over time. In: Proceedings of the 2018 CHI Conference on Human Factors in Computing Systems, pp. 1–13 (2018)
12. Jakob, M., Krcmar, H.: Which barriers hinder a successful digital transformation in small and medium-sized municipalities in a federal system? In: Central and Eastern European eDem and eGov Days, pp. 141–150 (2018)
13. Jan, S.T., Ishakian, V., Muthusamy, V.: AI trust in business processes: the need for process-aware explanations. In: IAAI 2020 (2020)
14. Kalia, A.K., Telang, P.R., Xiao, J., Vukovic, M.: Quark: a methodology to transform people-driven processes to chatbot services. In: Maximilien, M., Vallecillo, A., Wang, J., Oriol, M. (eds.) ICSOC 2017. LNCS, vol. 10601, pp. 53–61. Springer, Cham (2017). https://doi.org/10.1007/978-3-319-69035-3_4
15. Lacity, M., Willcocks, L.P., Craig, A.: Robotic process automation: mature capabilities in the energy sector. Technical report (2015)
16. Leopold, H., van der Aa, H., Reijers, H.A.: Identifying candidate tasks for robotic process automation in textual process descriptions. In: Gulden, J., Reinhartz-Berger, I., Schmidt, R., Guerreiro, S., Guédria, W., Bera, P. (eds.) BPMDS/EMMSAD -2018. LNBIP, vol. 318, pp. 67–81. Springer, Cham (2018). https://doi.org/10.1007/978-3-319-91704-7_5
17. Marrella, A.: What automated planning can do for business process management. In: Teniente, E., Weidlich, M. (eds.) BPM 2017. LNBIP, vol. 308, pp. 7–19. Springer, Cham (2018). https://doi.org/10.1007/978-3-319-74030-0_1
18. Matthies, C., Dobrigkeit, F., Hesse, G.: An additional set of (automated) eyes: chatbots for agile retrospectives. In: Proceedings of the 1st International Workshop on Bots in Software Engineering, pp. 34–37. IEEE Press (2019)
19. Moffitt, K.C., Rozario, A.M., Vasarhelyi, M.A.: Robotic process automation for auditing. J. Emerg. Technol. Account. **15**(1), 1–10 (2018)
20. Muise, C., et al.: Planning for goal-oriented dialogue systems. arXiv preprint arXiv:1910.08137 (2019)
21. Muthusamy, V., Slominski, A., Ishakian, V.: Towards enterprise-ready AI deployments minimizing the risk of consuming AI models in business applications. In: 2018 First International Conference on Artificial Intelligence for Industries (AI4I), pp. 108–109. IEEE (2018)
22. Papageorgiou, D.: Transforming the HR function through robotic process automation. Benefits Q. **34**(2), 27–30 (2018)
23. Rizk, Y., et al.: A unified conversational assistant framework for business process automation. In: AAAI IPA (2020)

24. Rizk, Y., Isahagian, V., Unuvar, M., Khazaeni, Y.: A snooze-less user-aware notification system for proactive conversational agents. In: Intelligent User Interfaces Workshop on User-Aware Conversational Agents (2020)

25. Rosemann, M.: Trust-aware process design. In: Hildebrandt, T., van Dongen, B.F., Röglinger, M., Mendling, J. (eds.) BPM 2019. LNCS, vol. 11675, pp. 305–321. Springer, Cham (2019). https://doi.org/10.1007/978-3-030-26619-6_20

26. Seeliger, A., Sánchez Guinea, A., Nolle, T., Mühlhäuser, M.: ProcessExplorer: intelligent process mining guidance. In: Hildebrandt, T., van Dongen, B.F., Röglinger, M., Mendling, J. (eds.) BPM 2019. LNCS, vol. 11675, pp. 216–231. Springer, Cham (2019). https://doi.org/10.1007/978-3-030-26619-6_15

27. Sen, J., et al.: Natural language querying of complex business intelligence queries. In: Proceedings of the 2019 International Conference on Management of Data, pp. 1997–2000. ACM (2019)

28. Stople, A., Steinsund, H., Iden, J., Bygstad, B.: Lightweight it and the it function: experiences from robotic process automation in a Norwegian bank. Bibsys Open J. Syst. **25**(1) (2017)

29. Tello, G., Gianini, G., Mizouni, R., Damiani, E.: Machine learning-based framework for log-lifting in business process mining applications. In: Hildebrandt, T., van Dongen, B.F., Röglinger, M., Mendling, J. (eds.) BPM 2019. LNCS, vol. 11675, pp. 232–249. Springer, Cham (2019). https://doi.org/10.1007/978-3-030-26619-6_16

30. Upadhyay, S., Agarwal, M., Bounneffouf, D., Khazaeni, Y.: A bandit approach to posterior dialog orchestration under a budget. In: NeurIPS Conversational AI Workshop (2019)

31. Weske, M.: Business Process Management (2012)

32. Wróblewska, A., Stanisławek, T., Prus-Zajączkowski, B., Garncarek, Ł.: Robotic process automation of unstructured data with machine learning. Ann. Comput. Sci. Inf. Syst. **16**, 9–16 (2018)

33. Wurm, B., Goel, K., Bandara, W., Rosemann, M.: Design patterns for business process individualization. In: Hildebrandt, T., van Dongen, B.F., Röglinger, M., Mendling, J. (eds.) BPM 2019. LNCS, vol. 11675, pp. 370–385. Springer, Cham (2019). https://doi.org/10.1007/978-3-030-26619-6_24

34. Yurochkin, M., Upadhyay, S., Bouneffouf, D., Agarwal, M., Khazaeni, Y.: Online semi-supervised learning with bandit feedback. In: LLD Workshop at ICLR (2019)

Is Robotic Process Automation Becoming Intelligent? Early Evidence of Influences of Artificial Intelligence on Robotic Process Automation

Johannes Viehhauser[✉]

Technical University of Munich, Arcisstraße 21, 80335 Munich, Germany
johannes.viehhauser@tum.de

Abstract. Advances in Artificial Intelligence (AI) are changing the nature of work and enable the increasing automation of tasks. The trend around AI technologies has also reached Robotic Process Automation (RPA). To date, RPA is known as a software solution that performs simple and routine tasks based on clearly defined rules. However, past research indicates that through the application of AI and Machine Learning technologies, RPA is starting to get "smart" by including intelligent features. Since little is known about the capabilities of intelligent RPA in academia, this paper examines how AI impacts the capabilities and applicability of RPA. Based on case studies with global RPA software providers and RPA integrators, evidence for cognitive capabilities within RPA is examined within the boundaries of a definition of cognitive intelligence. The paper also discusses the general necessity for cognitive intelligence within RPA software.

Keywords: Robotic Process Automation · Artificial Intelligence · Cognitive intelligence · Machine Learning · Intelligent Process Automation

1 Introduction

Artificial Intelligence (AI) is entirely changing the nature of work. Even complex tasks, which were previously performed exclusively by human knowledge workers, are increasingly being automated by machines [1]. The increasing automation is made possible by recent advances in AI technologies, the increasing processing power of computers, and the availability of vast amounts of data [2,3]. The trend around AI has also reached Robotic Process Automation (RPA). Various researchers indicate that sophisticated RPA solutions are starting to get "smart" and include AI and Machine Learning (ML) capabilities to recognize and process unstructured data or to learn in cooperation with human users [e.g., 4–6].

However, research on RPA mainly focuses on simple RPA. Per definition, RPA is an umbrella term for computer programs that mimic and replicate human

© Springer Nature Switzerland AG 2020
A. Asatiani et al. (Eds.): BPM Blockchain and RPA Forum 2020, LNBIP 393, pp. 101–115, 2020.
https://doi.org/10.1007/978-3-030-58779-6_7

activities by imitating manual, screen-based manipulations [7–9]. Simple RPA is limited to the execution of well-structured routine tasks based on explicit and predefined rules and substitutes for the "arms" and "legs" of human workers [5,6]. Little is known about RPA with intelligent capabilities, even though it appears to be a major trend in industry. Agostinelli et al. (2019) focus on intelligent RPA by analyzing different RPA software and identify limited self-learning abilities within the examined RPA solutions [10]. Other authors address intelligent RPA only marginally as an idea or early indication but do not provide in-depth analyses [5,8,11].

Given the increasing importance of and attention on RPA and AI in industry as well as the lack of research in academia, this paper raises the question of how intelligent RPA is and thus asks: *How does AI impact the capabilities of RPA as well as its applicability, with focus on suitable task characteristics?* Due to the limited theoretical understanding and present dynamics in the field of intelligent RPA, a multiple case study approach is applied to assess the level of intelligence of current RPA solutions [12]. Specifically, rich field and archival data from nine global RPA software providers and six RPA integrators are used.

This research comes with several contributions. First, based on an operationalized definition of cognitive intelligence as a subdomain of AI, the level of intelligence of RPA is assessed. It becomes clear that RPA has only very limited cognitive capabilities and, as per its nature, remains a rule-based execution engine. Only intelligence that enables RPA to work more efficiently and expand its applicability without affecting the predictability and accuracy of outcomes is built into RPA engines. Second, a platform approach to combine RPA with external cognitive capabilities is introduced and discussed. All examined RPA providers offer platforms to add intelligent capabilities from external solutions to RPA. Finally, the impact on process and task suitability is examined. The findings reveal that increasing intelligence expands the potential fields of application of RPA, since the necessity for structured data input, standardization, and process stability becomes less important.

The paper is organized as follows: Sect. 2 provides an overview of fundamental knowledge about RPA and AI, followed by the introduction of the research method in Sect. 3. The analysis of RPA robots and platforms and their level of cognitive intelligence as well as implications on the applicability are presented in Sect. 4. Finally, key findings, limitations, and future research opportunities are summarized in Sects. 5 and 6.

2   Background

2.1   Definition and Introduction to Simple RPA

RPA is part of the Business Process Management domain and aims to automate existing processes based on available IT infrastructure by applying robots to digitally perform tasks [7,8]. RPA is used as an umbrella term for a computer program or software based on scripted language that mimics and replicates human activities by imitating manual, screen-based manipulations and reacting to events on the screen [7–9]. The software can be configured by humans to capture and interpret existing applications, process transactions, manipulate data, trigger responses, or communicate with other systems. RPA robots can either be traditionally programmed, configured by using a graphical user interface, or trained based on recorded process steps [6]. The software operates on graphical user interfaces or computer systems in the way a human would and can, therefore, interact with a wide range of software systems without requiring changes to existing applications [4–6]. This definition of RPA is mainly valid for simple RPA solutions without any kind of cognitive intelligence, which was the primary focus of past research.

2.2   Artificial Intelligence in the Context of RPA

In order to decide whether a system or software is intelligent, one first needs to define the term "intelligence". For computer scientists, the term "intelligence" refers to AI, machine intelligence, or computational intelligence as a subset of human cognitive behavior [13]. It is common in research to apply the concept of human intelligence to approach the definition of AI as machines that exhibit aspects of human intelligence [13,14]. Intelligence is regarded as the ability to learn from experience and adapt to the environment [15]. This research refers to the definition of AI by Kaplan and Haenlein (2019), who define AI as "the ability [of a system] to correctly interpret external data, to learn from such data, and to use those learnings to achieve specific goals and tasks through flexible adaption" [16]. This definition is particularly suitable in the context of RPA, since it builds on management literature and specifically targets application in business environments. The authors introduce three types of intelligence: cognitive intelligence, such as pattern recognition or systematic thinking, emotional intelligence, such as adaptability or self-awareness, and social intelligence, such as empathy or teamwork. Since most of the AI systems used in the context of RPA aim to emulate cognitive intelligence by generating a cognitive representation of the environment as well as by learning from past experience to inform future decisions, it is sufficient to focus on cognitive intelligence to assess the degree of "intelligence" of RPA [5,8]. Humanized AI with emotional and social intelligence is not included in the analysis, since it is not available yet [16]. Moreover, intelligence can also be classified into weak and strong AI. The hypothesis of weak AI constitutes that machines act as if they were intelligent, apply AI only to specific areas, and are not able to solve problems autonomously [16,17]. In contrast, strong or general AI assumes that machines actually think and do not just imitate human intelligence [16,17]. In the context of intelligent RPA, cognitive intelligence is considered a form of weak AI [14].

2.3   Classification Framework for Cognitive Intelligence

To analyze cognitive capabilities of RPA, cognitive intelligence is operationalized by cognitive computing. The technology is inspired by the human mind and aims to interact with external sources, process and understand contextual meaning, learn from past experiences, and draw conclusions based on large volumes of data [3,18]. Cognitive computing includes technologies, such as Natural Language Processing (NLP), ML, Neural Networks, or Automated Reasoning [19].

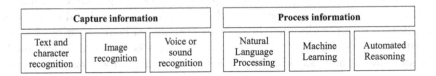

Fig. 1. Classification framework for cognitive intelligence

Cognitive computing comprises two core capabilities: information capturing and information processing [3,19]. For this research, they are applied as a framework to discuss and identify intelligent capabilities of current RPA software solutions in the context of implemented use cases (cf. Fig. 1). The first dimension, capturing information, includes the collection of data and information as well as the perception and observation of the environment. Data collection includes information from text, vision, sound, or voice. The second dimension, processing information, includes capabilities to analyze and interpret contextual meaning via NLP, to learn via ML capabilities, and to reason and take decisions via Automated Reasoning. NLP uses computational techniques to understand natural language and produce human language content. It thereby serves as a basis for human-machine or machine-machine communication [20]. ML solutions provide the ability to recognize patterns, to learn, to develop solutions, and to adapt to new circumstances based on the applied learning algorithm. In the context of RPA and this paper, ML refers to supervised learning methods that learn based on the mapping of a given set of input variables to a given set of predefined output variables [16]. Automated Reasoning allows computers to autonomously reason about knowledge they have gained completely, or almost completely, answer questions, and draw conclusions [21].

3   Research Method

Given the limited theoretical understanding and present dynamics in the field of intelligent RPA, this paper applies a multiple case study approach as described in [12] to assess the impact of AI on the capabilities and applicability of RPA. The multiple case study approach is broadly used in Information Systems research and is particularly suitable for research on newly emerging technologies in organizations, such as RPA in combination with cognitive intelligence [22,23].

As shown in Table 1, several data sources are included: semi-structured interviews with top management as well as technology and innovation managers from RPA software providers and RPA integrators, informal follow-up interviews, and archival data such as product specifications or case documentations. The sample

Table 1. Interview panel

Company	Origin	Position	Interview type	Duration (IV/FU)	Archival data
			Interview and archival data		
RPA provider A	North America	Director Partnerships	Phone call	75/15 min	6 PS, 1 PR, 2 CD
RPA provider B	North America	IT Solution Manager	Phone call	80/15 min	4 PS, 2 PR, 1 CD
RPA provider C	Europe	IT Solution Manager	Phone call	60/10 min	6 PS, 2 CD
RPA provider D	Europe	Business Development Manager	Phone call	75/20 min	2 PS, 2 CD
RPA provider E	Europe	IT Solution Manager	Phone call	60 min	2 PS, 2 CD
RPA provider F	Europe	Director RPA	Phone call	55 min	4 PS
RPA provider G	North America	Director RPA and AI	Phone call	70/15 min	1 PS, 1 PR, 5 CD
RPA provider H	Europe	Global Head IoT	Phone call	80/30 min	4 PS, 2 CD
RPA provider I	Europe	Account Manager	Phone call	50/10 min	3 PS, 1 PR
RPA integrator A	Europe	Managing Director	Phone call	50 min	2 PS
RPA integrator B	North America	Managing Director	Phone call	50 min	1 PS, 1 CD
RPA integrator C	Europe	R&D Manager	Phone call	55 min	1 PS, 1 CD
RPA integrator D	Middle East	Managing Director	Phone call	55 min	1 PS
RPA integrator E	Europe	Innovation Manager	Phone call	90 min	2 PS
RPA integrator F	Asia	Managing Director	Phone call	45 min	1 PS

Legend: IV = Semi-structured interview, FU = Follow-up interview, PS = Product specification, CD = Case documentation, PR = Press release

consists of nine RPA software providers, including three global market leaders, who provide a technology-driven perspective. For a bottom-up validation, six RPA integrators, who worked with the examined RPA software, are included. They provide an application-driven perspective and verify the technology view of the software providers.

The interview process consisted of three waves, starting with the three globally leading RPA providers, followed by six interviews with second and third tier RPA providers, and six interviews with RPA integrators. Follow-up interviews were used to clarify information. As proposed by Eisenhardt and Graebner (2007), the data analysis consisted of a within-case and a cross-case analysis of the transcribed interview and archival data from all RPA providers to detect patterns and to develop constructs [12]. Data from software integrators were used to refine, confirm, or reject the findings and emerging hypotheses.

To ensure data validity, a broad panel of RPA software providers was included. The technical capabilities were critically challenged and only accepted if use cases prove their successful application. Also, the interview transcripts were sent out and reviewed by the experts to ensure accuracy. To overcome a potential elite bias, interviewees from various functional areas and hierarchical levels were included. Finally, a detailed overview of the research project was given beforehand and anonymity was granted to overcome a potential lack of trust.

4   Classification and Analysis of RPA Software

The analysis of the conducted interviews and case studies based on a framework for cognitive intelligence, as introduced in Sect. 2.3, reveals two different approaches with regard to RPA and cognitive capabilities. The approaches are in line with past research [5,6,8]. On the one hand, RPA is defined as stand-alone software and any kind of cognitive intelligence is incorporated into the RPA software itself. This further development of RPA can be referred to as intelligent RPA and is detailed in Sect. 4.1. For the purpose of this research, all software that is defined as RPA without external solutions that are not incorporated into the software engine is regarded as intelligent RPA. On the other hand, features from cognitive intelligence can be combined with RPA using a platform approach. This means that the concept of simple RPA, as rule-based software, is not touched upon. The intelligence is added by external software, which is integrated into an RPA platform. The platform approach is detailed in Sect. 4.2 below. Academia and industry introduced Intelligent Process Automation or Intelligent Automation to specify this approach [4,24].

4.1   Examination of Cognitive Intelligence Within RPA Solutions

Based on the operationalized definition of cognitive intelligence from Sect. 2.3, Table 2 provides an overview of identified elements of cognitive intelligence that are incorporated into intelligent RPA solutions. They are derived from the analyses of the conducted case studies. The RPA robots A to I correspond to the solutions of the software providers A to I, as introduced in Table 1.

Capturing Information. Capturing information from digital text files with structured electronic text in the form of character recognition is regarded as a standard feature of RPA and included in all examined RPA solutions. The extraction of data from text files constitutes rule-based processing of information. It can be triggered either based on predefined rules within a process flow or based on events that are initiated by activities or keywords. The robots, for example, copy text strings and transfer them into other systems, classify documents based on specific keywords, or use keywords to extract text information.

Optical Character Recognition (OCR) enables the extraction of text from images, ranging from scanned printed documents to pictures with text elements such as traffic signs. Five of the examined robots are able to process images, i.e., robots A, B, C, E, and F. However, most of them are limited to basic OCR capabilities. Basic OCR provides the ability to process scanned, printed documents with a structured nature of text and printed fonts and convert the content into a digital text string. Only solution C contains advanced OCR capabilities. Advanced OCR technology enables texts within images or tables, texts that are randomly located, or texts that are hand-written to be processed and transformed into structured output with a high level of quality. All other vendors do not include OCR in their RPA, as software provider D described:

Table 2. Overview of incorporated cognitive capabilities within RPA solutions

Robot	Capture information				Process information	
	Text and character recognition	Image recognition	Voice or sound recognition	Natural Language Processing	Machine Learning	Automated Reasoning
RPA robot A	CR, KS	Basic OCR, CV	—	—	DC, TC, CV	—
RPA robot B	CR, KS	Basic OCR, CV	—	—	CV	—
RPA robot C	CR, KS	OCR, CV	—	—	DC, TC, CV, SH	—
RPA robot D	CR, KS	CV	—	—	CV	—
RPA robot E	CR, KS	Basic OCR, CV	—	—	CV	—
RPA robot F	CR, KS	Basic OCR	—	—	SH, RE	—
RPA robot G	CR, KS	CV	—	—	CV	—
RPA robot H	CR, KS	CV	—	—	CV	—
RPA robot I	CR, KS	—	—	—	—	—

Legend: CR = Character recognition, KS= Keyword search, OCR = Optical Character Recognition, CV = Computer Vision, DC = Document classification, TC = Text classification, RE = Recommendation engine, SH = ML-based scheduling

We do not include OCR in our RPA solution, because we want to keep our solution flexible and the results predictable. For us, RPA is the execution engine that performs rule-based tasks. If a client wants to extract unstructured data, they need to apply external software.

To verify the basic OCR capabilities, a use case with robot B from the banking industry is analyzed. After a new e-mail with scanned mortgage contracts arrives, the robot saves the files on a local drive and converts them into a digital text string by applying OCR. After identifying the corresponding contract number based on a predefined keyword search, the robot uploads the text into a data management system and completes the process.

Seven out of nine examined RPA solutions utilize Computer Vision technologies to identify, understand, and classify digital elements and objects on user interfaces, i.e., robots A, B, C, D, E, G, and H. The technology is based on similarity analysis and reacts to visual conformance. Computer windows and on-screen elements can be identified and used as a trigger for process activities. Computer Vision is regarded as an integral part of RPA and is used for applying RPA when underlying data cannot be accessed, as explained by provider E:

Computer Vision is a core feature of RPA. Our strategy is to make the RPA engine just as intelligent as necessary to detect and process elements on the screen. The purpose is really RPA, which is why it is embedded.

Computer Vision provides several advantages. First, the technology eliminates the reliance on selectors and underlying data, since it workswith visible screen elements. It is even possible to use screen elements as anchors and access User Interface (UI) elements that are located within a certain distance. This enables a broader integration of elements and applicability. Second, the flexibility of RPA processes increases. Elements can be accessed even after modifications of software or changes in homepage designs. Third, Computer Vision enables remote automation on a virtual screen based on graphical data. This serves as a fallback solution if other automation methods do not work.

None of the examined RPA solutions can process rich media, such as voice or sound. The technology is not regarded as an essential part of process automation with RPA. RPA provider F commented:

> *Processing of rich media is complex and a different technology than RPA. It is not part of our solution, since we see enough demand on the text side. In addition, some of the tools and technologies in the market are not as robust as required yet. If you want to achieve a sufficient accuracy level, it starts to get expensive. If required by a client, voice processing can be combined with RPA as third-party software.*

Processing Information. None of the examined RPA solutions contain incorporated NLP capabilities. Only basic NLP features in the form of keyword search are included. However, the keyword search is strictly rule-based and does not require any cognitive intelligence. In general, most RPA software providers do not regard NLP as a critical or core capability of RPA. NLP is utilized as separate technology and integrated into RPA processes as a distinct component.

Two of the examined RPA robots provide built-in ML capabilities for document and text classification (robots A and C). Document classification enables the assignment of labels of a document type based on a predefined selection of options. The technology is based on supervised ML and combines different document properties, such as document type, author, subject, or content data [25]. After the document type is identified, specific text classification modules are applied. This enables critical information to be extracted and converted into structured output. The text classification is also based on supervised ML and trained by human employees. The integration of document and text classification capabilities correlates with the integration of basic or advanced OCR capabilities. However, there are only two RPA solutions with inherent basic and advanced OCR capabilities that include classification mechanisms.

Computer Vision also contains ML features. Based on the shape and type of objects, ML is applied to determine the purpose and usage of objects. The algorithms are fed with a large amount of images and corresponding categories. Also, error reporting in interaction with human users is used to further develop the ML algorithm.

In addition, supervised ML is applied by RPA vendor F for exception management in the form of an ML-based recommendation engine (cf. "RE" in Table 2). The ML algorithm monitors exception handling activities of RPA users and learns based on their decisions. Thereby, changes on a code level or within workflows become superfluous, since RPA can automatically recommend configurations based on prior learnings and even perform them routinely. In the examined case, the characters "O" and "Q" cannot be assigned by the robot, which leads to an error. The algorithm monitors the human exception handling. If it detects a similar exception multiple times, it makes a recommendation to the human user, and, after approval, routinely performs the exception. Since it improves the performance of RPA, it is regarded as useful for RPA and included in the software as an intelligent component.

Scheduling is a critical part of RPA, especially if multiple robots are applied or if one robot performs multiple tasks. Most RPA solutions use a scheduler based on predefined rules about the priority of tasks, the timing, or the duration of the execution. Two RPA providers offer built-in ML-based scheduling modules (robots C and F). They enable the dynamic scheduling of robots and tasks based on multiple parameters, such as scope and time requirements of tasks, defined service levels, concurrent processes, and the performance of underlying applications. The ML algorithm takes into account the defined parameters, the former performance of the robot, and the relation between latency times of applications and the resulting robot performance and dynamically schedules multiple robots to meet the agreed service levels. This enables flexible application and reassignment as well as increased service level fulfillment and utilization.

None of the examined RPA solutions provide any kind of Automated Reasoning capabilities. The interview partners agreed that intelligence in the form of independent decision making should not be part of RPA. It weakens the ability of RPA to deliver accurate and predictable results based on explicit rules. RPA provider A distinguished between built-in intelligence in RPA solutions and intelligence outside the robot:

Automated Reasoning is not the kind of intelligence that we want to build into RPA. It is an external intelligence that can be leveraged to answer questions or to carry out decisions. What RPA can do is the subsequent execution.

4.2   Enhancement of RPA with External Cognitive Intelligence

Introduction of Platform Approach. All nine examined RPA providers pursue the strategy of incorporating cognitive intelligence via a platform. This means that RPA, as a rule-based execution engine, is combined with selected external solutions. The external technologies are incorporated into the RPA platforms and can be easily integrated into the workflows as modules. RPA steers the cognitive components and executes the structured output. If needed, further external technologies can be added via application programming interfaces (APIs).

The platform approach facilitates the integration of external technologies. This allows faster and more robust automation with little time required and no need for coding. The integration without coding is important in that it enables the application of RPA at a business level. By introducing a technology partner ecosystem and modular integration, RPA can be extended with best-in-class cognitive capabilities without the requirement for in-house solutions. This means that solutions from RPA providers, clients, or third parties can be leveraged and flexibility is increased.

Table 3. Overview of cognitive capabilities integrated into RPA platforms

RPA platform	Capture information				Process information	
	Text and character recognition	Image recognition	Voice or sound recognition	Natural Language Processing	Machine Learning	Automated Reasoning
Platform A	—	OCR	—	—	DC, TC	—
Platform B	—	OCR	—	—	DC, TC	—
Platform C	—	OCR	—	—	DC, TC	—
Platform D	—	OCR	—	NLP	DC, TC	—
Platform E	—	OCR	—	NLP	DC, TC	—
Platform F	—	OCR	—	—	DC, TC	—
Platform G	—	OCR	—	NLP	DC, TC	—
Platform H	—	OCR	—	NLP	DC, TC	—
Platform I	—	OCR	—	—	DC, TC	—

Legend: OCR = Optical Character Recognition, NLP = Natural Language Processing, DC = Document classification, TC = Text classification

Cognitive Intelligence Within Platforms. Table 3 provides an overview of external cognitive capabilities integrated into the RPA platforms. Platform A corresponds to robot A, as introduced in Table 2. The digitization of input by processing images via advanced OCR is identified as a standard feature of all nine RPA platforms, which can be integrated via drag-and-drop. The providers include prepackaged leading external software solutions from suppliers, such as Abbyy or Kofax. In doing so, the RPA software providers can utilize best-in-class solutions to address specific digitization problems and keep their RPA solution simple. In addition, some of the RPA platforms also provide interfaces to integrate open-source solutions on demand.

Four of the examined RPA platforms offer a built-in preselection of NLP solutions, which can be integrated via drag-and-drop (robots D, E, G, and H). The cases reveal that NLP is mainly used for contextual and sentiment analysis to understand the intent and body of texts. These platforms mainly originate from technology companies with competence in NLP and not from specialized RPA providers. The NLP software offered is either an internal solution or based on external software and, in any case, is not part of the license model. Even though it is regarded as a critical component, the majority of RPA platforms within the sample do not contain NLP capabilities as part of their platforms, as RPA software provider E emphasizes:

Within RPA itself, there are no NLP capabilities yet and it is not a core functionality of our RPA platform. Nonetheless, some RPA processes

include external NLP technologies based on license models or as open-source solutions to fulfill specific demands.

As described in Sect. 4.1, RPA engines themselves partially provide supervised ML capabilities. With the platform approach, all examined solutions provide ML capabilities in the form of text and document classification. They are added through the integration of external OCR solutions. Moreover, all platforms enable the integration of additional ML solutions via standardized interfaces. For example, the programming language Python can be applied to code ML capabilities or to use pre-trained Python models. Thus, the RPA robot or platform itself does not include ML capabilities other than those described in Sect. 4.1, but it enables the integration of external solutions. Automated Reasoning has not been part of any of the RPA platforms and examined cases.

4.3   Impact of Increasing Intelligence on Process and Task Suitability

The increasing level of cognitive intelligence within RPA software solutions or as integrated solutions within RPA platforms impacts the applicability of RPA. According to the experts, the process requirement that is affected most is the need for structured data input. Intelligent RPA can work with unstructured or fast changing data. RPA integrator E explains:

Unstructured data can be structured and made accessible based on intelligent RPA. The importance of standardization of data decreases as the level of cognitive capabilities increases.

The data first needs to be transformed and structured. RPA subsequently receives the structured data and processes it based on predefined rules. The requirement for structured data input decreases, although RPA still needs structured data to process tasks. Second, the requirement for a high degree of process standardization and clearly defined rules decreases. Intelligent RPA can perform processes with changing process steps or rules. However, rules remain critical and an important prerequisite for RPA. Intelligent RPA can, so far, only perform changes or exceptions with low complexity. Third, the requirement for process stability becomes less important. Exception management based on a supervised ML algorithm enables the handling of errors and exceptions during the process or within unstructured data input. Nevertheless, the software solution still requires human employees for decision making as well as for processing of critical tasks. Even though this impact has been confirmed by most experts, only one examined RPA robot provides ML-based exception handling capabilities.

Regardless of the increasing cognitive capabilities that impact decision criteria for RPA, basic process requirements remain unaffected. A process that is structured, simple, and mature is still more eligible than a process with less structure and with exceptions. Cognitive capabilities broaden the field of application of RPA at the cost of complexity and implementation effort.

5 Discussion

5.1 RPA and Built-In Cognitive Intelligence

This research reveals that RPA has only very limited cognitive capabilities, despite the contrary being argued by software providers and indicated by research. Almost all experts emphasize that RPA is not intelligent and does not need intelligent capabilities. It is, as per definition, a software for the rule-based processing of click sequences with predictable and stable outcomes. This has been confirmed by the interviews conducted and the analyses of nine RPA software solutions along a framework of cognitive intelligence. None of the RPA engines fulfill the prerequisites for cognitive intelligence and this therefore disproves the hypothesis of RPA being intelligent. Nevertheless, the findings show that all RPA solutions can process structured digital text and perform keyword search based on predefined rules. In addition, four of the examined RPA solutions have built-in basic OCR capabilities and one solution even provides advanced OCR. The findings are partially in line with prior research, which indicates that RPA is starting to get "smart" features, such as image recognition [4,5]. However, the results reveal that the extent to which OCR is part of RPA is very limited and the majority of RPA software providers do not regard OCR as an essential part of RPA. Additionally, none of the solutions are able to capture complex, unstructured data input from sources such as voice or sound. On the processing side, none of the RPA engines provide NLP or Automated Reasoning capabilities. They are regarded as complex and non-core technologies. According to the definition of cognitive intelligence, those components, however, would be critical to contribute machine intelligence to understand contextual meaning, reason, or draw conclusions [3,18]. Only the added value of ML is regarded as suitable to RPA. Therefore, ML in the form of supervised learning methods is incorporated in most of the examined RPA solutions, mainly through Computer Vision, document and text classification, and partially through scheduling and exception management. The findings are in line with existing research, which point out that learning capabilities should be incorporated into RPA solutions [6,8]. However, the extent to which ML is used for RPA is limited. The cases emphasize that only ML capabilities enabling RPA to work more efficiently and expand its applicability without affecting the predictability and accuracy of outcomes are built into RPA engines.

The separation of RPA and cognitive capabilities as well as the consequential lack of intelligence of RPA relies on a broadly accepted rationale. First, the definition of RPA as a rule-based execution engine sets limits, which would be undermined by an unpredictable operation. Second, RPA provides the mechanical foundation for process automation, which is a key advantage. RPA should remain with exactly these capabilities, since the demand for rule-based automation is likely to continue to exist. Besides, it is the same with RPA as with employees: building on basic requirements, companies recruit employees or train them to work on specific tasks. This flexibility can only be guaranteed with RPA if it remains an execution engine to which cognitive intelligence can be added flexibly. Third, most companies in the RPA market are RPA-only companies and have limited AI, OCR, or NLP capabilities. Since those technologies require a high degree of specialization, it is reasonable to integrate best-in-class external technologies instead of developing proprietary solutions. The integration of non-RPA technologies also drives the complexity with regard to integration, usability, and maintenance with varying update cycles and technical requirements. Fourth, commercial restrictions hinder the incorporation of cognitive capabilities within RPA. The concept of modular RPA platforms enables the flexible tailoring of solutions to customer demands and reduces the costs for simple RPA.

5.2 Development Towards Platform-Based Automation

All nine RPA providers offer RPA platforms to add cognitive intelligence to RPA as external elements. This indicates that the evolution of RPA towards more intelligent capabilities does not take place built into RPA but rather with external capabilities that can be bolted on to RPA in a modular fashion. The RPA software itself acts as an execution engine within the platform, which steers external components and processes structured outputs. The case studies reveal that mainly OCR and NLP are added via the platform. As such, the key contribution comes with the ability to process information in the form of content understanding and supervised learning. Four RPA platforms provide preselected NLP solutions and all platforms enable the simple integration of external NLP technologies. However, RPA platforms still lack key cognitive capabilities, mainly in the field of Automated Reasoning. The experts cited a lack of transparency and reliability, the level of development of AI solutions, and the reluctance of users as the main reasons against the deployment of Automated Reasoning.

In general, the development towards RPA platforms is driven by the dynamic nature of most processes, which calls for flexible and non-static solutions. The modular platforms provide interfaces and an open architecture to external solutions. Since cognitive technologies are highly sophisticated and are developing rapidly, built-in capabilities would not be reasonable. Integrating intelligence via programming interfaces makes the platforms more robust and improves the operational efficiency and stability. The modular integration also ensures simple usability. This is vital, since RPA is applied on an operational business level and needs to be set up and operated by non-IT employees.

6   Limitations and Future Research

By following the principles for data validity as stated in the methodology section, this paper aimed to prevent structural errors. Nevertheless, the research is not without limitations. First, the definition of RPA potentially differs across software providers. Even though this has been explicitly clarified, a divergent understanding of RPA could have led to missing or exaggerated capabilities, which may reduce comparability. Second, the selection of RPA software providers is not exhaustive and is limited to the globally leading providers plus a selection of additional RPA companies. Third, the experts could have potentially overstated the actual capabilities of their RPA software and platforms. To overcome this problem, a bottom-up perspective from RPA integrators is introduced and case documentations are used to confirm the capabilities. Fourth, the framework could potentially bias the results. However, core elements are included and no other features were mentioned during the interviews.

RPA and cognitive intelligence constitute interesting research opportunities. A general discussion about the definition and designation of RPA and cognitive intelligence would be needed to clarify the terminology used, since RPA is predefined and per definition rules out any kind of dynamic or intelligence. Since this research provides indications of influences on process suitability, future research could address the question of how decision support criteria are affected by intelligent RPA. Another interesting research opportunity is the question of which cognitive capabilities complement RPA best and should be integrated. Moreover, research could address the implications of RPA with cognitive intelligence on its applicability as well as the resulting effects on performance. Finally, the question of how AI could be used to understand and process exceptions and assist with coding without human intervention is of interest.

References

1. Dias, M., Pan, S.L., Tim, Y.: Knowledge embodiment of human and machine interactions: robotic process automation at the Finland government. In: Twenty-Seventh European Conference on Information Systems (ECIS 2019), Stockholm-Uppsala, Sweden (2019)
2. French, R.M.: Moving beyond the Turing test. Commun. ACM **55**(12), 74–77 (2012)
3. Gupta, S., Kar, A.K., Baabdullah, A., Al-Khowaiter, W.A.: Big data with cognitive computing: a review for the future. Int. J. Inf. Manage. **42**, 78–89 (2018)
4. Hofmann, P., Samp, C., Urbach, N.: Robotic process automation. Electron. Markets **30**(1), 99–106 (2019)
5. Plattfaut, R.: Robotic Process Automation - process optimization on steroids? In: Fortieth International Conference on Information Systems, Munich (2019)
6. Wanner, J., Hofmann, A., Fischer, M., Imgrund, F., Janiesch, C., Geyer-Klingeberg, J.: Process selection in RPA projects - towards a quantifiable method of decision making. In: Fortieth International Conference on Information Systems, Munich (2019)
7. Lacity, M.C., Willcocks, L.P.: Robotic process automation at telefónica O2. MIS Q. Execut. **15**(1) (2016)
8. van der Aalst, W.M.P., Bichler, M., Heinzl, A.: Robotic process automation. Bus. Inf. Syst. Eng. **60**(4), 269–272 (2018)
9. Penttinen, E., Kasslin, H., Asatiani, A.: How to choose between robotic process automation and back-end system automation? In: Twenty-Sixth European Conference on Information Systems (ECIS 2018) (2018)
10. Agostinelli, S., Marrella, A., Mecella, M.: Research challenges for intelligent robotic process automation. In: Di Francescomarino, C., Dijkman, R., Zdun, U. (eds.) BPM 2019. LNBIP, vol. 362, pp. 12–18. Springer, Cham (2019). https://doi.org/10.1007/978-3-030-37453-2_2

11. Syed, R., et al.: Robotic process automation: contemporary themes and challenges. Comput. Ind. **115**, 103162 (2020)
12. Eisenhardt, K.M., Graebner, M.E.: Theory building from cases: opportunities and challenges. Acad. Manag. J. **50**(1), 25–32 (2007)
13. Feigenbaum, E.A.: Some challenges and grand challenges for computational intelligence. J. ACM **50**(1), 32–40 (2003)
14. Huang, M.H., Rust, R.T.: Artificial intelligence in service. J. Serv. Res. **21**(2), 155–172 (2018)
15. Gardner, H.: Frames of Mind: The Theory of Multiple Intelligences. Basics, New York (1983)
16. Kaplan, A., Haenlein, M.: Siri, Siri, in my hand: who's the fairest in the land? On the interpretations, illustrations, and implications of artificial intelligence. Bus. Horiz. **62**(1), 15–25 (2019)
17. Russell, S., Norvig, P.: Artificial Intelligence: A Modern Approach. Pearson (2002)
18. Modha, D.S., Ananthanarayanan, R., Esser, S.K., Ndirango, A., Sherbondy, A.J., Singh, R.: Cognitive computing. Commun. ACM **54**(8), 62–71 (2011)
19. Davenport, T.H., Kirby, J.: Just how smart are smart machines? MIT Sloan Manag. Rev. **57**(3), 21 (2016)
20. Hirschberg, J., Manning, C.D.: Advances in natural language processing. Science **349**(6245), 261–266 (2015)
21. Rich, C., Feldman, Y.: Seven layers of knowledge representation and reasoning in support of software development. IEEE Trans. Software Eng. **18**, 451–469 (1992)
22. Conboy, K., Fitzgerald, G., Mathiassen, L.: Qualitative methods research in information systems: motivations, themes, and contributions. Eur. J. Inf. Syst. **21**(2), 113–118 (2012)
23. Orlikowski, W.J., Baroudi, J.J.: Studying information technology in organizations: research approaches and assumptions. Inf. Syst. Res. **2**(1), 1–28 (1991)
24. Kokina, J., Blanchette, S.: Early evidence of digital labor in accounting: innovation with robotic process automation. Int. J. Account. Inf. Syst. **35** (2019)
25. Sebastiani, F.: Machine learning in automated text categorization. ACM Comput. Surv. (CSUR) **34**(1), 1–47 (2002)

Automated Generation of Executable RPA Scripts from User Interface Logs

Simone Agostinelli, Marco Lupia, Andrea Marrella$^{(\boxtimes)}$, and Massimo Mecella

Sapienza Universitá di Roma, Rome, Italy
lupia.1694700@studenti.uniroma1.it,
{agostinelli,marrella,mecella}@diag.uniroma1.it

Abstract. Robotic Process Automation (RPA) operates on the user interface (UI) of software applications and automates - by means of a software (SW) robot - mouse and keyboard interactions to remove intensive routine tasks (or simply *routines*). With the recent advances in Artificial Intelligence, the automation of routines is expected to undergo a radical transformation. Nonetheless, to date, the RPA tools available in the market are not able to automatically learn to automate such routines, thus requiring the support of skilled human experts that observe and interpret how routines are executed on the UIs of the applications. Being the current practice time-consuming and error-prone, in this paper we present SmartRPA, a cross-platform tool that tackles such issues by exploiting UI logs to automatically generate executable RPA scripts that automate the routines enactment by SW robots.

Keywords: Robotic Process Automation (RPA) · Automated RPA script generation · User Interface (UI) logs · Process mining

1 Introduction

Robotic Process Automation (RPA) is a fast-emerging automation technology in the field of Business Process Management (BPM) that uses software (SW) robots to mimic and replicate the execution of highly repetitive routine tasks (we refer to them as *routines*) performed by human users in their applications' user interfaces (UIs). The RPA technology is still in its infancy [1], even if similar solutions have been around for a long time. For instance, closely related to SW robots, chatbots have been using for years to accept voice-based or keyboard inputs and guide customers to find relevant information in web-based applications [14]. Differently from chatbots, RPA can be seen as an evolution of screen scraping solutions [9], which sought to visualize screen display data from legacy applications (having no means for automated interfacing) to display such data using modern UIs. The strength of RPA is that it does not replace existing applications or manipulate their code, but rather works with them in a way similar to a human user.

In recent years there was an increased interest around RPA, resulting in many industry-specific deployments for financial and business services [5, 12, 19]. In this

© Springer Nature Switzerland AG 2020
A. Asatiani et al. (Eds.): BPM Blockchain and RPA Forum 2020, LNBIP 393, pp. 116–131, 2020.
https://doi.org/10.1007/978-3-030-58779-6_8

direction, according to [6], the market of RPA solutions has developed rapidly and today includes more than 50 vendors developing tools that provide SW robots with advanced functionalities for automating office tasks in operations like accounting, billing and customer service. Nonetheless, when considering state-of-the-art RPA technology, it becomes apparent that the current generation of RPA tools is driven by predefined rules and manual configurations made by expert users rather than automated techniques [3]. To be more specific, the traditional workflow to conduct a RPA project can be summarized as follows [18]:

1. Determine which routines are good candidates to be automated.
2. Record the mouse/key events that happen on the UI of the SW applications involved in a routine execution, i.e., the *UI logs*.
3. Model the selected routines in the form of flowchart diagrams, which involve the specification of the actions, routing constructs (e.g., parallel and alternative branches), data flow, etc. that define the behavior of a SW robot.
4. Develop each modeled routine by generating the SW code required to concretely enact the associated SW robot on a target computer system.
5. Deploy the SW robots in their environment to perform their actions.
6. Monitor the performance of SW robots to detect bottlenecks and exceptions.
7. Maintain the routines, which takes into account the SW robots performance and error cases to eventually enhance their behaviour.

The majority of the previous steps, particularly the ones involved in the early stages of the RPA life-cycle (i.e., steps 1 and 3), require the support of skilled human experts, which need to: *(i)* understand the anatomy of the candidate routines to automate by means of interviews, walk-troughs, and detailed observation of workers conducting their daily work; and *(ii)* define manually the flowchart diagrams representing the structure of such routines, which will drive the development of the SW code, often in form of executable scripts (also called *RPA scripts*), allowing the concrete enactment of SW robots at run-time (cf. step 4). While this approach is effective to execute simple rules-based logic in situations where there is no room for interpretation, it becomes time-consuming and error-prone in presence of routines that are less predictable or require some level of human judgment [4,25]. Indeed, the designer should have a global vision of all possible variants of the routines to define the appropriate behaviours of the SW robot, which becomes complicated when the number of variants increases. The issue is that in case where the flowchart diagram does not contain a suitable response for a specific situation, e.g., because of a shallow modeling activity, then the associated RPA scripts would not properly reflect the behaviour of the potential routine variant, forcing SW robots to escalate to a human supervisor at run-time, in contrast with the RPA philosophy.

To tackle and mitigate this issue, in this paper we develop a cross-platform software tool, called SmartRPA, to automatically generate executable RPA scripts directly from the UI logs that record the user interactions with the SW applications involved in a routine execution (cf. step 2), thus skipping completely the (manual) modeling activity of the flowchart diagrams (cf. step 3). SmartRPA involves five consecutive stages that enable to: *(i)* record the UI logs that keep

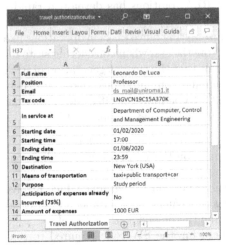

(a) Excel spreadsheet

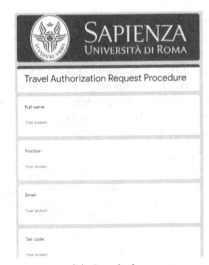

(b) Google form

Fig. 1. UIs involved in the running example

track of the different routine executions on the UIs of the involved SW applications; *(ii)* processing such UI logs in form of a single *event log* with additional execution properties; *(iii)* filtering out those events not relevant for the routine of interest and grouping together similar events; *(iv)* detecting the most frequent routine variant from the log, leveraging process discovery and abstraction techniques; and *(v)* generating the executable RPA scripts necessary to enact the SW robot that implements the selected routine variant. SmartRPA is available for download at https://github.com/bpm-diag/smartRPA/.

The rest of the paper is organized as follows. Section 2 presents a motivating running example. In Sect. 3, we analyze the architecture and the technical aspects of SmartRPA, together with the approach underlying the working of the tool. Section 4 examines the instantiation of SmartRPA on the running example. Finally, in Sect. 5 we present the related works, while Sect. 6 concludes the paper by discussing the weaknesses of the tool and the potential future works.

2   Running Example

Below, we describe an RPA use case inspired by a real-life scenario at Department of Computer, Control and Management Engineering (DIAG) of Sapienza Universitá di Roma. The scenario concerns the filling of the travel authorization request form made by professors, researchers and PhD students of DIAG for travel requiring prior approval.

The request applicant must fill a well-structured Excel spreadsheet (cf. Fig. 1(a)) providing some personal information, such as her/his bio-data and the email address, together with further information related to the travel, including the destination, the starting/ending date/time, the means of transport to be used, the travel purpose, and the envisioned amount of travel expenses, associated with the possibility to request an anticipation of the expenses already incurred (e.g., to request in advance a visa). When ready, the spreadsheet is sent via email to an employee of the Administration Office of DIAG, which is in charge of approving it and (only in this case) elaborating the request. Concretely, for each row in the spreadsheet, the employee manually copies every cell in that row and pastes that into the corresponding text field in a dedicated Google form (cf. Fig. 1(b)), accessible just by the Administration staff. Once the data transfer for a given travel request has been completed, the employee presses the "Submit" button to submit the data into an internal database. Once the form is submitted, a confirmation email is sent automatically to the applicant.

The above routine procedure is usually performed manually, it is tedious (as it must be repeated for any new travel request) and prone to errors. We will use it to show how the proposed SmartRPA tool is able to automatically develop the executable RPA scripts for automating the data transfer task of the routine, requiring in input just the UI logs that record the previous executions of such routine performed by several human users during dedicated training sessions.

3   SmartRPA Approach and Architecture

The architecture of SmartRPA integrates five main SW components developed in Python that enable to automatically generate executable RPA scripts that will drive the working of SW robots in emulating the users' observed behavior (previously recorded in dedicated UI logs) during the enactment of a routine of interest. An overview of the SmartRPA architecture is shown in Fig. 2.

The first SW component of the architecture is an **Action Logger** that can be used to record a wide range of UI actions from multiple SW applications during the enactment of a routine. This means that SmartRPA belongs to the category of those RPA tools that learn to automate routines "by examples" (see also our discussion in Sect. 5). To be more specific, a training session in which several users perform the routine to be automated is required to record the UI actions involved in its execution. To this aim, the Action Logger provides a Graphical User Interface (GUI) that allows a user to select which SW applications s/he wants to record UI actions on. All the applications that are not available in the host operating system of the user's PC/MAC are disabled by default. Then, the user can start the training session by clicking on the *"Start logger"* button (see Fig. 3). The Action Logger provides three categories of logging modules:

- *System Logger*: It detects those UI actions not related to specific SW applications, i.e.: copy and paste of files/folders; creation, renaming, movement and deletion of files/folders; usage of double-click and hotkeys; opening and closing of applications; printing activities; insertion/remotion of USB drives.
- *Office Logger*: It detects the UI actions performed within Microsoft Office applications, i.e.: Excel, Word and PowerPoint.

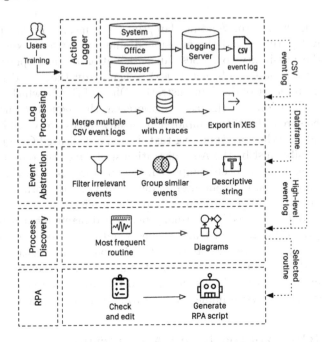

Fig. 2. SmartRPA architecture

– *Browser Logger*: It detects the UI actions performed on web browsers, i.e.: Google Chrome, Mozilla Firefox, Microsoft Edge and Opera.

Of course, multiple users can run the Action Logger on their PC/MAC many times performing the same routine in different training sessions. When a training session is completed, i.e., when the routine of interest has been executed from the start to the end, the user can push the *"Stop logger"* button to stop the recording of UI actions. The logging modules interact with a Logging Server implemented with the *Flask* framework,[1] which is in charge to store the UI actions captured by the logging modules and organize them as *events* into several CSV event logs. Each CSV event log contains exactly one (long) trace of UI actions performed in a single training session by a single user. From a technical point of view, *(i)* system events are recorded using different Python modules, including *PythonCOM* (to access the Windows APIs and COM objects like the Microsoft Office suite), and *MacFSEvents* for MacOS; *(ii)* events generated by Microsoft Office applications are recorded using the Office JavaScript APIs; and *(iii)* browser events are recorded using dedicated JavaScript web extensions developed for each supported web browser.

The second SW component of the architecture is a **Log Processing tool** that comes into play when any training session is considered as completed. Specifically, after *n* training sessions, the Logging Server will deliver the *n* created CSV

---

[1] https://palletsprojects.com/p/flask.

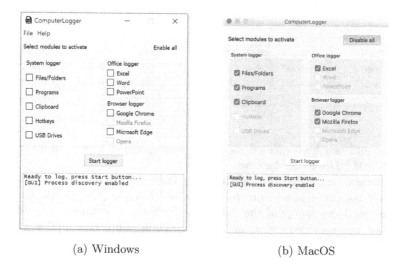

(a) Windows   (b) MacOS

Fig. 3. GUI of SmartRPA both on Windows and MacOS

event logs to the Log Processing tool, which uses Algorithm 1 to import them into a single Pandas dataframe.[2] A dataframe is a two-dimensional size-mutable and heterogeneous tabular data structure with labeled axes (rows and columns), which is used as the main artifact to represent event logs in SmartRPA. Of course, SmartRPA also produces an XES[3] (eXtensible Event Stream) version of the datastream, which will contain exactly n traces, one for each recorded CSV

Algorithm 1. Processing event logs

---

procedure HANDLELOG(*file_list*)
    create_directories()   ▷ where files will be saved
    for any CSV log in *file_list* **do**
        df ← import a CSV log into Pandas dataframe
        df ← rename columns to match XES standard
        df ← sort rows by timestamp
        df ← create *case:concept:name* column based on the first timestamp
        df ← generate a dataframe including the UI actions of the CSV log
    end for
    combined_df ← combine all dataframes into a single dataframe
    export(combined_df)   ▷ exported as XES file
end procedure

---

[2] https://pandas.pydata.org/.
[3] XES is the standard for the storage, interchange, and analysis of event logs [15].

Table 1. A partial view of a dataframe

case:concept:name	time:timestamp	org:resource	Category	Application	concept:name
429102859961	2020-04-29T10:29:33.887	marco	Office	Excel	editCell
429102859961	2020-04-29T10:29:34.583	marco	Browser	Chrome	mouseClick
429102859961	2020-04-29T10:29:35.401	marco	Browser	Chrome	changeField
429102859961	2020-04-29T10:29:36.119	marco	Clipboard	Chrome	paste

event log, and can be inspected using the most popular process mining tools, such as *ProM*,[4] *Disco*[5] or *Apromore*.[6]

The dataframe created by Algorithm 1 consists of low-level events with fine granularity associated one-by-one to a recorded UI action (e.g., mouse clicks, file selections, etc.). Each row of the dataframe includes 45 columns with relevant data about the recorded event, such as: the timestamp, the application that generated the event, the resources involved, etc. A partial view of a dataframe, describing only the first 6 columns recorded for each event, is shown in Table 1.

At this point, an **Event Abstraction component** is used to convert the low-level dataframe recording the event log (that will be used later for generating the excutable RPA scripts) into a high-level one to be exploited for diagnostic and analysis purposes by expert RPA analysts. In particular, the high-level event log can be used to derive the flowchart representing the abstract workflow underlying the routine execution. Specifically, the Event Abstraction component performs the following steps to produce a high-level event log:

1. *Filtering irrelevant events.* The Action Logger records many low-level events in the dataframe-based event log, such as the interaction with the browser windows (e.g., UI actions "resize", "open", "close"), tabs (e.g., UI actions "move", "open", "close") and content (page zoom, installing extensions). From a workflow perspective, these events are not relevant for any RPA analyst that aims to understand the general behaviour of the routine. For this reason, they are filtered out by the high-level event log under construction.
2. *Grouping similar events.* Within a dataframe-based event log, different low-level events can refer to the same high-level concept. For example, in a web page, the Action Logger can capture 7 different types of clicks, based on the element that's being clicked ("clickButton", "clickTextField", "doubleClick", "clickTextField", "mouseClick", "clickCheckboxButton", "clickRadioButton"). All these events just indicate that the user, during the training session, has clicked on an interactive element on the UI, thus the high-level workflow of the routine may just show the action "Click on button", because from the RPA analyst perspective it is not relevant what kind of click was performed.

---

[4] http://www.promtools.org/.
[5] https://fluxicon.com/disco/.
[6] https://apromore.org/.

3. *Creating descriptive labels.* Any recorded event provides a low-level description of the nature of the UI action performed. For example, if the user edits a
cell in Excel, the Action Logger records one of these events: "editCellSheet",
"editCell", or "editRange". From the RPA analyst perspective, all such events
refer to the same concept of "Editing a cell". To this aim, to make the UI
action underlying an event more descriptive for the RPA analyst, further
information (stored in the low-level dataframe-based event log) can be added
to its label, such as the cell and the sheet edited, the value inserted, etc. This
allows us to create a (more) descriptive label for any event in the high-level
event log, e.g., *"Edit cell B12 on Sheet 2 with value'test'"*.

Concretely, the Event Abstraction component is realized enacting the above
steps through Algorithm 2, and the outcome will be an high-level event log to
be used by the next component of the architecture.

Algorithm 2. Event Abstraction

---

   procedure GETHIGHLEVELEVENTS(*dataframe*)
       df ← filter irrelevant rows from the dataframe
       df ← group similar events in the dataframe
       for row in *df* **do**
          descriptive_row ← create descriptive string for each event
       end for
       return a high-level dataframe-based event log
   end procedure

At this point, the **Process Discovery** component of the architecture has a
twofold objective:

– It takes in input the high-level event log generated by the Event Abstraction component and applies the heuristic miner algorithm implemented in
  PM4PY [8] to derive the high-level workflow describing the overall users'
  observed behavior as a Directly-Follows Graph (DFG). This flowchart can
  be analyzed by an RPA analyst to investigate the high-level structure of the
  routine under analysis. The decision to employ the heuristic miner has been
  driven by its ability to discover highly understandable flowcharts from a BPM
  analyst perspective [2].
– It selects the most frequent routine variant among all the different execution traces stored in the low-level dataframe-based event log, as shown in
  Algorithm 3. On the one hand, if only traces having exactly the same flow
  are recorded, the one with the shortest duration is selected. If, on the other
  hand, every recorded trace is different by the others, they are compared using
  the Levenshtein distance algorithm [23], which defines the distance of the textual version of two traces (built by concatenating the actions' name associated
  to the events in the trace) as the minimal number of edit operations necessary to transform a (textual) trace into the other. The most similar traces

(a threshold percentage of similarity can be customized depending on the routine's context) are grouped into a single set, and the shortest trace (from the duration perspective) in that set is selected as the representative routine variant to be later enacted by a SW robot. If there are not similar traces in the log, the one with the shortest duration is selected among all the available ones.

The working of the Process Discovery component is shown in Algorithm 3.

Algorithm 3. Finding the most frequent routine variant

procedure SELECTMOSTFREQUENTVARIANT(*dataframe*, *threshold*)
    df ← flatten dataframe
    df1 ← group rows with same *caseID* into single row
    df1 ← calculate duration for each trace
    df2 ← compute variants
    if ∃ predominant variant with equal traces **then**
        min_duration_trace ← select trace in that variant with shortest duration
    else if ∃ similar traces (by a certain threshold) **then**
        df3 ← group similar traces into a single variant
        min_duration_trace ← select trace in that variant with shortest duration
    else   ▷ All traces are different
        min_duration_trace ← select trace with shortest duration among all variants
    end if
    return *min_duration_trace*
end procedure

Once the routine to automatize is selected, before its enactment with a SW robot, it is possible for a RPA analyst to personalize the values stored in its events through a custom dialog window (cf. Fig. 4). The tool automatically detects the events that can be edited, such as typing something in a web page, renaming a file, pasting a text or editing an Excel cell, and dynamically builds the GUI to let the RPA analyst editing them. After confirmation, the dataframe-based event log is updated.

Finally, the Python executable scripts based on the most frequent RPA routine (updated with the RPA analyst's edits) is generated by scanning the recorded low-level events in the dataframe-based log and converting them into executable pieces of SW code in Python. To properly work, the script generation algorithm (here omitted for the sake of space) relies on *Automagica*,[7] an Open Source framework for process automation, and *Selenium*,[8] a popular suite of tools for automating web browsers. Note also that the script generation algorithm takes into account only the platform where the SW robot is going to be run, regardless of the operating system used to capture the log. For example, if

---

[7] https://github.com/automagica/automagica.
[8] https://www.selenium.dev/.

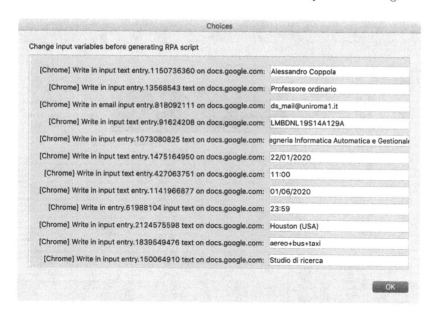

Fig. 4. Custom dialog window to personalize editable fields of a routine variant

the (selected) most frequent routine variant was recorded on a Windows operating system, but the tool is being executed on macOS, the RPA scripts will be generated taking into account this aspect, e.g., by converting the information about the system paths. This guarantees cross-platform compatibility across event logs recorded on different platforms.

4 SmartRPA in Action

SmartRPA was tested with the running example presented in Sect. 2. We provided the tool to 25 different end users that were instructed to fill the Google Form using the data from the Excel spreadsheet containing the information to apply for a travel request. We selected this routine because, for recording the UI actions to emulate, it is required to exploit all the logging modules provided by the Action Logger. Specifically, *(i)* actions to copy and paste data from the spreadsheet to the web form (System Logger), *(ii)* web navigation actions to access to Google Form (Browser Logger), and *(iii)* actions for moving between the cells of the spreadsheet to access the single values of the travel request (Office Logger). The exact steps to correctly perform the routine and record the UI actions involved are the following ones:

1. Open the Action Logger, tick the checkboxes related to Clipboard, Excel and the browser installed on the applicant's PC/MAC, and click *"Start logger"*.
2. Open the Excel spreadsheet that contains the data of a travel request.
3. Open Google Form.

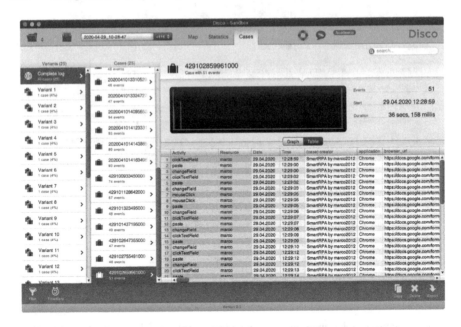

Fig. 5. An overview of the low-level event log opened in Fluxicon Disco

4. Copy and paste each value from the Excel spreadsheet to its respective field on the web form.
5. Submit the form. Once done, a confirmation email is sent to the applicant.

All the UI actions were recorded on 25 different computer systems having different features and operating systems, and stored in 25 event logs in CSV format. Then, we merged the CSV event logs into a single dataframe-based event log (and a corresponding XES file) using the Log Processing tool. An overview of the final event log has been analyzed through Disco, as shown in Fig. 5. In our test, we found 25 slightly different execution traces, resulting in 25 potential variants to properly complete the routine.

At this point, according to the working of SmartRPA, the Process Discovery component executed Algorithm 3, grouping together 7 traces out of the 25 available because they were similar by at least 90%. It is worth to notice that this particular threshold was set by us a-priori, and it is customizable depending on the specific routine's application context. Finally, among the 7 variants selected, the one having the shortest duration was chosen by the tool (specifically, the one with case ID 429102859961000 in Fig. 5). Figure 4 shows the custom dialog window to personalize the editable values of the most frequent routine variant of the running example. Taking into account the last edits made, SmartRPA can finally generate the required executable scripts to run the SW robot that emulates the routine execution on the UI. A screencast with installation instructions and showing the working of SmartRPA against the running example is available in the github repository of the tool at: https://github.com/bpm-diag/smartRPA/.

5 Related Work

The state-of-the-art in RPA is plenty of recent works that are focused on optimizing specific BPM aspects of a RPA project. In the literature, there exist three main groups of approaches that are targeted to automatically derive the behaviour of SW robots.

The first group of approaches aims at learning how to automate routines by observing human users that perform routine tasks in their computer systems. SmartRPA falls in this category. Specifically:

– The works [10,21] present a method to record UI actions performed within Excel and Google Chrome into an event log, and enable the use of process mining techniques to detect which fragments of a routine can be automated. Conversely, SmartRPA records only those UI actions that is known at the outset that can be automated, and consequently the associated routines. In addition, SmartRPA enables to record a much larger spectrum of UI actions, not just limited to Excel and Google Chrome (cf. Sect. 3).
– The work [18] proposes a method to improve the early stages of the RPA life-cycle by reducing the effort to analyze the actual system using process mining techniques based on a-priori models. SmartRPA focuses on automating the best (in terms of frequency and time duration) recorded routine variant without requiring any a-priori model.
– In [24], the authors present the *Desktop Activity Mining* tool, which records the desktop-based UI actions of users performing an office-based routine task, and employs process mining techniques to discover an integrated process model describing the behaviour of such routine. However, Desktop Activity Mining does not use events to keep track of UI actions, but it is based on recording the mouse click coordinates on the screen, and thus it can not replicate the same user's observed behavior performed in different computer systems. On the contrary, SmartRPA records the events happened during a UI interaction, so it can work across different computer systems. In addition, the identification of similar routine variants is not done using the screenshots of the user's desktop (like happens in [24]) that may differ between different computer systems, but it is performed in a way that guarantees cross-platform compatibility of the recorded event logs.
– In [11], the authors propose a self-learning approach to automatically detect high-level RPA-rules from captured historical low-level behaviour logs. An if-then-else deduction logic is used to infer rules from behaviour logs by learning relations between the different routines performed in the past. Then, such rules are employed to facilitate the SW robots instantiation. A similar approach is adopted in [20], where the *FlashExtract* framework is presented. FlashExtract allows to extract relevant data from semi-structured documents using input-output examples, from which one can derive the relations underlying the working of a routine. SmartRPA adopts a different approach: multiple variants of a routine execution are considered and the most frequent one is chosen for being executed by a SW robot, with the possibility of customizing some of its input values.

– The work [26] identifies repetitive edits to text documents by keeping track of a graph of edits and suggests automation rules for SW robots. While this work focuses on supporting expert users in the manual development of SW code, SmartRPA is targeted to automatically generate executable scripts for SW robots.

It is worth to quickly discuss the other two groups of approaches towards SW robots automation, even if they focus on different challenges than SmartRPA. The *second* group of approaches focus on learning the anatomy of routine tasks from natural language descriptions of the procedures underlying such routines. In this direction, the work [16] defines a new grammar for complex workflows with chaining machine-executable meaning representations for semantic parsing. In [22], the authors provide an approach to learn activities from text documents employing supervised machine learning techniques such as feature extraction and support vector machine training. Similarly, in [13] the authors adopt a deep learning approach based on Long Short-Term Memory (LSTM) recurrent neural networks to learn the relationship between activities of a routine task.

Finally, a *third* group of approaches exist that aim to eliminate human-dependent training [7,17]. They rely on probabilistic and machine learning algorithms to automatically train SW robots, so that any manual effort is avoided. These approaches are currently the least mature if compared with the others discussed above, but potentially with the best promises for realizing fully automated intelligent RPA approaches.

6   Discussion and Concluding Remarks

While RPA is currently used for automating routines and high-volume tasks requiring a manual intervention of expert users, the aim of SmartRPA is to automatically develop SW robots directly from the user's observed behavior. SmartRPA offers an innovative contribution to RPA technology with the goal of mitigating some of its core downsides. Notably, using SmartRPA, all the routine executions recorded by the tool can be automated, an high-level flowchart diagram is presented to expert users for potential diagnosis operations, and the executable RPA scripts to drive the working of a SW robot are generated based on the most frequent routine variant. In addition, the tool is cross-platform and allows to personalize some input fields of the selected routine variant before executing the related RPA scripts, thus supporting those steps that require manual user inputs. As a consequence, this makes the working of SW robots more flexible and adaptable to several real-world situations.

Thanks to its Action Logger, SmartRPA aims also at improving the *auditability* of RPA tools, since all routine tasks executed by human users on a UI are previously recorded in dedicated event logs, making them auditable to external users. It is worth to notice that the logs produced by the state-of-the-art RPA tools have usually a poor quality (actions may be missing or not recorded properly), since they are mainly used for debugging purposes [4]. Conversely,

SmartRPA aims at logs at the highest possible quality level thanks to its detailed recording phase performed during the training sessions.

Of course, the tool presents some weaknesses that we are tackling as future works. First of all, the executable RPA scripts for implementing SW robots are developed based on the most frequent routine variant recorded in a dataframe-based event log. However, a more accurate approach to derive the SW robot's behaviour would consist of interpreting at run-time the flowchart discovered from many routine executions stored in the event log, and selecting step-by-step the most suitable flowchart fragment (i.e., the sub-routine) to be executed by the SW robots. A second weakness, which strongly depends by the first one, relies on the fact that SmartRPA is currently able to emulate routines where the procedure to be automated is the same for all applicants, i.e., the only difference is in the values entered by the users performing the training session into fixed pre-defined fields. This limitation can be observed also in the running example, where the fields to be filled in the Excel sheet are static (they are always the same ones), and only their content can vary from applicant to applicant.

Despite the weaknesses, we consider this work as an important first step towards a more complete approach and tool towards the fully automated generation of executable RPA scripts.

Acknowledgments. This work has been supported by the "Dipartimento di Eccellenza" grant, the H2020 projects DESTINI and FIRST, the Italian project RoMA - Resilience of Metropolitan Areas, and the Sapienza grant BPbots.

References

1. van der Aalst, W.M.P., Bichler, M., Heinzl, A.: Robotic process automation. Bus. Inf. Syst. Eng. **60**(4), 269–272 (2018)
2. Agostinelli, S., Maggi, F.M., Marrella, A., Milani, F.: A user evaluation of process discovery algorithms in a software engineering company. In: 2019 IEEE 23rd International Enterprise Distributed Object Computing Conference (EDOC), pp. 142–150 (2019). https://doi.org/10.1109/EDOC.2019.00026
3. Agostinelli, S., Marrella, A., Mecella, M.: Research challenges for intelligent robotic process automation. In: Di Francescomarino, C., Dijkman, R., Zdun, U. (eds.) BPM 2019. LNBIP, vol. 362, pp. 12–18. Springer, Cham (2019). https://doi.org/10.1007/978-3-030-37453-2_2
4. Agostinelli, S., Marrella, A., Mecella, M.: Towards Intelligent Robotic Process Automation for BPMers (2020). http://arxiv.org/abs/2001.00804
5. Aguirre, S., Rodriguez, A.: Automation of a business process using robotic process automation (RPA): a case study. In: Figueroa-García, J.C., López-Santana, E.R., Villa-Ramírez, J.L., Ferro-Escobar, R. (eds.) WEA 2017. CCIS, vol. 742, pp. 65–71. Springer, Cham (2017). https://doi.org/10.1007/978-3-319-66963-2_7
6. AI-Multiple: All 52 RPA Software Tools & Vendors of 2020: Sortable List (2019). https://blog.aimultiple.com/rpa-tools/
7. Ayub, A., Wagner, A.R.: Teach Me What You Want to Play: Learning Variants of Connect Four through Human-Robot Interaction (2020). https://arxiv.org/abs/2001.01004

8. Berti, A., van Zelst, S.J., van der Aalst, W.: Process Mining for Python (PM4Py): Bridging the Gap Between Process- and Data Science (2019). http://arxiv.org/abs/1905.06169

9. Bisbal, J., Lawless, D., Wu, B., Grimson, J.: Legacy information systems: issues and directions. IEEE Softw. **16**(5), 103–111 (1999)

10. Bosco, A., Augusto, A., Dumas, M., La Rosa, M., Fortino, G.: Discovering automatable routines from user interaction logs. In: Hildebrandt, T., van Dongen, B.F., Röglinger, M., Mendling, J. (eds.) BPM 2019. LNBIP, vol. 360, pp. 144–162. Springer, Cham (2019). https://doi.org/10.1007/978-3-030-26643-1_9

11. Gao, J., van Zelst, S.J., Lu, X., van der Aalst, W.M.P.: Automated robotic process automation: a self-learning approach. In: Panetto, H., Debruyne, C., Hepp, M., Lewis, D., Ardagna, C.A., Meersman, R. (eds.) OTM 2019. LNCS, vol. 11877, pp. 95–112. Springer, Cham (2019). https://doi.org/10.1007/978-3-030-33246-4_6

12. Geyer-Klingeberg, J., Nakladal, J., Baldauf, F., Veit, F.: Process mining and robotic process automation: a perfect match. In: 16th International Conference on Business Process Management (BPM 2018), Dissertation/Demos/Industry track (2018)

13. Han, X., et al.: Automatic Business Process Structure Discovery using Ordered Neurons LSTM: A Preliminary Study (2020). https://arxiv.org/abs/2001.01243

14. Hill, J., Ford, W.R., Farreras, I.G.: Real conversations with artificial intelligence: a comparison between human-human online conversations and human-chatbot conversations. Comput. Hum. Behav. **49**, 245–250 (2015)

15. IEEE Digital Library: Standard for eXtensible Event Stream (XES) for Achieving Interoperability in Event Logs and Event Streams. IEEE Std 1849–2016 (2016). https://doi.org/10.1109/IEEESTD.2016.7740858

16. Ito, N., Suzuki, Y., Aizawa, A.: From natural language instructions to complex processes: issues in chaining trigger action rules (2020). https://arxiv.org/abs/2001.02462

17. Jenkins, P., Wei, H., Jenkins, J.S., Li, Z.: A Probabilistic Simulator of Spatial Demand for Product Allocation (2020). https://arxiv.org/abs/2001.03210

18. Jimenez-Ramirez, A., Reijers, H.A., Barba, I., Del Valle, C.: A method to improve the early stages of the robotic process automation lifecycle. In: Giorgini, P., Weber, B. (eds.) CAiSE 2019. LNCS, vol. 11483, pp. 446–461. Springer, Cham (2019). https://doi.org/10.1007/978-3-030-21290-2_28

19. Kirchmer, M.: Robotic Process Automation-Pragmatic Solution or Dangerous Illusion. BTOES Insights, June 17 (2017)

20. Le, V., Gulwani, S.: FlashExtract: a framework for data extraction by examples. In: ACM SIGPLAN PLDI 2014, pp. 542–553 (2014)

21. Leno, V., Polyvyanyy, A., Rosa, M.L., Dumas, M., Maggi, F.M.: Action logger: enabling process mining for robotic process automation. In: Proceedings of the Dissertation Award, Doctoral Consortium, and Demonstration Track at 17th International Conference on Business Process Management (BPM 2019), pp. 124–128 (2019)

22. Leopold, H., van der Aa, H., Reijers, H.A.: Identifying candidate tasks for robotic process automation in textual process descriptions. In: Gulden, J., Reinhartz-Berger, I., Schmidt, R., Guerreiro, S., Guédria, W., Bera, P. (eds.) BPMDS/EMMSAD -2018. LNBIP, vol. 318, pp. 67–81. Springer, Cham (2018). https://doi.org/10.1007/978-3-319-91704-7_5

23. Levenshtein, V.: Efficient implementation of the levenshtein-algorithm, fault-tolerant search technology, error-tolerant search technologies (2007). http://www.levenshtein.net/

24. Linn, C., Zimmermann, P., Werth, D.: Desktop activity mining - A new level of detail in mining business processes. In: Workshops der INFORMATIK 2018 - Architekturen, Prozesse, Sicherheit und Nachhaltigkeit, September 26–27, pp. 245–258 (2018)

25. Marrella, A., Mecella, M., Sardiña, S.: Supporting adaptiveness of cyber-physical processes through action-based formalisms. AI Commun. **31**(1), 47–74 (2018). https://doi.org/10.3233/AIC-170748

26. Miltner, A., et al.: On the fly synthesis of edit suggestions. ACM Program. Lang. **3**(OOPSLA), 1–29 (2019)

Integrating Robotic Process Automation into Business Process Management

Maximilian König[(✉)], Leon Bein[(✉)], Adriatik Nikaj, and Mathias Weske

Hasso Plattner Institute, University of Potsdam, Potsdam, Germany
{Maximilian.Koenig,Leon.Bein}@student.hpi.de,
{Adriatik.Nikaj,Mathias.Weske}@hpi.de

Abstract. As of today, robotic process automation (RPA) is a prominent process automation technology, which uses software to replace humans at operating graphical user interfaces. However, RPA is limited in scope and, in order for it to be established successfully, its environment must meet many requirements. The more mature research field of business process management (BPM) has the potential to provide the environment for RPA to thrive. We present an approach for embedding RPA into BPM in order to link their technologies and combine their systematic methods. The approach allows RPA to synergize with capabilities and insights provided by BPM.

Keywords: Robotic process automation · Business process management · RPA architectures

1 Introduction

Robotic process automation (RPA) is an emerging technology to automate business processes that are driven by user interaction with software systems. It is characterized as generic term for software that mimics human interaction with graphical application interfaces [1]. Thus, human resources are replaced by software robots, which results in decreasing costs and increasing efficiency and consistency [5]. The emergence of RPA is an important development in process automation, labeled as "fastest-growing software subsegment" in 2018 by the IT market research company Gartner[1].

However, RPA is limited in that many techniques required to successfully implement it lay outside its scope. This includes gathering the necessary information for automation enactment, dealing with exceptions during the execution of automated processes, and managing process automation on an organizational level.

Existing research suggests to solve these problems by combining RPA with business process management (BPM). More specific, most works propose integrating RPA with BPM. RPA is considered more successful, or even only successful, when combined with BPM [5,6,8,9]. While Kirchmer et al. [5] already

---

[1] https://www.gartner.com/en/newsroom/press-releases/2019-06-24-gartner-says-worldwide-robotic-process-automation-sof.

© Springer Nature Switzerland AG 2020
A. Asatiani et al. (Eds.): BPM Blockchain and RPA Forum 2020, LNBIP 393, pp. 132–146, 2020.
https://doi.org/10.1007/978-3-030-58779-6_9

present a so-called value-driven robotic process automation approach, including formal methods for RPA enactment and suggesting to integrate them into BPM, no concrete solution for the integration is described.

In this paper, we propose an integration solution, from a software architecture as well as a methodology perspective, to position RPA into BPM. To evaluate our approach, we implemented a prototypical software solution and applied our approach to a use case scenario.

The remainder of this paper is structured as follows: Sect. 2 describes the fundamentals of RPA and BPM. Following, Sect. 3 lists the limitations of RPA to motivate the need for putting it into a larger context and allow for a discussion of our work. In Sect. 4, we explore the existing work that suggests an RPA-to-BPM integration, and examine the proposed approaches. Section 5 and Sect. 6 present our main contribution: A concrete integration solution, consisting of software architectural and methodological means to implement RPA processes in a BPM context. Section 7 evaluates the technological feasibility, applies our solution to a use case, and discusses general findings and shortcomings. In Sect. 8, the main results are summarized and future work is investigated.

2   Preliminaries

This section outlines our understanding and assumptions about BPM and RPA. A general architecture of the underlying systems of BPM and RPA is detailed as it serves the upcoming sections.

2.1   Business Process Management

According to the definition provided by Weske, "BPM includes concepts, methods, and techniques to support the design, administration, configuration, enactment, and analysis of business processes" [10]. It is a mature research area that encompasses rich knowledge from academia and industry as well.

The methods needed for conducting a successful BPM project can be structured into the BPM lifecycle. The lifecycle provides an iterative methodology for the enactment of BPM on the level of business processes. While the exact phases differ from source to source, the included activities and their order stay the same. In this paper, we will follow the definition by Weske [10], which

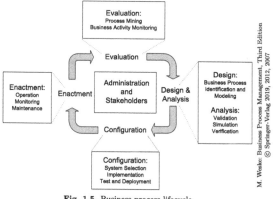

Fig. 1. BPM lifecycle taken from [10]

is depicted in Fig. 1. It is structured as follows: The entry point to the cycle is the *design and analysis* phase, where the business processes are identified and provided with a formal representation. Newly created models and models from past iterations are verified and validated against current process requirements. In the *configuration* phase, the systems to use are selected, and the business processes identified before are implemented, tested, and deployed. During the *enactment* phase, the processes are operated, and the process execution is monitored and maintained. The resulting execution data is processed by the techniques of the *evaluation* phase, for example process mining. Using the knowledge gained from one iteration, the next iteration can be started by redesigning the business processes.

Business process management is realized by business process management systems (BPMS). Their generic architecture is shown in Fig. 2.

A BPMS consists of a collection of tools that allow the model-driven enactment and operation of business processes. It includes a business process modeler, which allows a process designer to model and configure business processes and to deploy them, a process engine, which executes the process models with the help of external applications, and a graphical user interface, which allows process participants to operate and monitor this execution. Analysis and evaluation tools like process miners and other peripheral tools are often shipped with BPM systems and are

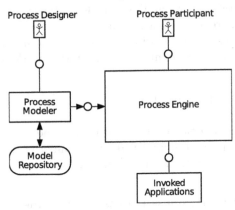

Fig. 2. BPMS architecture adapted from [10]

an important part of BPM tooling. A BPMS allows for automation of business processes by delegating the execution of specific tasks to software with APIs. It further enables process orchestration, resource management, process monitoring and process analysis.

2.2   Robotic Process Automation

Defined by van der Aalst, "RPA is an umbrella term for tools that operate on the user interface of other computer systems in the way a human would do" [1]. RPA is an upcoming "hot topic" for research and companies. Many projects and research works have been realized in this context within the last few years. RPA aims at automating business processes that consist of human interaction with software, such as transferring data from an ERP system to a web application form. Thereby, human involvement is reduced to starting and supervising the automated processes, a role which will be called *operator* in the course of this paper. Processes automated with RPA will be referred to as *RPA processes*. As there is no standardized formalization yet, their model representations depend on the RPA provider.

RPA is enacted by robotic process automation systems (RPAS). The basic structure of an RPAS, described in Fig. 3, looks similar to that of a BPMS: The modeler allows an RPA process designer to create RPA process models and to deploy them to a model repository. The controller holds the repository and orchestrates running robots as resources to execute RPA process instances. It provides an interface to the operator to start and monitor RPA process instances. This interface is generally graphical, but most systems also provide an API. Robots are programs that run on a physical or virtual machine. They execute RPA process instances, meaning that they emulate

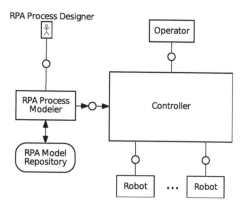

Fig. 3. RPAS architecture

user interaction on the machine they run on. The controller distributes the jobs of running certain RPA process instances among a pool of robots that are connected to it.

Generally speaking, RPA is usually applied to processes that are too infrequent for traditional process automation to be profitable, but are still repetitious enough to be formalized into an RPA process model [1]. Several criteria for RPA applicability are widely accepted [1,2,5,6,8]: Process in- and outputs must be in a machine readable format. As machine recognition capabilities greatly increase due to upcoming advancements in AI technologies, so does RPA applicability. A process to be automated must be well-defined and have a low change rate. Otherwise, inconsistencies between process model and actual process inhibit RPA success drastically. In addition, a low decision complexity is required for RPA processes, as robots cannot (yet) fully replace human decision making.

In comparison to traditional process automation, RPA is cheaper to establish and provides a much faster return on investment [2,6,7]. RPA enables the automation of processes that could not be traditionally automated, as it does not require any APIs [5]. In comparison to human execution of processes, RPA saves lot of time. Together with the fact that RPA workforce can easily be scaled up, this allows for a much greater number of cases to be handled [5]. Additionally, robots execute processes consistently and avoid human errors, therefore increasing effectiveness and process compliance [6].

3   Problem Statement

Despite all benefits, RPA has strong limitations: In order to identify and implement an RPA process, extensive process knowledge is required. Existing work has shown that, if no such knowledge is available (e.g. no other systems for gathering it are in place), the benefits of RPA are far less significant, as much time and effort has to be put into gaining that knowledge [5,6]. RPA is often considered a risk, due to the fact that it is hard to test and, once deployed, the robots execute a potentially faulty process at very high rate with high consistency [5,8]. Testing RPA requires setting up test environments for all software dependencies. While initial work has been done recently [4], no standard testing mechanisms have been established yet. In addition, whereas humans check each of their steps in each process instance, RPA has only few built-in error recognition algorithms [5,8]. The largest identified flaw of RPA is that its scope is too limited and therefore insufficient to manage and automate business processes on an organizational level. RPA orchestration is usually limited to orchestrating the robots, but does not allow to orchestrate large-scale or end-to-end processes [8] in the scope of a whole organization. RPA systems lack the ability to execute activities that are not automated with robots: Human elements cannot be completely removed from all processes of an organization, but RPA does not provide concepts to execute tasks that have to be done manually. Likewise, executing larger software and coordinating services is outside the scope of operating a user interface. Moreover, resource management is crucial for larger companies to maximize the efficiency of the employees and use their full potential. Contrary to BPM, RPA does not include research on this topic.

To cope with all the limitations of RPA, related work suggests to embed RPA into BPM [2,5,6,8]. However, the nature of this integration has not yet been investigated. A concrete integration approach needs to be developed to serve as basis for RPA projects and further research.

4   Related Work

Although not much work has been done on the integration of RPA into BPM, existing work on RPA often suggests that such an integration is desirable, and describes the relation between the two approaches.

One possible approach to enact RPA was described by Kirchmer et al. in [5]. They introduce the value-driven robotic process automation approach that includes criteria for the identification of processes which can be automated, and basic methods for design and deployment of RPA processes. Although they suggest to integrate this approach into the larger BPM context, they do not describe how to realize the integration or which benefits and synergies arise from this combination. They identify the need for BPM to be set up or already running in order to increase reliability and enable exception handling. Additionally, the need for the combination is motivated with process governance, which is provided by BPM and required for RPA. As entry point for further research and development, they suggest the integration of RPA into a larger automation context.

According to [8], BPM is a prerequisite for implementing RPA successfully. This is based mainly on capabilities that BPM has over RPA: BPM includes monitoring and process improvement techniques and makes in-depth process knowledge available. This knowledge is required for RPA process identification and implementation. It can also be used for communication about the processes, allowing to attune activities on an organizational level.

Further work on the relation between RPA and BPM include the following: Kroll et al. state that RPA draws advantages from process standardization provided by BPM [6]. Aguirre et al. encourage the combination of RPA tools and BPM systems, demanding for further studies on it [2]. Lacity et al. describe a case study on the integration of RPA in a company, which states that establishing RPA profited a lot from having a BPMS running in the background [7].

While existing work presents methods for RPA process configuration and enactment, and motivates their integration into the BPM methodology, it does not describe how to accomplish the integration. Therefore, we propose below a solution to realize RPA processes inside a BPM context.

5   Architectural Integration

In this section, we propose an architecture to link RPA and BPM systems. This architecture aims to provide a technological foundation for RPA-to-BPM integration, give an execution context for RPA systems, and facilitate the implementation of RPA processes in an organizational setting.

It already is technologically possible to call an RPAS from a BPMS. For instance, REST calls can be sent from script tasks to RPAS APIs. However, these solutions expose implementation details of the link between the two systems. In order to avoid a massive development effort each time a company wants to automate an RPA process, implementation details should be encapsulated in BPMS abstractions. Therefore, this section aims at providing an architecture that allows the systematic use of RPA and BPM systems in tandem.

The integrated architecture specifies a system that acts as a bridge between the RPA and BPM systems. The system enables the instantiation and execution of a robotic-automated activity (by an RPAS) during the run of a higher-scope business process (by a BPMS) without the intervention of a human. Configured process models should not include the configuration of the actual implementation but only the configuration of the process to automate. Therefore, process designers only need to specify activity inputs and outputs and do not have to deal with technical details.

Assuming that both, RPA and BPM, systems are already set up independently and could run on their own, the system design conforms to the following rationales: It is non-invasive in that it does not limit the capabilities of either of the standalone systems. The design is also independent of specific BPMS or RPAS vendors. In order to minimize the effort for an organization, deploying the bridge should only include a single setup and configuration step. Regarding the separation of concerns between the RPAS and BPMS, each system manages what it is designed for. The system's design does not put constraints on the abstraction level of the processes that are to be automated. Rather, the organization decides on which business process abstraction level the RPA process shall be implemented. We assume, however, that the top process level is managed by the BPMS.

The concrete design solution is depicted in Fig. 4. It introduces an additional component between the BPM and RPA systems: This bridge system connects to the BPMS as external application that the execution of a task can be delegated to. On the other side, it uses the API provided by the RPAS as interface to act as RPA operator. The bridge system is split into specific adapters for the BPM and RPA systems and a core system in between.

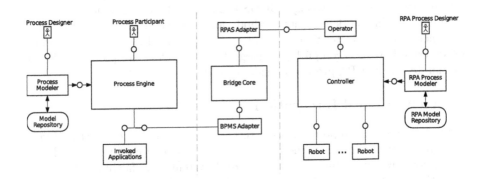

Fig. 4. Architecture of bridge system

In accordance with the rationales, we made the following design decisions: To guarantee the rationale of vendor independence, the bridge is composed of two interchangeable adapters, and a core system, which contains the functionality that can be used for all pairs of vendors. By using existing interfaces of the BPMS, namely the activity execution delegates, and of the RPAS, namely the operator API, the systems remain untouched. Thus, the bridge does not induce any constraints to them. The RPA controller is designed to orchestrate the robots and distribute jobs amongst them. Consequently, we preserve this responsibility, following the separation of concerns rationale. As a result, the single robots are unknown to the BPMS because the controller acts as a mediator. Furthermore, a BPMS offers the ability to define reactions to business exceptions and errors. Therefore, exceptions that occur during the execution of RPA processes are forwarded to the BPMS to be handled.

The system behavior for executing an RPA activity is depicted in Fig. 5 as an UML sequence diagram. The bridge is deployed into the BPMS as delegate for the execution of a defined type of activity. Therefore, the configuration of the activity to automate must include the information required to configure and execute the RPA process. Once the BPMS starts an activity instance of the specified type, it delegates the execution to a BPMS-specific adapter. This adapter converts the BPMS process information and activity inputs to a standardized RPA process input format. The core system distributes this information to an RPAS-specific adapter and governs the execution of the RPA process. This governing is phased in starting the RPA-process, waiting for its termination, and retrieving the output. The RPAS adapter implements this governing interface, interacts with the robot controller via the controller API, and converts the RPAS-specific process results to a standardized RPA process result format. The retrieved results are first passed to the core and then to the BPMS adapter, which updates the BPMS process and its variables accordingly before terminating the activity.

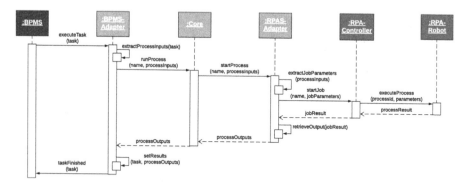

Fig. 5. Sequence of the execution of one RPA activity

6 Methodological Integration

This section addresses the research gap on how to embed RPA process configuration and enactment into the BPM methodology by combining the RPA methods with the BPM lifecycle. It further describes the synergies arising from this combination.

The resulting methodology provides a standardized approach for RPA-to-BPM integration. It allows to use existing techniques of BPM in order to design, configure, enact, and evaluate RPA processes. We approach the design of our methodology by transferring the existing BPM methodology to realizing RPA. The resultant RPA realization methods are then reintegrated into the BPM methodology.

The business process lifecycle described in Sect. 2.1 provides a detailed standard methodology for managing business processes on different levels of abstraction. We therefore chose it to be our base and adapt it to form an RPA-aware BPM lifecycle. As RPA systems can only automate processes on a low level of abstraction, RPA processes can be considered activities of a parent business process. They can therefore be handled as such and whenever operations on activities would be performed by the surrounding BPM framework, they are also performed on the RPA processes. This way, information and tools available to methods on the outer process are also available for the methods on RPA processes.

The adaptions to the BPM lifecycle (depicted in Fig. 6), which form the RPA-aware lifecycle, are structured as follows:

In the *design and analysis* phase, RPA processes are identified and modeled, following the criteria from Sect. 2.2. Important aspects for the identification are process repetitiousness, in- and outputs, and the necessity for human involvement. Information on these aspects is provided by techniques from the BPM design and analysis phase, allowing better judgment about the applicability of RPA to certain activities. Additionally, thorough process knowledge gained in past iterations is provided by the BPM evaluation phase, which

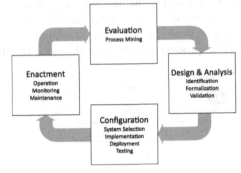

Fig. 6. RPA-supporting or -enacting methods of the RPA-aware BPM lifecycle

eases the modeling of RPA processes, and gives leverage points for improving existing RPA processes. This design results in a semi-formal representation of the processes to automate, which can be validated against execution data and interviews gathered by BPM techniques.

In the *configuration* phase, an organization selects their RPA system to use, and how to deploy the robots. The robots can either run on physical or virtual machines. The semi-formal process representation is then implemented as an executable RPA process model. In the next step, the controller is set up and configured, the model is deployed to the controller, and the robots are installed. The existing infrastructure of BPM deployment can be utilized therefor. The set up RPA system must now be tested before being released. The configuration results in implemented robot process models and a running RPAS infrastructure.

In the *enactment* phase, the RPA processes are operated. The operators start RPA process instances via the RPA controller. In our embedded context, the operator role is adopted by the BPMS through the bridge system described in Sect. 5. As RPA process execution is prone to errors, it needs detailed monitoring during operation. The monitoring and exception handling mechanisms of the BPMS can be used to support this. In addition to the data collected by the RPAS, the BPMS gathers further information about the execution, for example, the duration of execution, or compliance and conformance properties. This helps monitoring by revealing when an RPA process does not behave as expected. Maintenance needs to be performed when bugs are detected or changing requirements exact immediate fixes. The enactment results in raw execution data.

In the *evaluation* phase, information about how the robot performed is derived from the raw data of the enactment, in order to use it as basis for the next (re-)design phase. For this, BPM provides access to its tools such as process mining, which has already been shown in related work [3].

Summing up, the RPA-BPM technological integration imposes the need for a careful methodological integration, which is introduced in this section on the bases of the more mature area of BPM.

7   Evaluation

To evaluate the proposed overall BPM-RPA integration, we developed a prototypical implementation to evaluate the architectural integration and applied the methodological integration to an use case scenario. The evaluation section is concluded with discussion on the results.

7.1   Architectural Integration Feasibility

To prove the concept of the architectural integration we created a prototypical implementation as Java Maven library. The system is called Talos and is available on GitHub[2]. Talos provides two interfaces, one for BPMS adapters and one for RPAS adapters. The Talos repository also includes an example implementation of those two interfaces using Camunda BPMN Workflow Engine[3] as BPMS and UiPath Community Cloud[4] as RPAS.

The prototype provides the *RPADelegate* class as implementation of a delegate for service tasks. When a service task that has been configured with this class is executed in Camunda, UiPath is automatically called to execute a specified RPA process. Thus, the only configuration required inside the process model is using this delegate and the RPA process identifier. This fulfills our main design goal of automatic delegation, while also not revealing bridge implementation details, hence retaining abstraction.

Alternative implementations of the interfaces allow a seamless change of BPM or RPA systems. Therefore, Talos is independent of vendors. To deploy the bridge, it is only necessary to download the latest build from the repository and deploy it to Camunda. For other BPM systems, there exist similar deployment mechanisms for applications to delegate the execution of tasks. Summarizing, the deployment effort can be considered as low.

To conclude, we showed how RPA processes can be technologically integrated into a BPMS with low effort and without violating process management abstractions.

7.2   Application to Use Case

This section provides an example application of our proposed integration solution in a company.

Assume a company which provides financial services on application. In the past, incoming applications were inserted into a web interface by a clerk. To

---

[2] https://github.com/LeonBein/Talos.

[3] https://camunda.com/de/products/bpmn-engine/.

[4] https://www.uipath.com/de/.

improve this time consuming, repetitive, and error-prone task, the company decides to introduce process automation with business process management.

The original process (depicted in Fig. 7) starts when an application form is received by mail. A clerk then manually validates the information contained in the application. If it is valid, he inserts all information into an online form. If the information is not valid, the clerk prepares a request for a valid application that is sent to the applicant afterwards.

Due to the introduction of BPM, the company now follows the BPM lifecycle:

During *design and analysis* phase of the original business process, it has been discovered. BPM process analysis via process mining and employee interviews has shown that the process is time-consuming, thus posing a bottleneck. Furthermore, employees tend to make typing mistakes, as the task is highly repetitive. Therefore, the process has proven to be error-prone.

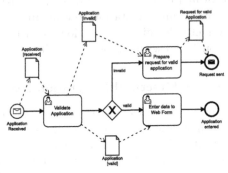

Fig. 7. Original application process without RPA

To improve performance, the company has decided to automate the process as far as possible. As the original process has already been discovered and modeled, information like involved data objects is known. Text from scanned paper-based documents can be extracted with RPA [9] and entering data into web forms is one of the classical use cases of RPA. Therefore, the company decides to use RPA to automate the interaction with the incoming document and the web form used to submit the application to their system. Additionally, validating the data and preparing requests for valid applications are automated by means of traditional process automation.

The new process (depicted in Fig. 8) is structured as follows: As before, it starts when an application has been received by mail. The clerk scans the application to make it machine readable. One robot then uses text recognition to automatically extract the form data and writes it to a CSV file. If the robot cannot parse the text, the clerk has to create it manually. The CSV file is now validated by a validation service. If the data is valid, a second robot inserts it into the web interface automatically. Otherwise, a service is used to prepare a request for valid application that is then sent to the applicant.

In addition to the business process model, the company creates textual documentations as semi-formal representation of the robotic-automated tasks.

In the *configuration* phase, the company selects an RPA provider and sets the system up. Robots can run in virtual machines on the same server infrastructure where the BPMS is put in place. Talos is deployed to the BPMS as execution delegate and configured to use the specific RPAS for task execution. The company then implements the redesigned process in their BPMS, configuring Talos

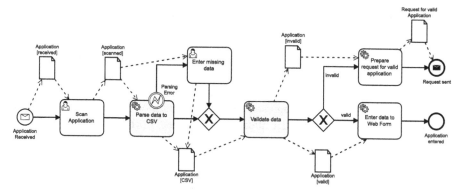

Fig. 8. Application process with RPA. Tasks that are automated with RPA are coloured gray

to handle the execution of the designated RPA tasks. The RPA task models that are used are implemented with the corresponding RPA process modeler. The business process model can then be deployed to the BPMS the same way as if RPA was not introduced.

Together with Talos, the BPMS assumes the operation of the RPAS during the *enactment* phase. If the robot cannot parse the document, the system allows to switch back to manual execution, thus putting the exception into a process context. Process monitoring additionally helps the company to ensure that the robots behave as expected.

During *evaluation* phase, logs of process executions are analyzed with process mining. This includes data on the execution of the RPA tasks, allowing to measure the time improvements compared to the original process and also to detect if further optimization is needed. The company also identifies more processes which should be improved and are potential candidates for RPA solutions.

7.3   Discussion

The main benefit of the RPA-aware BPM lifecycle is that it describes a concrete approach for realizing RPA in a BPM context, addressing the research gap. This allows RPA to be introduced to and used in organizations more easily, especially when BPM infrastructure and knowledge are already in place. In contrary to ad-hoc usage, not every organization needs to define their own methodology. Instead, they can build on the RPA-aware BPM lifecycle. Together with further research, the organizational experience can help to improve the methodology. Using a proven set of methods decreases the risk of project failure for the organizations [5]. As BPM techniques and technologies are well tested and therefore efficient and stable, these risks are further reduced. Furthermore, BPM scales well, allowing to handle numerous processes. The RPA-aware BPM lifecycle also provides the means to handle multiple RPA processes, as they are fully integrated. The fact that RPA scales with BPM renders RPA scalable as well.

The RPA-aware lifecycle deals with the shortcomings of RPA:

The knowledge created during the BPM lifecycle is necessary or at least beneficial for RPA. This minimizes the overhead created when running both systems concurrently, as the process knowledge needs to be gathered either way. BPM provides information about process attributes, inputs, and outputs in the analysis phase and about the execution in the enactment phase. As shown in the example, this information can be used to identify and model new RPA processes and to improve existing ones. In addition to process optimization, the BPMS provides documentation and standardization for all processes not managed by the RPAS.

The RPA-aware lifecycle also helps to cope with the RPA faultiness. BPM exception handling provides a standardized and well-tried approach to handle business exceptions, thus unburdening employees. BPMS monitoring accelerates finding errors in the RPA processes. Technical checking mechanisms incorporated into the BPMS catch execution errors and provide basic handling for them. Data gathered from enactment phases can be used to improve RPA processes in further iterations, thus making the processes more stable and eliminating errors [8].

Integrating the RPAS into a BPMS complements the capabilities an RPAS lacks. High level process orchestration, the execution of non-RPA activities, resource management, process monitoring, process mining, and additional features are assumed by the BPMS and its periphery tools.

Despite the benefits, some aspects of RPA-to-BPM integration are not yet covered. While this solution provides means for an integration on the software architectural and methodological level, it does not consider change management like employee training and changes on an organizational level. The example company must convince the clerks of the change and find new occupations for them. The given approach also does not build up a solution tailored to the needs of RPA. Therefore, some RPA specific issues might not be examined and addressed. An example is the issue of RPA process testing, which requires the development of specialized environments. Additionally, the lifecycle does not provide new RPA-specific error and exception handling mechanisms. Furthermore, this solution is limited in the level of detail it provides for each phase. For instance, no pre-implementation formalization approach is given for the design of RPA processes.

8 Conclusion

An RPA integration into BPM can break up RPA limitations and provide the process knowledge required for a successful RPA realization. In this paper, we presented an integration solution, which provides the basic means to implement RPA processes inside BPM environments. Our solution consists of a software architectural bridge and an RPA-aware BPM lifecycle which link the RPA and BPM systems and integrate their methodologies. The architectural bridge has been evaluated with a working prototype that allows the technological integration of RPA processes into a BPMS with low effort, preserving business process management abstraction. The RPA-aware BPM lifecycle describes RPA methods that are embedded to the larger BPM discipline, thus profiting from synergies drawn from BPM tooling and methodology.

With our work, we integrate RPA into the larger BPM automation scope. Thereby, we follow the research proposal of Kirchmer et al. [5]. In return, their RPA process configuration and enactment methods can be used to provide another view on the respective RPA lifecycle phases. We discussed a further approach to combine RPA and BPM, providing foundations for further studies, as proposed by Aguirre and Rodriguez [2].

Future work on the exemplary bridge implementation includes realizing concepts to catch RPA process execution exceptions and forward them to the BPMS to handle them. Future research should explore the impact of integrated RPA on an organizational level, including change management and workforce training. For example, according to [5], inappropriate preparation of employees may lead to a significant reduction of the efficiency benefits gained by introducing RPA. It may also be worth to investigate approaches for standalone RPA that are specifically tailored to it, and to compare these to our solution. Dedicated testing strategies need to be examined and developed to further decrease the error rate of RPA process executions. For the RPA-aware lifecycle, much work can be done by exploring the details of its phases, further improving it, and defining it more precisely.

References

1. van der Aalst, W.M.P., Bichler, M., Heinzl, A.: Robotic process automation. Bus. Inf. Syst. Eng. **60**(4), 269–272 (2018). https://doi.org/10.1007/s12599-018-0542-4
2. Aguirre, S., Rodriguez, A.: Automation of a business process using Robotic Process Automation (RPA): a case study. In: Figueroa-García, J.C., López-Santana, E.R., Villa-Ramírez, J.L., Ferro-Escobar, R. (eds.) WEA 2017. CCIS, vol. 742, pp. 65–71. Springer, Cham (2017). https://doi.org/10.1007/978-3-319-66963-2_7
3. Jimenez-Ramirez, A., Reijers, H.A., Barba, I., Del Valle, C.: A method to improve the early stages of the robotic process automation lifecycle. In: Giorgini, P., Weber, B. (eds.) CAiSE 2019. LNCS, vol. 11483, pp. 446–461. Springer, Cham (2019). https://doi.org/10.1007/978-3-030-21290-2_28
4. Jiménez-Ramírez, A., Chacón-Montero, J., Wojdynsky, T., González Enríquez, J.: Automated testing in robotic process automation projects. J. Softw. Evol. Process e2259 (2020). https://doi.org/10.1002/smr.2259
5. Kirchmer, M., Franz, P.: Value-driven Robotic Process Automation (RPA). In: Shishkov, B. (ed.) BMSD 2019. LNBIP, vol. 356, pp. 31–46. Springer, Cham (2019). https://doi.org/10.1007/978-3-030-24854-3_3
6. Kroll, C., Bujak, A., Darius, V., Enders, W., Esser, M.: Robotic process automation - robots conquer business processes in back offices (2016). https://www.capgemini.com/consulting-de/wp-content/uploads/sites/32/2017/08/robotic-process-automation-study.pdf
7. Lacity, M.C., Willcocks, L.P.: Robotic process automation at telefónica O2. MIS Q. Exec. **15**(1) (2016). http://misqe.org/ojs2/index.php/misqe/article/view/620

8. Signavio Whitepaper: Putting the 'P' in RPA: overcoming the challenges of RPA Implementation. Technical report, Signavio GmbH (2019). https://www.signavio.com/downloads/white-papers/overcoming-challenges-rpa-implementation/
9. Tornbohm, C.: Market guide for robotic process automation software (2017). Gartner.com
10. Weske, M.: Business Process Management, 3rd edn. Springer, Heidelberg (2019). https://doi.org/10.1007/978-3-662-59432-2

How to Trust a Bot: An RPA User Perspective

Rehan Syed[(✉)] and Moe Thandar Wynn

Queensland University of Technology, Brisbane, Australia
{r.syed,m.wynn}@qut.edu.au

Abstract. Robotic Process Automation (RPA) has taken the industry by storm in recent years. Many organisations are keen to adopt RPA technology to dramatically improve their operational efficiency and digitally transform their business operations. However, industry reports and early academic research papers on RPA have highlighted various challenges associated with the use of RPA. Trust is one of the key factors that poses a challenge on the organisational acceptance of RPA. In this paper, we analysed the IS literature on trust to build an initial RPA-trust conceptual model. We then collected primary data from a selected group of RPA users to explore, explain, and confirm the factors that hinder building the user trust in bots using IT-artefact and Integrative model of organisational trust theories. The outcomes of this study are summarised in a conceptual model for RPA trust that will help organisations to build their strategies to effectively introduce and sustain RPA technology in their daily operations.

Keywords: Trust · Robotic Process Automation · IT-artefact · Qualitative case study · RPA-trust conceptual model

1 Introduction

In order to remain competitive and increase market share, organisations continuously seek out various opportunities to achieve service delivery excellence, cost efficiencies, profit maximisation and product innovation. Robotic Process Automation (RPA) is a recent automation technology that has created ripple effects in today's industry. Many organisations have been keen to adopt RPA technology to dramatically improve their operational efficiency.

RPA technology uses software to perform mundane and repetitive operational tasks by mimicking actions of a human user. This software (a.k.a. bots) can be used to follow a workflow with predefined steps, rule-based instructions and inbuilt functions to perform tasks such as copying data, sending emails, filling forms, going through verification and compliance checks, and updating different types of records. RPA has been termed as "macros on steroids" [23], as a bot can perform highly repetitive tasks with a high efficiency rate.

RPA is marketed as an ideal solution for organisations with labour-intensive processes that are high-volume and repetitive [1,17,22]. From an architectural

© Springer Nature Switzerland AG 2020
A. Asatiani et al. (Eds.): BPM Blockchain and RPA Forum 2020, LNBIP 393, pp. 147–160, 2020.
https://doi.org/10.1007/978-3-030-58779-6_10

perspective, RPA software does not integrate with an organisation's IT infrastructure; it works independently by using user-credentials to gain access to the required data and execute related software applications. This non-invasive nature of RPA results in a low turnaround time and less risks of unauthorised data access without the need for a major system or enterprise architecture modification. Not surprisingly, the promises made by RPA vendors managed to convince the industry to consider RPA technology as a serious contender for automation solutions.

A recent industry report mentioned a 30.14% RPA market growth rate that will lead to a $US 2.5 billion market size by the year 2022 [19]. A recent Forrester report [14] also confirms the high level of efficiency and improved customer services as key outcomes of RPA. Despite the high projection of success, RPA adoption is facing a number of challenges. Enterprise-wide stakeholder acceptance was mentioned as one of the key success factors for RPA [5,7]. Major consultancy firms also reported an estimated 50% failure rate, the inability to achieve the expected profitability targets, the lack of mastering RPA resilience, constant bot failures, and scalability problems [14].

User trust is one of the key challenges among many for RPA adoption [12] and plays an important role for organisational buy-in of RPA [4,23]. Automation carries a negative connotation from the users' perspective and is associated with resistance to change due to fear of job losses and redundancies.

With the introduction of RPA software, various human users and bots need to share the process and task responsibilities. More importantly, in line with Lee and See [18], the argument for increasing controlling roles of IT artefacts, bots are expected to take over a majority of mundane yet important process tasks previously performed by human users. As a bot takes over a significant amount of responsibilities from human users, the bot's performance is vital for the successful acceptance of RPA by users. It also requires a certain level of delegation between human users and bots to access the required corporate systems and data, and perform the assigned tasks. Hence, RPA must produce visible and tangible outcomes to build user trust [13]. We contend that the social acceptance of a bot as a "digital colleague" requires a deeper understanding of users' perspectives.

The insights gathered from recent RPA literature highlight the gaps in the viability of RPA technology to deliver the expected outcomes and raise concerns to investigate the notion of trust in RPA. We embarked on this study to understand "How trust is formed between human users and RPA technology?" We first analysed the IS literature on trust to build an initial RPA-trust conceptual model. We then collected primary data from a selected group of RPA users to explore factors that hinder building the user trust in bots. We positioned our findings using the IT-artefact and the Integrative model of organisational trust theories and proposed a conceptual model for RPA trust to assist organisations in developing strategies to effectively introduce and sustain RPA technology.

The rest of the paper is organised as follows. Section 2 provides a brief overview of trust in the Information Systems and RPA literature. Section 3 outlines the proposed two-staged constructivist grounded theory based research design. Section 4 presents our synthesis from user interviews whereas Sect. 5 provides a brief discussion. Section 6 concludes the paper.

2   A Brief Overview of Trust in Information Systems

The relationship between user trust and information system artefacts has been discussed extensively in past studies. The most common definition used by IS researchers for trust [18,28] is provided by Mayer et al. [20] which states that trust is the "willingness of a party to be vulnerable to the actions of another party based on the expectation that the other will perform a particular action important to the trustor, irrespective of the ability to monitor or control that party" . Trust has been a key factor in major IS theories to analyse the behavioural intention and technology adoption and acceptance [24,32]. There are a number of studies measuring trust ranging from e-commerce, e-government, social media, to a variety of software systems [25,26].

Our search for literature related to RPA and trust was not able to find sufficient published research in this domain. RPA is a software artefact; therefore, we opted to extract the literature that explained the interrelationships between user trust and software/IT artefacts. In [9], the authors argued that trust in technology artefacts is equitable to inter-personal trust. The quality of the system, technical infrastructure, and the system's performance were identified as influencing factors for user trust [29].

A recent study on IoT and consumer acceptance [2] argued the importance of trust for IoT acceptance due to the novelty associated with the emerging domain. Along similar lines, understanding the effect of trust for RPA is required since it is an emerging technology and like any emerging trend, it suffers from limited user confidence in the promised technical capabilities as well as the socio-cultural aspects. A recent Forrester Consulting report [14] highlighted that the frequent bot failure is a key concern for the early adopters of RPA, hence the concerns with bot performance and reliability have a high potential to negatively influence user trust.

Most IS research on studying trust used Mayer et al.'s three dimensions of trustworthiness; namely, "ability, benevolence, and integrity" [20]. The **ability** dimension includes skills, competencies, and characteristics of a trustee (i.e., a bot) that enable it to influence a certain area of operations [20,28]. The **benevolence** dimension explains the perception of a trustee's intentions to bring genuine benefits to the trustor (i.e., a human user) beyond mere focus of financial and operational motives [20,28]. The **integrity** dimension explains the trustee's attitude towards adhering to certain principles that are important from the trustor's perspective. Furthermore, the vital impact of contextual factors (such as social influence, corporate policies, competitive pressure, etc.) on user trust has been extensively discussed in IS literature on technology adoption and acceptance [6,11,30]. Therefore, we opt to explore the contextual influences in the initial model to validate if there is any relationship between contextual influences and RPA user trust.

Figure 1 illustrates the initial framework developed as the synthesis of the trust factors identified in the literature.

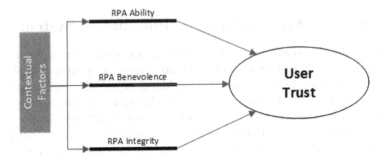

Fig. 1. An initial RPA-trust conceptual framework adapted from Mayer et al. [20].

3   Study Design

This study adopts a grounded theory approach [3, 8, 15, 16] to explore the user trust factors for RPA. The constructivist grounded theory guidelines of [8] were used to design the research process. As suggested in [8], the constructivist design is useful to build theory by analysing systematically collected data using constant comparative analysis techniques. The constructivist grounded methodology is suitable to explore how social actors construct meaning in a selected domain of inquiry to build conceptual frameworks or theories using inductive analysis of qualitative data [8]. We collected data in two stages.

In stage one we performed a thorough literature review on IT trust and confidence factors by identifying 158 research articles available on Scopus. Each article was fully read and 33 articles with a focus on IT artefacts and user trust were extracted from the pool for deeper analysis. Selected articles were analysed using NVivo 12 as the data management software. The results of the literature review were used to define four dimensions for user trust in IT-artefacts and used to build an initial conceptual framework for user trust and RPA adoption.

In stage two we used a purposive sample to select our study participants. We invited selected staff from different organisations representing different industries, who have been using RPA for at least one year. The selected participants represented different roles and designations in their organisations; however, all participants closely engaged with the RPA software in their day-to-day operations. Five out of six interview participants belong to Banking, Financial Services, and Insurance (BFSI) domains in Australia and Sri Lanka. Each participant was actively engaged in RPA planning, design, and implementation activities in their organisations, whereas one participant was from an RPA consultant organisation.

Data was collected using semi-structured interviews. Six interviews were conducted with an average duration of 90 min. Each participant was requested to answer a set of open ended questions developed using the outcomes of stage one. Additional factors that did emerge from the primary data and not discussed in the literature were also accommodated. The details of the various dimensions of user trust and the areas for interview questions are provided in Table 1.

All primary data was then inductively analysed to explore the interrelationships and their dependencies. Data coding was performed in three iterations. In qualitative research, the coding is an analytical process to explore concept similarities, categorisation, and recurrence in data. In the first iteration, open coding was performed using the verbatim interview quotes. Coded data was compared and analysed to explore concept similarities. Next, focused coding was applied by labeling and re-grouping the coded data into suitable categories. The process was repeated after each interview to compare the coded data with the new data and categories were constantly redefined using inductive, deductive, and abductive reasoning [31]. The process continued until theoretical saturation was reached where no new categories emerged from the data. Next, theoretical coding was applied to synthesise and discover relationships and inter-dependencies between coded data. Theoretical coding is the process to explore and identify pattern and clues in analysed data [21]. Section 4 details the final deliberations and findings of the data analysis.

Table 1. Key dimensions of RPA-user trust.

Dimensions	Definitions	RPA trust construct
Abilities	This dimension includes skills, competencies, and characteristics of a trustee (i.e. the RPA Bot) that enables it to influence a particular area of operations [1, 2]	– Responsibility – Information Accuracy –Reliability
Benevolence	This dimension explains the perception of a trustee's intention to bring genuine benefits to the trustor (i.e. the end-user) beyond the mere focus of financial and operational motives (i.e. a mentoring relationship between a mentor (trustee) and a mentee (i.e. trustor) [1, 2]	– Authorised Data Usage – Designer Benevolence – User Understandability – Faith
Integrity	This dimension explains the trustee's attitude towards adhering to certain principles that are important from the trustor's perspective [1, 2]	– Predictability – Confidentiality – Data Integrity – User Authenticity
Context	The organisation factors that influence a trustor's perception of a trustee. The context may affect the other dimensions as a moderating factor	– Strategic needs – Policies – Associated risks

4   Findings

The following section provides a summary of the key themes that emerged from the interview data categorised into the four dimensions shown in Table 1. The findings are supported by selected interview quotes from different participants and evidences. The bold text refers to the main themes that emerged under each dimension of trust.

4.1 User Trust and Bot Ability

The **over expectation** relates to the users' perception on the bots' ability to perform an assigned task. It was mentioned as one of the main issues that influences user trust in RPA. The promises and hype created by the RPA vendors, market vibes, and organisational units responsible for implementing RPA solutions, as well as the management result in users developing high expectations of a bot's capabilities to perform the assigned tasks quite independently and with a high level of accuracy and reliability. However, as explained by the participant, when bots fail to perform due to several reasons, users get frustrated, they lose trust in the bots' capabilities. *"they thought it was going to be a lot more capable than it actually was so I think that people had very high expectations whether that came from the consultants or from their own imagination I don't know but they expected that the robot would know better"* (Participant 1); *"the concern is they will start the bot and they will lock their screen and go somewhere for a break, now bot is not able to recognise the screen elements, because system is locked, it will start showing errors, so according to them they are like the bot is not performing as expected"* (Participant 2).

Participants highlighted the vital role of the **consistency of data** and dependency of a bot on well defined data inputs. Inconsistent data sources severely hamper the bots' ability to process assigned tasks and result in users spending extra time and effort in cleaning up the data definitions. An oversight on effective data quality will result in users building negative perceptions and the loss of trust on the bots' ability. *"there was no discipline around it and I'll give an example of that is that the robot was checking names in the system to see whether it was already a customer and the people didn't adhered to a naming convention, so the robot would go in search for customer Jane Doe, but oh no, she's not there, people might have entered it as J Doe or Doe J or you know Doe Jane or whatever it might be and created a duplicate so then that's when trust again failed because they tried to implement something and there wasn't the discipline up front to set it up for success so that definitely was a problem"* (Participant 1). *"they haven't uploaded the file, bot was not able to extract the data and they were like no bot is not working today it's down, how do you process this many transactions? so it was the issue from their end"* (Participant 2); *"most of the issues were actually either the wrong process has been communicated to the bot or you know the whole hybrid coexistence issues where the bot is expecting a certain file or process to start from a particular location but that's missing, so we went through some of these issues"* (Participant 4).

Task visibility refers to the internal operations of a bot to process data. In a human-task environment, a user can comfortably send a request to another user to check the progress of an assigned task. However, a user expecting an output from a bot cannot view or query the status of a transaction. The 'black-box' nature of a bot, user curiosity and 'waiting' for an answer/output was explained as a contributing factor mentioned by the participants in building user trust. *"they lost visibility so they perceived the robot can do 8 things, so they would think you know, somethings gone into the bot and "I don't see it for 24 hours I* *don't know what's going on with it"* so that kind of lack of visibility was definitely an issue. They were very much frustrated by that lack of visibility and I did not necessarily trust that what went in would be what came out"* (Participant 2).

4.2   User Trust and Bot Benevolence

Design effectiveness refers to the bot designers' ability to accurately design and program a bot incorporating the users' key process requirements. The design effectiveness was explained as a critical issue since bots are personified and users literally blame the bot for a task failure even though the main issue lies with the programming and design of the bot. *"...they programmed it incorrectly, they personified the bot in a way that they were blaming the bot for getting things wrong. Now clearly it's not a bot that's got things wrong, its the programming of the bots by a human got it wrong in terms of not understanding the requirements"* (Participant 1). *"the performance of the bot depends on the developers who are building the bot, initially when they started building the bots, they were not using correct frameworks"* (Participant 2).

The interview participants strongly agreed that effective end-user engagement is crucial for building trust in bots. **End-user engagement** refers to the identification and involvement of key stakeholders during the design and productions stages of a bot. An oversight will result in an inefficient bot design and add to the users' frustration. *"if they had engaged the person [actual user] directly, she would have been able to give them a lot more information that would have made them be able to build the bot more effectively and would have preempted a lot of the problems, but they held back because I assumed that they thought she would be threatened by the bot"* (Participant 1).

Awareness of process complexity refers to the ability of RPA designers and business analysts to comprehend the scope, cross-functionality, steps involved in a process, and users' expectations from a particular bot. As mentioned by a participant, a key reason for lost user trust was related to the external consultants' inability to understand the context and complexities involved in a process. *"it was a more complex process then they thought and certainly initially the people who programmed it were external consultants and they were going by a standard that didn't apply in the context.... and so they wanted to impose a standard that just didn't work"* (Participant 1).

Another factor that emerged from the interviews relates to the technology support. **Technology support** refers to provision and availability of the required technical staff to provide hands-on assistance when a bot breaks down. *"we made sure that we got into details, vendor was literally you know on the floor throughout these three months, and hands-on, basically behind the persons' back, so something pops up, we addressed the issue then and there, so that's how we build user confidence and successfully transitioned"* (Participant 3).

4.3   User Trust and Bot Integrity

Data security refers to the users' trust in a bot's access to corporate data. The participants were from the BFSI industry that extensively comes under strict data security regulations and compliance requirements. However, these aspects of data security were not mentioned as an anxiety factor for user trust since a bot does not share their access credentials. *"from a security perspective, bots had their own logins so that there was no sharing in that respect, so that didn't become an issue"* (Participant 1). *"initially I was a bit concerned but then it was assured that bot can only access a team folder, it won't go beyond anywhere to just extract data from the portal, write it into the shared drive within a particular template. so yeah through this streamlined process the team was pretty much comfortable with that and now we're not facing issues like this"* (Participant 2).

Task delegation explains a user's perception towards sharing the assigned tasks with a bot. The participants were quite positive about sharing the workload with a bot, however, their main concern was about the availability of the required technical support to ensure task completion in case of a bot failure. *"I don't think they minded so much at the coalface, so I think that people who were receiving the output from the bot, their main concern was if the people [technical support] would be there for them"* (Participant 1).

4.4   User Trust and Contextual Influences

Fear of job loss was mentioned as one of the main factors that negatively associate with users' trust in bots. Not surprisingly, the participants unequivocally mentioned this factor as the main cause for resistance to change. The strategies to introduce automation and RPA are considered as ways to reduce cost by the management. *"I thought people will be threatened by it because that's what we have been told that it will take over jobs And all this kind of stuff"* (Participant 1).

Industry pressure refers to the organisations' response to industry-wide adoption of RPA to gain competitive advantage. The manner in which organisations pursue and introduce RPA in their operations varies from being a 'trend' follower to actually using the technology to genuinely develop their staff's job enrichment features. The participants explained this aspect as a driver for building staff's trust in corporate intentions for introducing RPA as a productivity tool rather than a cost minimisation tactic. *"I think there was almost like an industry pressure, certainly a senior who was the catalyst of the change was like 'well you know this competitor has done it, the big boys have done it, you know we should be doing it'. I think that was kind of potentially a driver or the desire to go in there plus I think it was a case of this is trendy we should be doing it"* (Participant 1).

Strategic direction refers to organisational focus on pursuing RPA as a robust strategy to improve staff capabilities and operational efficiency. The participants from the organisations where RPA faced stiff resistance to change and loss of user trust highlighted the absence of a cohesive and focused strategy as a result of senior management's lack of vision for RPA. *"a lot of the problems seem to be with the higher ups. Because there seemed to be a kind of almost like a turf war going on between senior levels, because you know they wanted to control the bot, they wanted it as their initiatives"* (Participant 1). On the other hand, the participants appreciated a well defined RPA strategy that created positive impression amongst the users. *"in our messaging we positioned RPA properly as an enhancement and industry first initiative which will give us a competitive edge, rather than we are going to replace you guys sort of thing"* (Participant 3).

The **top management support** was referred as a key driving factor to build user trust. Top management support involves the leadership from the senior management, and the provision of required resources for RPA adoption. The performance of RPA heavily depends on the technical infrastructure and the availability of technical support staff. Both aspects were mentioned as critical by the participants. Participants with a positive attitude towards RPA were quite appreciative of the level of technical support provided during the introduction stage. On the contrary, the absence of a good IT infrastructure and technical support worked negatively. *"they kind of brought together a kind of team, they weren't really IT but they were kind the robotics team, but they were understaffed, so the fact that they were understaffed again... they felt that they weren't able to support them well enough"* (Participant 1).

Data channel variations refers to the inconsistent document formats used by different sources that provide data for a bot. These variations tend to result in either process or business exceptions. The inflexibility of an associate organisation to align their reporting or document formats with a bot's process requirement can result in serious failures. Also, the bargaining power of an associate can determine the terms of engagement with a bot's processes. As mentioned by a participant, their organisation was in a high bargaining position and was able to demand their associates to sync their formats with the bots' required process. It is this variation that positively or negatively influences a bot's performance and affects the user trust. *"there were issues with the data formats... some of the payment channels [banks] were changing the way the files are, the templates that the statements are being delivered, so if the bot has been programmed to capture in one way and if the bank does the change, that will also impacting our day-to-day processes because then we have to retrain the bot to adjust to the new templates that being done at the payment channel level"* (Participant 4). *"if we are talking about volume, 20% of their volume came from branches and 80% came from brokers. The robot was only implemented for multiple reasons with the branches... and they couldn't even roll it out to the brokers because the brokers would have just said no I'll give you my form it's up to you to deal with it but there was also that level of trust and repeat business because brokers would give lots and lots of business. And if you mucked that up then they would just go to a different provider"* (Participant 1).

Awareness of RPA capabilities refers to the users' understanding of the links between the complexities associated with process executions and RPA capabilities. This lack of understanding creats higher expectations amongst RPA users. In general, users tend to believe that a bot has intelligent capabilities and is able to work quite independently even though their organisation uses an attended bot that requires users' intervention to complete an assigned task. *"they lack the understanding in technical terms, what a bot can access what a bot can't access. so that is the issue and since it is a very new term for almost all the organisations right now they don't know that deep understanding how this whole automation works behind the scenes"* (Participant 2).

5   Discussion

In this section, we provide a brief discussion on the factors identified and the interrelationships between different aspects. In general, the factors explained in Sect. 4 are quite close to the general causes for any standard software application. However, the key differences lie with the manner in which organisations approach RPA technology adoption. The participants with a high degree of trust acknowledged that a robust change management strategy is vital to build user trust in RPA. The training of a bot as well as the users was mentioned as the winning strategy. The quality assurance and testing of a bot's performance was key to build user trust. During the production phase, the target should be on achieving a high level of performance validation with an 85 to 100% bot accuracy. The bot designers' technical skill levels and comprehension of an end-to-end process can directly effect the users' trust in a bot.

As explained by a participant, *"Initially some of the teething issues were mainly related to training, on two sides you see the bot had to be properly trained. Because like with any other business case, the initial requirement gathering you may not gather 100% of the requirement on day one...then we had to train obviously the same set of users. We can't be parallel running with the bot since the bot is obviously faster so we narrowed down those number of users, I think we ended up with only one or two users maximum and we got them to shadow the bot until the errors were zeroed and as of today, the number of errors are zero and the number of human errors also are zero"* (Participant 3).

The lack of awareness and knowledge of RPA and its capabilities was another important factor that must be considered before deployment of a bot. The business teams without having a deep understanding of their processes and contexts in which a process is performed, and associated complexities will produce insufficient or incomplete requirements needed for a bot developer. The processes to automate belongs to the operations team in most organisations. The operations team must develop their technical understanding and the internal details of how a whole process works and integrates with a bot to overcome performance issues. As mentioned by a participant, a well defined process is the key for an effective bot design which will in turn be able to perform as per the user's expectations. *"we took around two months time to develop the process, it was very difficult, so many applications, national applications were involved, we delivered that as well. Even though that bot was only producing around 70% accuracy of the task, but still they were very happy because we have reduced their time, so I think this is the thing, mutual understanding between the team, when they start understanding the capability of the bot and start trusting it after the first use of their product"* (Participant 2). The findings reflect that the human personification of bots (i.e., creating a human identity for a bot) without creating proper awareness can also result in negative consequences and confusions (see, Sect. 4.1 - Over expectations and Sect. 4.2 - Design effectiveness). The personification created a false assumption amongst human users that a bot is equivalent to humans in terms of its capabilities and its ability to make critical decisions.

The issue of user trust is also attributed to the development of attended bots where the coexistence between human users and a bot was required due to the nature of the process. Interestingly, the implementation teams did not come across user trust issues and in fact mentioned their own confidence on the abilities, and integrity of a bot. *"For compliance it was much smoother because there was no human interventions. Yes, there is no human intervention, it is the bot runs as scheduled"* (Participant 5). A bot will perform the way it is designed to perform, therefore, the notion of trust actually depends on the manner in which the requirements are identified by the business analyst/operations team, the accurate identification of required inputs, the data format, training of the bot to reach a comfortable level of accuracy, and the users' training and awareness.

6   Conclusions and Future Research

Advances in digital technologies also introduce new challenges regarding their adoption within an organisation. For organisations keen to adopt RPA technology, the social acceptance by human users of a RPA bot as a "digital colleague" is crucial to ensure smooth and seamless operations. Current literature on RPA demonstrates that user trust is one of the key challenges of RPA adoption.

This paper proposes a conceptual model for the RPA-trust framework, which is built on the three dimensions of trustworthiness, namely "ability, benevolence and integrity" [20]. Primary data from interviews with six RPA experts is then used to analyse key factors that hinder building users' trust in bots using the IT-artefact and the Integrative model of organisational trust theories. The first set of interview findings shows that organisations embarking on their RPA journey should pay attention to building a mutual understanding between the operations teams and RPA designers; ensuring relevant stakeholders are identified and closely engaged with; building the confidence of human users by providing much needed technical support; and implementing an effective change management plan. Furthermore, the deployment of a bot to handle actual tasks must only be performed after a rigorous quality assurance and performance assessment. Our findings also point out that most of issues can be addressed by existing knowledge (see [10]) related to software design, testing and implementation.

This study has several limitations. The data was collected from a small number of respondents from similar industries and therefore, lacks the generalisability of key findings. The interview participants were from technical backgrounds and provided their views from a technical perspective. In future, we aim to alleviate these limitations by following a mixed method approach. In line with Shenton [27], the credibility will be achieved by interviewing additional participants from different domains to increase the richness and variety of data. For triangulation, a Delphi study approach will be pursued to get the 'expert' consensus on findings. In addition, the findings will be confirmed by using a quantitative survey approach with a large sample size.

References

1. Aguirre, S., Rodriguez, A.: Automation of a business process using robotic process automation (RPA): a case study. In: Figueroa-García, J.C., López-Santana, E.R., Villa-Ramírez, J.L., Ferro-Escobar, R. (eds.) WEA 2017. CCIS, vol. 742, pp. 65–71. Springer, Cham (2017). https://doi.org/10.1007/978-3-319-66963-2_7
2. Aldossari, M.Q., Sidorova, A.: Consumer acceptance of internet of things (IoT): smart home context. J. Comput. Inf. Syst., 1–11 (2018)
3. Barney, G., Anselm, S.: The Discovery of Grounded Theory, pp. 1–19. Weidenfield & Nicolson, London (1967)
4. Bawack, R.E., Samuel, F.W., Kevin, C.: Artificial intelligence in practice: implications for is research. In: 25th Americas' Conference on Information Systems (AMCIS), pp. 1–10. Association of Information Systems (2019)
5. Beers, A., Heijndijk, R., van Dalen, C.: Understanding the challenge of implementing your virtual workforce: Robotic Process Automation as part of a new social-technological paradigm (2018). https://www2.deloitte.com/content/dam/Deloitte/nl/Documents/strategy/deloitte-nl-so-understanding-challange-of-implementing-rpa.pdf
6. Bunker, D., Kautz, K., Anhtuan, A.: An exploration of information systems adoption: tools and skills as cultural artefacts-the case of a management information system. J. Inf. Technol. 23(2), 71–78 (2008)
7. Carden, L., Maldonado, T., Brace, C., Myers, M.: Robotics process automation at techserv: an implementation case study. J. Inf. Technol. Teach. Cases 9(2), 72–79 (2019). https://doi.org/10.1177/2043886919870545
8. Charmaz, K.: Constructing Grounded Theory: A Practical Guide Through Qualitative Analysis. Sage, London (2006)
9. David, G., Paul, P., Izak, B., Harrison, M., Katherine, S., Detmar, S.: ICIS panel summary: should institutional trust matter in information systems research? Commun. Assoc. Inf. Syst. 17(1), 9 (2006)
10. Davis, F.D., Venkatesh, V.: Toward preprototype user acceptance testing of new information systems: implications for software project management. IEEE Trans. Eng. Manage. 51(1), 31–46 (2004)
11. Dayan, M., Di Benedetto, C.A.: The impact of structural and contextual factors on trust formation in product development teams. Ind. Mark. Manage. 39(4), 691–703 (2010). https://doi.org/10.1016/j.indmarman.2010.01.001

12. Dintrans, P., Anand, A., Ponnuveetil, M., Dash, S., Ray, K.: How digital 2.0 is driving banking's next wave of change (2017). https://www.cognizant.com/whitepapers/how-digital-2-0-is-driving-banking-s-next-wave-of-change-codex2865.pdf

13. Dunlap, R., Lacity, M.: Resolving tussles in service automation deployments: service automation at Blue Cross Blue Shield North Carolina (BCBSNC). J. Inf. Technol. Teach. Cases **7**(1), 29–34 (2017)

14. Forrester Research: Barriers and best practices for scaling RPA: centralized automation, resiliency, and low-maintenance bots pave the way to RPA success. Technical report, Forrester Consulting (2020)

15. Glaser, B.G.: Advances in the Methodology of Grounded Theory: Theoretical Sensitivity. Sociology Press, Mill Valley (1978)

16. Kathy, M., Linda, J., Josselson, R., Anderson, R., McSpadden, E.: A constructivist grounded theory analysis of losing and regaining a valued self. In: Five Ways of Doing Qualitative Analysis. Phenomenological Psychology, Grounded Theory, Discourse Analysis, Narrative Research, and Intuitive Inquiry, pp. 165–204. The Guilford Press, New York (2011)

17. Lacity, M., Willcocks, L.: Robotic process automation at Telefonica O2. MIS Q. Execut. **15**(1), 21–35 (2016)

18. Lee, J.D., See, K.A.: Trust in automation: designing for appropriate reliance. Hum. Factors **46**(1), 50–80 (2004). https://doi.org/10.1518/hfes.46.1.50_30392. PMID: 15151155

19. Markets, Markets: RPA market global forecast to 2022, markets and markets, March 2017 (2017). https://www.marketsandmarkets.com/Market-Reports/robotic-process-automation-market-238229646.html?

20. Mayer, R.C., Davis, J.H., Schoorman, F.D.: An integrative model of organizational trust. Acad. Manage. Rev. **20**(3), 709–734 (1995). http://www.jstor.org/stable/258792

21. Melanie, B., Jane, M.: Grounded Theory: A Practical Guide. Sage, Los Angeles (2015)

22. Mendling, J., Decker, G., Hull, R., Reijers, H.A., Weber, I.: How do machine learning, robotic process automation, and blockchains affect the human factor in business process management? Commun. Assoc. Inf. Syst. **43**(1), 19 (2018)

23. Mitra, S.: RPA's adoption challenges & how to solve them (2019). https://it.toolbox.com/guest-article/rpas-adoption-challenges-how-to-solve-them

24. Oliveira, T., Martins, M.F.: Literature review of information technology adoption models at firm level. Electron. J. Inf. Syst. Eval. **14**(1), 110 (2011)

25. Pang, M.S., Lee, G., DeLone, W.H.: It resources, organizational capabilities, and value creation in public-sector organizations: a public-value management perspective. J. Inf. Technol. **29**(3), 187–205 (2014). https://doi.org/10.1057/jit.2014.2

26. Qin, L.: A cross-cultural study of interpersonal trust in social commerce. J. Comput. Inf. Syst. **60**(1), 26–33 (2020)

27. Shenton, A.K.: Strategies for ensuring trustworthiness in qualitative research projects. Educ. Inf. **22**(2), 63–75 (2004)

28. Söllner, M., Hoffmann, A., Hoffmann, H., Wacker, A., Leimeister, J.M.: Understanding the formation of trust. In: David, K., et al. (eds.) Socio-Technical Design of Ubiquitous Computing Systems, pp. 39–58. Springer, Cham (2014). https://doi.org/10.1007/978-3-319-05044-7_3

29. Vance, A., Elie-Dit-Cosaque, C., Straub, D.W.: Examining trust in information technology artifacts: the effects of system quality and culture. J. Manage. Inf. Syst. **24**(4), 73–100 (2008)

30. Venkatesh, V., Morris, M.G., Davis, G.B., Davis, F.D.: User acceptance of information technology: toward a unified view. MIS Q. **27**(3), 425–478 (2003). http://www.jstor.org/stable/30036540

31. Ward, K., Gott, M., Hoare, K.: Analysis in Grounded Theory-How Is It Done? Examples From a Study That Explored Living With Treatment for Sleep Apnea. SAGE Publications Ltd., London (2017)

32. Li, X., Valacich, J.S., Hess, T.J.: Predicting user trust in information systems: a comparison of competing trust models. In: Proceedings of the 37th Annual Hawaii International Conference on System Sciences, p. 10 (2004)

Towards a Taxonomy of Cognitive RPA Components

Antonio Martínez-Rojas, Irene Barba, and José González Enríquez[✉]

Departamento de Lenguajes y Sistemas Informáticos, Escuela Técnica Superior de
Ingeniería Informática, Avenida Reina Mercedes, s/n, 41012 Sevilla, Spain
antonio.martinez@iwt2.org, {irenebr,jgenriquez}@us.es

Abstract. Robotic Process Automation (RPA) is a discipline that is
increasingly growing hand in hand with Artificial Intelligence (AI) and
Machine Learning enabling the so-called cognitive automation. In such
context, the existing RPA platforms that include AI-based solutions classify their components, i.e. constituting part of a robot that performs a
set of actions, in a way that seems to obey market or business decisions instead of common-sense rules. To be more precise, components
that present similar functionality are identified with different names and
grouped in different ways depending on the platform that provides the
components. Therefore, the analysis of different cognitive RPA platforms
to check their suitability for facing a specific need is typically a time-
consuming and error-prone task. To overcome this problem and to provide users with support in the development of an RPA project, this
paper proposes a method for the systematic construction of a taxonomy
of cognitive RPA components. Moreover, such a method is applied over
components that solve selected real-world use cases from the industry
obtaining promising results .

Keywords: RPA · Artificial intelligence · Taxonomy

1 Introduction

The term Robotic Process Automation (RPA) refers to a software paradigm
where robots are programs which mimic the behavior of human workers interacting with information systems (ISs) [17,18,26,31], i.e. sets of components that
perform actions that solve a particular RPA task. Such a paradigm has become
increasingly popular due to RPA is of much interest to organizations. In such
context, solutions that are based on Artificial Intelligence (AI)—called cognitive
RPA [21] solutions—are receiving increasing attention since the combination of
both disciplines offers several advantages. On the one hand, AI methods enhance
RPA solutions by providing new capabilities. On the other hand, RPA solutions produce data regarding the own execution of the processes, that allows for
improving the performance and accuracy of AI-based proposal, i.e., they enable
a continuous training of the AI models. Therefore, main RPA platforms [20]

© Springer Nature Switzerland AG 2020
A. Asatiani et al. (Eds.): BPM Blockchain and RPA Forum 2020, LNBIP 393, pp. 161–175, 2020.
https://doi.org/10.1007/978-3-030-58779-6_11

(e.g., BluePrism[1], UiPath[2], and Automation Anywhere[3]) already offer a battery of components that are based on AI techniques.

In the context of an RPA project, the RPA developer[4] should take several decisions related to the robot design. Such decisions need to be based on the target RPA platform where robots are being developed. For this, the RPA developer needs to clearly understand such platforms, since one of the key factors which lead to the failure of RPA projects is the lack of understanding of these platforms [3]. This is especially important in the context of AI-based RPA solutions since they classify their AI-based RPA components in a way that seems to obey market or business decisions instead of common-sense rules. That is, components that present similar functionalities (e.g., "character recognition" is similar to "text language detection") that are identified with different names and grouped within different categories depending on the platform that provides the components. For instance, UiPath platform considers that a task related to the recognition of a document element is classified as part of the group named *Document understanding*, while the BluePrism platform classifies such task within a group named *Document processing*. Therefore, analysing different RPA platforms to check their suitability for facing a specific need is typically a time-consuming and error-prone task.

This problem has been also pointed out by industry. To be more precise, the Servinform S.A. company, which considers AI-based RPA solutions as one of their strongest business lines, has identified a series of components that solve common use cases, in which the application of AI techniques is required. When developing these components, two main problems were found: (1) the task of selecting the most suitable platform is very challenging due to the heterogeneity of names and grouping of components, and (2) the task of training experts within the team to master one kind of component, such as *detecting elements in documents* or *natural language processing for conversations*, since these categories do not exist or are not easy to identify among the platforms. As a consequence, Servinform S.A. together with the IWT2 research group[5] is currently involved in a research project, called AIRPA[6], that is focused in the integration of AI techniques and RPA.

Figure 1 shows a graphical description of the motivation of this work. The RPA developer should decide how to design a robot to solve a cognitive task. For this, the developer has to analyze several AI-based RPA components that provide a solution to the problem. As can be observed, this component is identified with different names in each RPA platform which, moreover, present heterogeneous taxonomies. To provide support to RPA developers in the context of an

---

[1] https://www.automationanywhere.com.

[2] https://www.uipath.com.

[3] https://www.automationanywhere.com.

[4] https://www.edureka.co/blog/rpa-developer-roles-and-responsibilities/.

[5] http://iwt2.org.

[6] https://www.servinform.es/wp-content/uploads/2020/02/Servinform-AIRPA-Publicidad-web-corporativa.pdf.

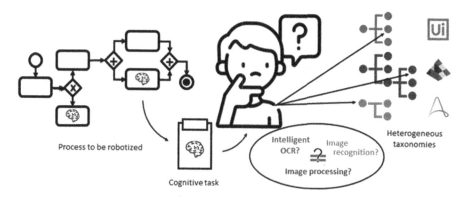

Fig. 1. Problem motivation

AIRPA project, this paper proposes a method for the systematic construction of a taxonomy of cognitive RPA components. This method is based on an incremental taxonomy which evolves a base taxonomy as needed. To be more precise, the application of the proposed approach leads to an initial taxonomy that can be extended and updated by following the incremental approach of the methodology. In addition, the proposed approach has been applied over a selection of RPA components that solve real-world use cases from industry. With such an application, it could be observed that the results that were obtained are very promising.

The rest of the paper is organized as follows. Section 2 describes the proposed method for the systematic construction of a taxonomy of cognitive RPA components. Section 3 presents the application example. Section 4 briefly summarizes related work. Finally, Sect. 5 concludes the paper and describes future work.

2 Systematic Construction of a Taxonomy of Cognitive RPA Components

To achieve a common classification for cognitive RPA components, named *AI-RPA taxonomy*, the following procedure has been carried out. Firstly, the available knowledge sources were identified. The sources that are considered are: (1) RPA platforms and organizations, and (2) human-knowledge that is provided by experts in such field. For example, in the application example described in Sect. 3, the sources are the UiPath, BluePrism and Automation Anywhere (hereafter AA) platforms, and experts from Servinform S.A. and IWT2 group.

The proposed approach considers a tree structure for the resulting taxonomy. In such a structure each node corresponds to a category. For defining the first level of the tree, taking as reference [28], a literature review on cognitive RPA taxonomies has been carried out. In such review, the works [9–11,15,24,27] have been analyzed. It can be observed that [9] is the only work that provides an AI classification by type of application. It proposes a first level for the taxonomy tree that covers all fields related to the application of AI to RPA. To be more precise, [9] proposes four categories: (1) classification, (2) skill acquisition, (3) continuous estimation, and (4) clustering. Considering these categories, a study was conducted to determine whether this classification could be used to group the studied AI-based RPA components. As a result, *classification* remains intact, *skill acquisition* and *continuous estimation* were adapted to *processing* and *governance* respectively, to bring their definition closer to RPA field. Meanwhile *clustering* is eliminated as a category, since it is considered as a technique used transversely in the other categories. This fact is justified by the very definition of the term given in this quotation *"Clustering is one of the most widely used techniques for exploratory data analysis. Across all disciplines, from social sciences to biology to computer science, people try to get a first intuition about their data by identifying meaningful groups among the data points"* [25]. Thus, it is an AI technique that will be the basis for the construction of components that are grouped in other categories, e.g. *classification* [19], but it cannot be defined as a category itself since this taxonomy does not group by technique but by application or functionality.

Thereafter, each of the categories was adapted to bring their definition closer to RPA field as described below.

- *Classification*: this term is used in both AI and RPA in the same way. As its name suggests, it comprises everything that encompasses a classification, from the traditional one by file type, to detection or recognition.
- *Processing*: includes functionality that requires skills acquisition, i.e., natural language *processing* [23] or intelligent image *processing* [7] to obtain a specific output.
- *Governance*: IT governance enables the effective use of IT which has a substantial impact on the value generated by IT investments [30,32]. In RPA, continuous estimation, similar to prediction and analysis—that is the basis of decision-making—are focused on process governance. The term governance is widely used in the field of RPA, as seen in [5,29]. One of the most representative examples of this is to determine which will be the next component to be used or if extra instances of a robot will be needed to cover the demand.

In the proposed approach, these categories will compose the first level of the AI-RPA taxonomy. In such taxonomy, when trying to classify a component, the aim will be to try to find the deepest possible category since the tree structure gives the taxonomy a hierarchical perspective. However, all the categories are defined by following the same procedure and have the same importance, including the ones that are placed in the first level.

This means that a component can be located in any of the nodes of the taxonomy, even if it is not a leaf node. This hierarchical structure will evolve dynamically, including new categories, for which these steps are followed[7]:

---

[7] A similar procedure for classification was successfully applied previously in the context of Machine Learning knowledge [13].

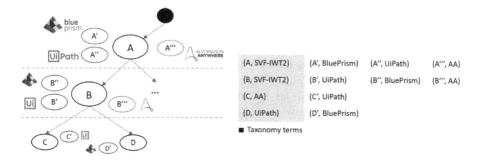

Fig. 2. AI-RPA unified knowledge store

1. A new term referring to an $AI - RPA$ category is taken from one of the sources.
2. This term is compared to existing terms in the taxonomy. If the taxonomy is empty or there are no equivalent terms—a term that refers to the same category—, it is added as a child of the most similar category. Conversely, if an equivalent term is found, it is compared with the current category and, if it is considered that conveys the concept better than the current one, the latter is replaced.
3. Whenever a new term is added to the taxonomy, (1) the knowledge source from which it comes is saved (cf. Fig. 2), (2) the characteristics that make a component to belong to a category must be entered or updated, and (3) if it corresponds to a leaf of the tree that forms the taxonomy, the type of input that supports that category it is also indicated. For instance, if the term *Document Understanding* is added, it would be related to the term *Classification* $\rightarrow$ *Detection* $\rightarrow$ *Elements*, storing that it supports *Documents* as input and its origin lies in $UiPath$.

To better understand the structure of the *AI-RPA taxonomy*, each of its component elements is defined below.

Definition 1. *An **AI-RPA taxonomy** AIRPAT = (KnowlSources, Category-Terms, TaxCategs, CategoryChars) consists of*

- *KnowlSources: a set of tuples $\langle source_{id}, source_{name} \rangle$ which contains a unique id in the AIRPAT, and the name of the knowledge source.*
- *CategoryTerms: a set of tuples $\langle categoryTerm_{id}, categoryTerm_{name}, source_{id}, taxCategory_{id} \rangle$ which contains a unique id in the AIRPAT, the name of the category which is given in the knowledge source, an id of a knowledge source in KnowlSources which this category term comes from, and an id of a taxonomic category in TaxCategs. The latter attribute aims to keep a synonymous relationship.*
- *TaxCategs:*
  a set of tuples $\langle taxCategory_{id}, taxCategory_{name}, parentTaxCateg_{id} \rangle$ which contains a unique id in the AIRPAT and a name of the taxonomic category, i.e., the category term that stands as the representative of the others.

- *CategoryChars: a set of tuples* $\langle categoryChars_{id}, categoryChars_{description},$ $taxCategory_{id} \rangle$ *which contains a unique id in the AIRPAT, the description in* $categoryChars_{description}$ *of the characteristic that must be fulfilled by a component to belong to this category of the taxonomy, and an id of the taxonomic category in TaxCategs.*
- *InputFormatSupported: a set of tuples* $\langle inputFormSup_{id}, inputForm -$ $Sup_{name}, taxCategory_{id} \rangle$ *which contains a unique id in the AIRPAT, the taxonomic category to which this property points in* $taxCategory_{id}$, *and the name of the type of input that can support the taxonomic category in* $inputFormSup_{name}$.

It is important to point out that each taxonomic category will have one or more characteristics or properties associated with it. For instance, for a single *TaxCateg*, there can be several *categoryChars* that define which characteristics a component must have to belong to it. Furthermore, it can support more than one input format, so it may have more than one *inputFormatSupported* associated. It can be deduced that in the case where no *TaxCateg* have been added to the taxonomy, only the first levels will be present. So a new category will always be added associated with one of the first levels, which are indispensable when initializing the taxonomy.

Thus, having defined all the elements to form the AI-RPA taxonomy, the incremental process to include new terms, described above in textual form, can now be defined in the form of an algorithm (cf. Algorithm 1).

Algorithm 1: How to increase the terms of the taxonomy

---

  input : New CategoryTerm n , AI-RPA taxonomy at, n origin source s

  if *n not added to at* **then**

    taxCategory $c \leftarrow$ *more similar category*

    if *s does not exist on at* **then**

      | up s as (s_{id}, s_{name})

    end

    if *n better represents the concept than c* **then**

      up n as $(n_{id}, n_{name}, s_{id}, c_{id})$

      up c with (c_{id}, n_{name})

    end

    if *c is null* **then**

      $p \leftarrow$ *more suitable parent*

      up n as $(n_{id}, n_{name}, s_{id}, p_{id})$

    end

  end

In summary, using this taxonomy, the RPA developer will be able to find the component she needs or classify a given one according to its characteristics or *CategoryChars* (cf. Fig. 3). To find them, she only has to follow three steps: (1) go from the first level of the taxonomy downwards, checking which of the categories have characteristics that fit with the component ones; (2) filter the taxonomic categories whose characteristics are not fulfilled, and (3); go down to

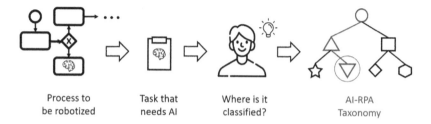

Fig. 3. Clear procedure to classify AI-RPA components

lower levels, doing the same with all the categories for each level, until reaching the deepest level of the tree. This way, the component to be found belongs to the categories that have not been filtered out after following these steps.

Thanks to the maintenance of traceability between the platforms and the terms of the taxonomy, it is also possible to automatically link each taxonomic category with the category in the own classification of each platform. Thus, the RPA developer will be able to find where the component that solves her problem is located, regardless of the platform the developer uses to build robots.

Consequently, seeking to unify cognitive RPA knowledge to facilitate this task to RPA developers, in the following section, it will be possible to see how the application of this methodology results in an initial and useful taxonomy. In addition, it can be extended due to the incremental nature of the proposed approach. Hence, the procedure described in this section can be further extended by performing successive iterations. Then, it is possible to perform a better classification of a great variety of cognitive RPA components.

3   Application Example

This section details the application of the proposed approach to selected real-world use cases from industry. Section 3.1 introduces the cognitive RPA platforms that have been selected. Section 3.2 describes the taxonomy that is obtained after applying the proposed approach to such selected platforms.

3.1   Selected Cognitive RPA Platforms from Industry

The cognitive RPA platforms that are selected are the following: UiPath[8], Automation Anywhere[9] and BluePrism[10]. We carefully reviewed the documentation of these platforms to obtain their cognitive categories and components, that are detailed in Table 1.

---

[8] https://docs.uipath.com/activities.

[9] https://docs.automationanywhere.com/bundle/enterprise-v2019/page/enterprise-cloud/topics/aae-client/bot-creator/using-the-workbench/cloud-commands-panel.html.

[10] https://digitalexchange.blueprism.com/dx/search.

Table 1. Heterogeneous taxonomies of selected cognitive RPA platforms

Platform	Category	Example of component
UIPath	UI automation (Computer vision)	CV Screen Scope
	Cognitive	Google Text translate or IBM Watson Text Analysis
	Document understanding	ML extractor
	Intelligent OCR (Document processing and PDF)	Intelligent form extractor
	ML services	ML Skill
	OCR	UiPath Screen OCR
BluePrism	Computer vision/Image processing	Tencent Cloud OCR
	Document processing	Elis Document Data Extraction
	Natural language processing	Natural Language Skill Google Cloud
	Expert Systems/Knowledge Base	Automated Fraud Investigation
	Machine learning	ML Engine Skill Google Cloud
	Workflow and decision engines	Appian Robotic Workforce Manager
	Visualization, monitoring reporting	ClearWork Process Orchestrator
	BI, Analytics and Big Data	Intelligent Decision Automation
	Conversational AI/Bots/Virtual Agents	Human-Robot Conversations
Automation Anywhere	There are no categories, it offers directly a list of components named "packages"	Fuzzy match
		IBM Watson Speech to Text
		Image recognition
		Microsoft LUIS NLP
		OCR
		IQ Bot

For instance, considering an intelligent document processing problem, UiPath classifies it as *Document understanding* or *Intelligent OCR*, BluePrism as *Document Processing* and Automation Anywhere as *IQ Bot* [14]. Some even refer directly to the name of the component instead of categorizing it. For example, Automation Anywhere, where these do not belong to any category (*Microsoft LUIS*) or Speech-Text (*IBM Watson Speech*). As can be observed in Table 1, the taxonomies of the different cognitive RPA platforms that were analyzed are heterogeneous. Therefore, in this scenario, the application of the proposed approach is desired to obtain a homogeneous taxonomy of cognitive RPA components.

3.2 Resulting Taxonomy

The proposed taxonomy (cf. Fig. 4) is put into practice considering the knowledge of Servinform and IWT2 and the review performed in Sect. 2. The taxonomy follows a tree structure, whose nodes represent the taxonomic categories and the black circles attached to the leaf nodes correspond to the type of input they support. Even though, only a part of it is shown in the category tree, is composed of four parts that give content and accumulate the knowledge hidden behind the nodes.

1. The first one composed of the terms *classification, processing,* and *governance.* Firstly, these terms will be instantiated as the first step in defining any $AI - RPA$ taxonomy. Their objective is to cover all areas of application of AI in the RPA, as well as carrying out pruning to achieve a quick classification.
2. The second part is formed by the rest of the nodes, which are more specific categories, hanging from the nodes of the first level. These categories may be modified or even increased being able to have as many children as terms can be included from available knowledge resources.
3. The third part corresponds to the maintenance of traceability of the terms added in the second part. Thus, the equivalent terms to each taxonomic category and the knowledge sources from which they come will be stored (cf. Fig. 2).
4. Finally, the fourth part is formed by the black-colored properties, corresponding to the input format supported by the category. These nodes do not belong to the tree structure, but they describe properties that allow differentiating the components according to the supported input type. For example, it can be distinguished between components that take *Text, Documents* or *Audio* as input. Note that these nodes will be conditioned by the category to which it belongs. For example, the *Image* option will not be included for a *Translation* category.

Note, that, since the information available to determine the belonging to the categories in the main platforms is minimal, the *CategChars* of each *TaxCateg* are being obtained as an effort from both Servinform and IWT2.

Hence, each of the *TaxCategs* presented in Fig. 4 are listed in order from left to right, in which the *CategoryChars* correspond to the items under each of them.

1. **Classification**
    - It takes as input a list of classes.
    - It takes a set of elements as input.
    - It finds association between classes/categories and elements.
    I Detection
        - It takes an input from which a specific classification is extracted.
        - The input can be a file from which it is necessary to deduce to which specific class it belongs or to identify the entities within it that comply with a specific classification.
        i. Elements
            - It extracts the elements that meet specific characteristics that have been taken as input.
        ii. Anomalies
            - Characteristics of a non-anomalous element as input.

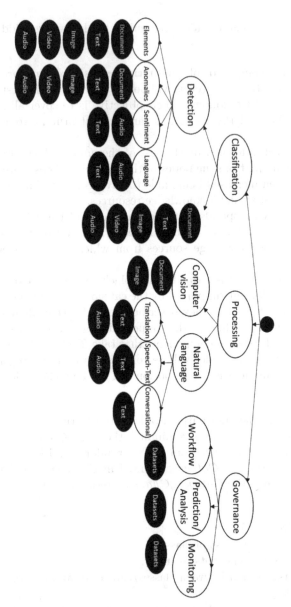

Fig. 4. Resulting taxonomy

- Of the elements it takes in the entry, it performs a binary classification between two classes, yes/no anomalous.
iii. Sentiment
    - It takes as input audio or text.

- It takes as classes a list of possible feelings, and gets as output one of them.

iv. Language
 - It takes as input audio or text.
 - It takes as classes the existing languages and gets as output one of them.

2. Processing
 - The output is obtained by transforming or modifying the input.

   I Computer vision
    - It takes as input an image or a document.
    - It extracts from the input, concrete information that is visually inferred.

   II Natural language
    - It takes as input an image or a document.
    - It transforms the input according to some of its. characteristics, such as language or format, or makes an interpretation of the input to obtain a coherent output to it.

   i. Translation
    - As its name suggests, performs an interpretation of its input to translate it into a specified language.

   ii. Speech-Text
    - It extracts the message contained in the entry, and transforms it into another format.
    - If it is an audio input, it transforms the input into text.
    - If it is a text input, it transforms it into audio.

   iii. Conversational
    - It takes an input from interaction with a human through language, either written or spoken.
    - According to the input, it interprets its meaning and generates as output a coherent response.

3. Governance
 - It takes as input a set of data concerning a decision
 - The outputs obtained are aimed at optimizing.
 - It is on a higher level than other instances or components, so that it carries out control over them.

   I Workflow
    - The component takes as input the data related to the process, such as the result of the last action.
    - The component determines which is the best action to take next according to the parameters.

   II Prediction/Analysis
    - It takes as input the historical and/or environmental data of the prediction.
    - It makes a forecast or regression of what is going to happen.

   III Monitoring

- It carries out a real-time control of the process.
- It is waiting for a failure to appears during the execution of the process when this happens it decides resolve it.

As mentioned above, for this taxonomy, the classification of a given component would be as simple as checking which of the characteristics it meets. It is important to note that it may belong to several of the taxonomic categories.

Making it easier for the RPA developer to find a component, simply by continuing to check which of the categories ($TaxCateg$) cover the characteristics of its problem (cf. Fig. 3). In this way, following the procedure defined in Sect. 2, RPA developers will be able to find out exactly which categories a component corresponds to.

4   Related Work

Some previous works related to addressing the problem of classifying AI techniques and RPA components have been found. This is the case of the taxonomies or classifications proposed for AI according to their application, the learning paradigm, or the algorithm used [6, 9, 11, 12, 15, 22, 24, 27, 33].

Even though all the work present taxonomies applied to different areas of AI or automation, the only one in which a taxonomy explicitly aimed at RPA is proposed is in this [8]. Two proposes [1, 2] that present specific taxonomies of cognitive RPA components are the closest ones related to the approach presented in this paper. However, unlike the proposed approach, they do not allow the dynamic generation of taxonomies.

Initial proposals for taxonomies can also be found in papers from more specific fields [4, 16]. In such context, all proposals follow the same form of definition, i.e., a classification that is not iterative, incremental nor extensible. Initial proposals for taxonomies can also be seen both in the papers mentioned above and those from other specific fields as [4, 16]. However, all proposals follow the same form of definition, i.e., again an unchanging classification is proposed that is not iterative, incremental or extensible.

To summarize, although the works [1, 2] are close to the topic of this paper, to the best of our knowledge, any previous work proposes an incremental classification for the cognitive components in RPA. And this is where the need identified by [28] comes up. *"There is a strong interest in taxonomies in Software Engineering, but few taxonomies are extended or revised. Taxonomy design decisions regarding the used classification structures, procedures and descriptive bases are usually not well described and motivated"*. This need is addressed in the proposed approach since it does not only proposes a classification for cognitive RPA components, but an extensible taxonomy is proposed following a defined procedure. Hence, such taxonomy can be updated and incrementally extended when necessary. Note that for the development of this work, the resources available in the literature related to the terms *robotic process automation, taxonomy, cognitive, machine learning* have been reviewed and only the papers that are listed in the references have been found.

5   Conclusions and Future Work

In the context of AI-based RPA solutions, the manual design of cognitive tasks is currently a time-consuming and error-prone task due to the heterogeneity that is given in the names and classifications of the different RPA platforms. To support RPA developers in this task, this work presents an approach for the systematic construction of a taxonomy of cognitive RPA components that are offered by different AI-based RPA platforms. Such approach is framed within a research project that is the result of a collaboration between the Servinform S.A. company and the IWT2 research group. The proposed approach is applied over selected components that solve real-world use cases from industry, and very promising results are obtained.

Unlike previous related work (e.g., [1,2]), the proposed approach does not propose a specific taxonomy but a method for systematically generating such taxonomy from the information that is provided by the different RPA platforms. Therefore, the taxonomy can be generated as many times as required, resulting in a dynamic process in which the resulting taxonomy can be extended and updated when necessary. Note that this is a great added value since the cognitive RPA market is growing by leaps and bounds. Furthermore, unlike previous related work, the proposed approach is focused on specific RPA platforms, i.e., on platforms that provide AI-based solutions.

For future work, we intend to consider the specification of the characteristics of the categories of the cognitive taxonomies as defined rules, to be able to use them for objective classification by a software system. In addition, an automatic classification of cognitive tasks in the resulting taxonomy according to using AI techniques is intended to be analyzed.

Acknowledgements. This research has been supported by the Pololas project (TIN2016-76956-C3-2-R) of the Spanish Ministry of Economy and Competitiveness, the Trop@ project (CEI-12-TIC021) of the Junta de Andalucía, and the AIRPA (P011-19/E09) project of the Centro para el Desarrollo Tecnológico Industrial (CDTI) of Spain.

References

1. IEEE guide for terms and concepts in intelligent process automation. IEEE Std 2755–2017, pp. 1–16 (2017)
2. IEEE guide for taxonomy for intelligent process automation product features and functionality. IEEE Std 2755.1-2019, pp. 1–53 (2019)
3. ABBYY. State of Process Mining and Robotic Process Automation 2020 (2020). www.abbyy.com/en-us/solutions/process-intelligence/research-report-2020. Last Accessed May 2020
4. Alaydie, N., Reddy, C.K., Fotouhi, F.: Exploiting label dependency for hierarchical multi-label classification. In: Tan, P.-N., Chawla, S., Ho, C.K., Bailey, J. (eds.) PAKDD 2012. LNCS (LNAI), vol. 7301, pp. 294–305. Springer, Heidelberg (2012). https://doi.org/10.1007/978-3-642-30217-6_25

5. Teemu, P.E.A., Aleksandre, K.: Unexpected problems associated with the federated it governance structure in robotic process automation (RPA) deployment. D4 julkaistu kehittämis- tai tutkimusraportti tai -selvitys (2019)
6. Baltrušaitis, T., Ahuja, C., Morency, L.-P.: Multimodal machine learning: a survey and taxonomy. IEEE Trans. Pattern Anal. Mach. Intell. **41**(2), 423–443 (2018)
7. Batchelor, B.G.: Intelligent Image Processing in Prolog. Springer Science & Business Media, London (2012). https://doi.org/10.1007/978-1-4471-0401-8
8. Beerbaum, D.: Artificial intelligence ethics taxonomy-robotic process automation (RPA) as business case (2020)
9. Golstein, B.: SharperAI, CEO. A Brief Taxonomy of AI (2018). https://www.sharper.ai/taxonomy-ai/. Last Accessed May 2020
10. Bkassiny, M., Li, Y., Jayaweera, S.K.: A survey on machine-learning techniques in cognitive radios. IEEE Commun. Surv. Tutor. **15**(3), 1136–1159 (2013)
11. Davis, J., Hoffert, J., Vanlandingham, E.: A taxonomy of artificial intelligence approaches for adaptive distributed real-time embedded systems. In: 2016 IEEE International Conference on Electro Information Technology (EIT), pp. 0233–0238. IEEE (2016)
12. Ding, R.-X., et al.: Large-scale decision-making: characterization, taxonomy, challenges and future directions from an artificial intelligence and applications perspective. Inf. Fusion **59**, 84–102 (2020)
13. Enríquez, J.G., Martínez-Rojas, A., Lizcano, D., Jiménez-Ramírez, A.: A unified model representation of machine learning knowledge. J. Web Eng. **19**, 319–340 (2020)
14. Everest Group Research. Everest Group PEAK Matrix^{TM} for Intelligent Document Processing (IDP) Technology Vendors 2020, March 2020
15. Feldt, R., de Oliveira Neto, F.G., Torkar, R.: Ways of applying artificial intelligence in software engineering. In: 2018 IEEE/ACM 6th International Workshop on Realizing Artificial Intelligence Synergies in Software Engineering (RAISE), pp. 35–41 (2018)
16. Fernández, A., García, S., Luengo, J., Bernadó-Mansilla, E., Herrera, F.: Genetics-based machine learning for rule induction: state of the art, taxonomy, and comparative study. IEEE Trans. Evol. Comput. **14**, 913–941 (2010)
17. Fung, H.P.: Criteria, use cases and effects of information technology process automation (ITPA). Adv. Robot. Autom. **3**, 1–10 (2014)
18. Jimenez-Ramirez, A., Reijers, H.A., Barba, I., Del Valle, C.: A method to improve the early stages of the robotic process automation lifecycle. In: Giorgini, P., Weber, B. (eds.) CAiSE 2019. LNCS, vol. 11483, pp. 446–461. Springer, Cham (2019). https://doi.org/10.1007/978-3-030-21290-2_28
19. Larson, R.R.: Classification clustering, probabilistic information retrieval, and the online catalog. Libr. Quart. **61**(2), 133–173 (1991)
20. Le Clair, C., O'Donnell, G., Lipson, A., Lynch, D.: The forrester wave^{TM}: robotic process automation, Q4 2019. The Forrester Wave (2019)
21. NASSCOM. Cognitive RPA, The Future of Automation (2019). https://www.nasscom.in/knowledge-center/publications/cognitive-rpa-future-automation. Last Accessed May 2020
22. Olsson, H.H., Crnkovic, I.: A taxonomy of software engineering challenges for machine learning systems: An empirical investigation. In: Agile Processes in Software Engineering and Extreme Programming: 20th International Conference Canada, 21–25 May 2019, Proceedings (2019)
23. Rainey, S.K., Brown, B., Kirk, D.B.: Bots, natural language processing, and machine learning. Tax Executive **69**, 39 (2017)

24. Ramírez-Gallego, S., García, S., Mouriño-Talín, H., Martínez-Rego, D., Bolón-Canedo, V., Alonso-Betanzos, A., Manuel Benítez, J., Herrera, F.: Data discretization: taxonomy and big data challenge. Wiley Interdisc. Rev. Data Min. Knowl. Discov. **6**(1), 5–21 (2016)
25. Shalev-Shwartz, S., Ben-David, S.: Understanding Machine Learning: From Theory to Algorithms. Cambridge University Press, New York (2014)
26. Slaby, J.R.: Robotic automation emerges as a threat to traditional low-cost outsourcing. HfS Res. Ltd **1**(1), 3 (2012)
27. Unterkalmsteiner, M., Feldt, R., Gorschek, T.: A taxonomy for requirements engineering and software test alignment. ACM Trans. Softw. Eng. Method. (TOSEM) **23**(2), 1–38 (2014)
28. Usman, M., Britto, R., Börstler, J., Mendes, E.: Taxonomies in software engineering: a systematic mapping study and a revised taxonomy development method. Inf. Softw. Technol. **85**, 43–59 (2017)
29. Vasarhelyi, M.A.: Formalization of standards, automation, robots, and IT Governance. J. Inf. Syst. **27**(1), 1–11 (2013)
30. Weill, P., Ross, J.: A matrixed approach to designing it governance. MIT Sloan Manage. Rev. **46**(2), 26 (2005)
31. Willcocks, L., Lacity, M., Craig, A.: Robotic process automation: strategic transformation lever for global business services? J. Inf. Technol. Teach. Cases **7**(1), 17–28 (2017)
32. Wu, S.P.J., Straub, D.W., Liang, T.P.: How information technology governance mechanisms and strategic alignment influence organizational performance: insights from a matched survey of business and it managers. MIS Q. **39**(2), 497–518 (2015)
33. Zaidan, A.A., Zaidan, B.B.: A review on intelligent process for smart home applications based on IoT: coherent taxonomy, motivation, open challenges, and recommendations. Artif. Intell. Rev. **53**(1), 141–165 (2020)

Towards an OpenSource Logger
for the Analysis of RPA Projects

José Manuel López-Carnicer, Carmelo del Valle,
and José González Enríquez[(✉)]

Computer Languages and Systems Department, Escuela Técnica Superior de
Ingeniería Informática, Avenida Reina Mercedes, s/n, 41012 Sevilla, Spain
joslopcar@alum.us.es, {carmelo,jgenriquez}@us.es

Abstract. Process automation typically begins with the observation of
humans conducting the tasks that will be eventually automated. Similarly, successful RPA projects require a prior analysis of the undergo-
ing processes which are being executed by humans. The process of collecting this type of information is known as user interface (UI) logging
since it records the interaction against a UI. Main RPA platforms (e.g.,
Blueprism and UIPath) incorporate functionalities that allow the recording of these UI interactions. However, the records that these platforms
generate lack some functionalities that large-scale RPA projects require.
Besides, they are only understandable by the proper RPA platforms.
This paper presents an extensible and multi-platform OpenSource UI
logger that generate UI logs in a standard format. This system collects
information from all the computers it is running on and sends it to a
central server for its processing. Treatment of the collected information
will allow the creation of an enriched UI log which can be used, among
others purposes, for smart process analysis, machine learning training,
the creation of RPA robots, or, being more general, for task mining .

Keywords: RPA · Computer-human interaction · OpenSource
project · Process discovery · Task mining

1 Introduction

The emerging technology of Robotic Process Automation (RPA) is said to enable
the automation of the most repetitive, tedious, and mundane digital tasks that
people are suing to do [1,25]. However, not every task is suitable to be robotised
since, besides these characteristics, it should (1) have a low level of exceptions,
(2) require an enclosed cognitive effort, and (3) be susceptible to human errors
[8]. Therefore, successful RPA projects require to start with an analysis phase
[7] which identify those candidate processes—or part of them—which have more
chances to be robotised in a cost-effective way, i.e., those which guarantees the
highest return of the inversion with the lowest risk. Although most of the time
this analysis mainly rely on interpreting process documentation, the latter may

© Springer Nature Switzerland AG 2020
A. Asatiani et al. (Eds.): BPM Blockchain and RPA Forum 2020, LNBIP 393, pp. 176–184, 2020.
https://doi.org/10.1007/978-3-030-58779-6_12

be of poor quality and may require substantial effort to understand [11]. In consequence, there is an increasing trend to capture the actual behaviour of the people interacting with real information systems (ISs) to amend the documentation problems, i.e., recording interaction events like mouse clicks or keystrokes.

Both academia and industry have acknowledged this issue and provide a variety of approaches. On the one hand, vendor-specific platforms (e.g., BluePrism [5], AutomationAnywhere [2], and UIPath [22]) offer tools to record macroslike scripts from the computer of a user executing the process tasks [23]. The obtained script can be analyzed later through the own vendor platform to discover the candidate process and, even, to support the robot code development. On the other hand, proposals can be found in the literature that suggest the creation of a standard log of events related to the interaction of the user with the graphical user interface, the so-called UI Log [6,11,12]. Obtaining this kind of log enables using the Process Mining paradigm [24] to disclose the knowledge that the log contains, among other things, the candidate processes to robotize. These proposals fall under the paradigm of Task Mining [16].

Although these solutions are reasonably mature, they lack support for real-world problems like those existing in the Business Process Outsourcing (BPO) industry, which presents one of the most suitable settings for conducting successful RPA projects [9]. The back-office of BPO departments is composed by large teams of workers performing digital processes through ISs of external companies. Creating a UI Log that comprises the behaviour of the whole team is a challenge for a series of reasons. Firstly, the distributed logging must be centralized in a common event log whose size increases with the size of the team. Secondly, the log of each member of the team may have some differences since not all the team share the same environment, e.g., screen resolution, text editor, WEB browser, etc. And, finally, each member of the team may perform the same processes differently than their teammates. Nowadays, this kind of distributed logging is not supported and, solutions that can be extended in this direction are not intended to be used in RPA, i.e., the generated log lacks detailed information for a thorough RPA analysis.

This paper motivates the minimum requirements that a UI logger should have in a distributed context based on an industrial collaboration with a company belonging to the BPO sector. In addition, software design is proposed to develop this logger as an Open Source project aiming to enable researchers and practitioners to easily get into RPA.

The rest of the paper is organized as follows. Section 2 describes the BPO context and identifies the fundamental requirements of this proposal. Section 3 describes a classification scheme where the most important features of the above requirements, and the tools related to this proposal, are categorized. Section 4 describes the proposed solution provided in this proposal. Finally, Sect. 5 summarises the work and presents some future work.

2 BPO Context

This section describes the knowledge flow which drives the interaction between all the participants in a BPO context which plan to acquire RPA capabilities.

In the context of the back-office employees, different training sessions provide them with the knowledge to perform an outsourced process against some ISs through their own computers. Different challenges are faced during the execution of such process since the real systems tend to present slight differences from the one learnt during the training, or even completely new process whose behavior is similar and they can adapt themselves to accomplish it. In addition, other issues may arise out of the processes like networking problems, operating system errors, etc. These challenges are typically addressed using their common sense and sharing the newly acquired knowledge with the rest of the back-office team.

In the context of the RPA analyst, similar training lessons are provided along with detailed documentation which is typically delivered by the company which host the process to outsource. This information is thoroughly analysed to (1) to understand the workflow and depict the *as-is* process, (2) to identify which parts of this process would be a good candidate to robotise, and (3) to provide a design of the robotised process to continue the RPA development. In this path, the RPA analyst recognises that there are chances that the prescribed process is not fully aligned with the real process. For this, this analyst uses to have periodic and informal interviews with some back-office employees to contrast to assimilate the on-the-field knowledge of them. Nonetheless, most of the details remain undisclosed within the back-office know-how.

For all these reasons, undesired effects occur from both perspectives, the RPA analyst and the back-office employees. RPA projects start with a higher uncertainty after long analysis periods and employees are sued to do mundane tasks for longer and unpredictable periods. For this, RPA analyst must be supported with a formal way to capture the back-office knowledge and which does not require intensive efforts from the back-office employees. Behavioural loggers present a suitable candidate that would be highly welcome by RPA analyst or the back-office employees.

After analysing this context, the following advanced requirements have been identified that are not typically offered by common loggers and that are the motivation of this paper: (1) The scalability level, i.e. the number of computers that can be monitored simultaneously, depending on the execution context, without impacting the system; (2) the method of sending the captured information to the user; (3) the facility to data processing, either through a database or some data structure that can be processed (log) and (4), the possibility of editing or complementing the features offered by the tool with the new software.

3 Related Work

Nowadays, different proposals provide the possibility of creating logs recording the behavior of a human interacting against a computer. In this sense, this section

Table 1. Classification scheme

	Keyboard	Mouse clicks	Mouse position	Clipboard	Screenshot	Foreground application	Capture moment	Specification	Multiplatform	Open source	Server	Remote control	Data access	Totals
Spyrix [18]	1	1	0	1	1	1	1	1	1	0	1	1	0.5	10.5
Spytech SpyAgent [19]	1	1	1	1	1	1	1	1	0	0	1	1	1	11.0
Action logger [13]	1	0	0	1	1	1	1	0	1	0	1	1	0.5	8.0
Best free keylogger [4]	1	0	0	1	1	1	1	0	0	0	1	0	1	7.0
Black cat [15]	1	1	0	0	1	1	1	0	0	1	1	0	1	8.0
UIPath [22]	1	1	1	1	0.5	1	0	1	1	0	0	0	0	7.5
OpenRPA [14]	1	1	1	1	0.5	1	0	1	1	1	0	0	0	8.5
Taskt [3]	1	1	1	1	0	1	0	0	1	1	0	0	0	7.0
Totals	8.0	6.0	4.0	7.0	6.0	8.0	5.0	4.0	5.0	3.0	5.0	3.0	4.0	

aims to describe the state-of-the-art regarding this topic, listing and categorizing the proposals found into a classification scheme.

In the context of parental and company employees control, many keylogger tools offer solutions for monitoring the activity of their users [4,15,18,19]. In addition, platforms with broader objectives, such as the creation and management of RPA projects, also offer users the possibility of recording their activity [3,20,21]. However, the generated logs are frequently understandable only in the context of the platform itself. The closest solution to the proposal presented in this paper is the one presented by Volodymyr et al. [13]. In this work, authors propose a logger to generate results ready to be processed by process mining techniques with RPA purposes. Considering the requirements listed in Sect. 2 and the related tools mentioned above, a mapping between them was executed resulting in Table 1.

In the classification scheme, for each of the tool or platform, each requirement receives a weight. If the tool provides full support to the requirement, it is weighed as 1. If the tool provides partial support to the requirement (e.g., limitations by payment license), it is weighed as 0.5. If the tool does not provide support to the requirement, it is weighed as 0.

As can be seen in Table 1, all the analyzed tools or platforms provides functionalities to record the keyboard strokes and the name of the application that is being executed on the moment of the capture. The vast majority of them allows the capture of clipboard content. Very close by are those platforms that allow the capture of mouse clicks and screenshots. Slightly above average are the tools or platforms that let the user recording the moment of the capture and send all the information collected to a server. In addition, these tools can be executed in different operative systems. Capturing the mouse position or the

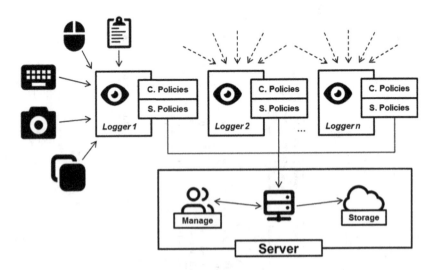

Fig. 1. Logger server

computer's characteristics that is being monitored can be only registered by half of the tools. Less than half of the proposals let the users make remote control of the computer that is being monitored. Finally, only three of the eight tools that have been analyzed have been classified as OpenSource (Fig. 1).

Although some OpenSource projects have been found, results show that most of them are independent modules that can be incorporated into other broader platforms. Thus, they only meet one or more of the defined requirements without completing the full set of them. The two best tools resulting from this classification are Spyrix and SpyAgent. However, they are not OpenSource. In addition, they do not cover important requirements like the possibility of being executed in diverse operating systems or recording the mouse position, among others.

To the best of our knowledge, none of the analyzed tools or platforms satisfies all the requirements defined, this paper presents the foundations of an OpenSource Logger to cover this gap.

4   RPA Logger

4.1   Endpoint Logger

The endpoint logger is focused on gathering enough information for a future RPA analysis. It captures the position and the button type of a mouse click, the keystrokes, and the screen captures. It provides three mechanisms of extension:

- Capture extensions. For specific context, the logger can be extended with a scraper component which adds more information for each event, e.g., web page changes in the context of an RPA project where only web pages are used.
- Capture policies. They are differentiated into two types. First, policies to capture mouse and keyboard events. The current mechanism is to capture one event per mouse click or keystroke. However, it would be interesting to define a policy where a set of keystrokes are grouped in only one event if they are within a defined time window. And secondly, policies to capture screen captures. The current policy capture one image per click or keystroke. However, some scenario that would not afford so many images can decide to make captures in a frequency basis, e.g., one capture every 30 s.
- Send policies. A big amount of data is sent to the central server and, in some context, strict policies must be defined. The current policy sends the event once it occurs. However, in a context where network restrictions apply, a common policy would be to send all the events at the end of the day.

4.2   Central Server

The central server is in charge of storing all the events associated with each monitored computer. In addition, the heavy processing is performed to extract information from the events to be more useful for future RPA analysis.

For example, comparing the similarities between images to detect which ones correspond to the same activity. This comparison may be done by the use of image-similarity techniques [11]. More precisely, an efficient bit-wise comparison [10] between images fingerprints (i.e., short hashes which are obtained from each image in a deterministic way) used to state that two screen captures are related to the same activity according to some prefixed similarity threshold [26]. Another example is to extract patterns or texts from the images applying image processing techniques like Object Character Recognition (OCR) [17].

Data processing in the central server will be performed on demand. At this point, the information being collected does not have to be processed at runtime. Moreover, this way of processing the information can be beneficial to prevent database overloads by avoiding unnecessary iterations.

A simple process, i.e, a teacher that has to consolidate the results of the exams that she marked on her institution website, has been the reference to illustrate how the log should look like. Figure 2 illustrates a simplified log with some of the most interesting fields to be considered. Among them: a global identifier, another one that identifies which computer the capture came from, the timestamp of the capture, the action and the window where the actions are executed.

ID	Computer ID	Timestamp	Action	...	Window
1	1	2020/06/10-0:4:32	Text "Tari Tavarez"	...	Student profile
2	1	2020/06/10-0:4:35	Left click on (100,200)	...	Student profile
3	1	2020/06/10-0:4:50	Text "9.5"	...	Student profile
4	2	2020/06/10-0:5:05	Text "Burton Bertram"	...	Student profile
5	2	2020/06/10-0:5:10	Left click on (115,206)	...	Student profile
6	2	2020/06/10-0:5:20	Left clic on (10, 240)	...	Student
...	...	...	...	...	...

Fig. 2. Log example

5   Conclusions and Future Work

This paper presents the foundations of an OpenSource project which aims to serve as a logger for the analysis phase of RPA projects. After introducing a motivation scenario where the critical requirements have been identified, the closet works related to this proposal have been presented. Although similar proposals have been found, it has been noticed that: (1) they do not cover all the requirements or (2), they are private. Thus, none of the proposals is suitable for giving a solution to the described scenario.

In this context, this paper presents a proposal covering all the aspects mentioned. The proposed solution consists of: (1) a logger capable of collecting information from different events and equipment and sending it to a server and (2), a central server that is responsible for processing this information and converting it into an enriched log so that the data can be processed later.

The immediate future work is focused on preparing the data for processing by data mining techniques. Moreover, an in-depth definition of the requirements will be studied to improve the connection meaning between the requirements and the ones used for the classification scheme. Finally, another important aspect is to manage the data processing itself on the central server.

Acknowledgements. This research has been supported by the Pololas project (TIN2016-76956-C3-2-R) of the Spanish Ministry of Economy and Competitiveness, the Trop@ project (CEI-12-TIC021) of the Junta de Andalucía, and the AIRPA (P011-19/E09) project of the Centro para el Desarrollo Tecnológico Industrial (CDTI) of Spain.

References

1. Aguirre, S., Rodriguez, A.: Automation of a business process using robotic process automation (RPA): a case study. In: Figueroa-García, J.C., López-Santana, E.R., Villa-Ramírez, J.L., Ferro-Escobar, R. (eds.) WEA 2017. CCIS, vol. 742, pp. 65–71. Springer, Cham (2017). https://doi.org/10.1007/978-3-319-66963-2_7

2. Automation Anywhere. Automation Anywhere: Global RPA Solutions (2020). www.automationanywhere.com. Accessed June 2020

3. Bayldon, J.: SharpRPA, a free and open-source RPA solution powered by the.net framework. http://www.taskt.net/. Accessed May 2020

4. Bestxsoftware. Best free keylogger. https://bestxsoftware.com/es/. Accessed May 2020

5. Blue Prism. Blue prism, intelligent RPA platform (2020). www.blueprism.com. Accessed June 2020

6. Dumais, S., Jeffries, R., Russell, D.M., Tang, D., Teevan, J.: Understanding user behavior through log data and analysis. In: Olson, J.S., Kellogg, W.A. (eds.) Ways of Knowing in HCI, pp. 349–372. Springer, New York (2014). https://doi.org/10.1007/978-1-4939-0378-8_14

7. Enríquez, J.G., Jiménez-Ramírez, A., Domínguez-Mayo, F.J., García-García, J.A.: Robotic process automation: a scientific and industrial systematic mapping study. IEEE Access **8**, 39113–39129 (2020)

8. Fung, H.P.: Criteria, use cases and effects of information technology process automation (ITPA). Adv. Robot. Autom. **3**(3), 1–10 (2014)

9. Geyer-Klingeberg, J., Nakladal, J., Baldauf, F., Veit, F.: Process mining and robotic process automation: a perfect match. In: International Conference on Business Process Management, pp. 1–8 (2018)

10. Gusfield, D.: Algorithms on Strings, Trees, and Sequences: Computer Science and Computational Biology. Cambridge University Press, New York (1999)

11. Jimenez-Ramirez, A., Reijers, H.A., Barba, I., Del Valle, C.: A method to improve the early stages of the robotic process automation lifecycle. In: Giorgini, P., Weber, B. (eds.) CAiSE 2019. LNCS, vol. 11483, pp. 446–461. Springer, Cham (2019). https://doi.org/10.1007/978-3-030-21290-2_28

12. Leno, V., Polyvyanyy, A., Dumas, M., La Rosa, M., Maggi, F.M.: Robotic process mining: vision and challenges. Bus. Inf. Syst. Eng. 1–14 (2020)

13. Leno, V., Polyvyanyy, A., La Rosa, M., Dumas, M., Maggi, F.M.: Action logger: enabling process mining for robotic process automation. In: Proceedings of the Dissertation Award, Doctoral Consortium, and Demonstration Track at 17th International Conference on Business Process Management (BPM 2019), Vienna, Austria, pp. 124–128 (2019)

14. OpenRPA. Open source robotic process automation software (2020). https://openrpa.openrpa.dk/. Accessed June 2020

15. Randhawa, A.: Blackcat keylogger. https://github.com/ajayrandhawa/Keylogger. Accessed May 2020

16. Reinkemeyer, L.: Process Mining in Action. Principles, Use Cases and Outlook. Springer, Heidelberg (2020)

17. Singh, S.: Optical character recognition techniques: a survey. J. Emerg. Trends Comput. Inf. Sci. **4**(6), 545–550 (2013)

18. Spyrix Inc.: Spyrix. parental & employees monitoring software. http://www.spyrix.com/. Accessed May 2020

19. Spytech Software and Design, Inc.: Spytech, providing computer monitoring solutions since 1998. https://www.spytech-web.com/spyagent.shtml. Accessed May 2020

20. Taulli, T.: Open source RPA. The Robotic Process Automation Handbook, pp. 259–272. Apress, Berkeley, CA (2020). https://doi.org/10.1007/978-1-4842-5729-6_11

21. UiPath. The UiPath Activities Guide (2020). https://docs.uipath.com/activities. Accessed June 2020

22. UiPath. UiPath enterprise RPA platform, where the future of RPA arrives first (2020). www.uipath.com. Accessed June 2020

23. UiPath. UiPath recording types (2020). http://docs.uipath.com/studio/docs/about-recording-types. Accessed June 2020

24. Aalst, W.: Data science in action. Process Mining, pp. 3–23. Springer, Heidelberg (2016). https://doi.org/10.1007/978-3-662-49851-4_1

25. Willcocks, L., Lacity, M., Craig, A.: Robotic process automation: strategic transformation lever for global business services? J. Inf. Technol. Teach. Cases **7**(1), 17–28 (2017)

26. Wong, C., Bern, M.W., Goldberg, D.: An image signature for any kind of image. In: International Conference on Image Processing, pp. 409–412 (2002)

Beyond the Hype: RPA Horizon for Robot-Human Interaction

Rafael Cabello[1], María José Escalona[2], and José González Enríquez[2(✉)]

[1] Servinform, S.A. Parque Industrial PISA, Calle Manufactura,
5, 41927 Mairena del Aljarafe, Sevilla, Spain
rcbello@servinform.es
[2] Computer Languages and Systems Department, Escuela Técnica Superior de
Ingeniería Informática, Avenida Reina Mercedes, s/n, 41012 Sevilla, Spain
{mjescalona,jgenriquez}@us.es

Abstract. Medium and big organizations have embraced RPA in the last years bringing to light the high maturity of the technology. Current trends are towards including "human-in-the-loop" which promotes efficient ways for robot-human interaction. This is especially relevant since most real RPA projects require a collaboration between the human and the robot leading to hybrids approaches. The challenges that arise from this line can be addressed by both asynchronous (i.e., landing area or task queues where robots and humans share information) and synchronous solutions (i.e., human digital augmentation where robots provide immediate support). This paper goes in deep elaborating in these two alternatives by setting the benefits, requirements, and future research lines which are envisioned through industrial experiences. In addition, this work exposes the role of process mining in this journey since it allows for the necessary efficiency in the process analysis, time-to-market reduction, and continuous improvement that this robot-human collaboration requires.

Keywords: RPA · Computer-human interaction · Process mining

1 Introduction

Currently, the concept of Robotic Process Automation (RPA) is an accepted concept that has been maturely deployed in medium-large organizations where it has focused mainly on efficiently and automatically solving large administrative and back-office processes [9]. In this context, there has been a very high initial hype because very high returns were expected in the short term. However, and after a landing phase of unrealistic expectations, the RPA movement has taken significant traction [13]. In recent years, its technology has matured rapidly, while it has become sophisticated in different lines [2]:

- Incorporate more "low code" approach elements. Thus, construction agility, deployment control, component reuse and "developer independence" (increasingly relevant factor in the software industry) are an improvement.

© Springer Nature Switzerland AG 2020
A. Asatiani et al. (Eds.): BPM Blockchain and RPA Forum 2020, LNBIP 393, pp. 185–199, 2020.
https://doi.org/10.1007/978-3-030-58779-6_13

- Incorporate machine learning elements that allow the systematic actions to be extended to others where cognitive elements have intervened to date.
- Facilitate the scalability and governance of numerous robotic processes; the existence of hundreds of robot farms requires control + command elements similar to the SCADA systems of an electrical network.
- Incorporate "human in the loop", promoting human-robot collaboration.

This last point is especially relevant since RPA was initially oriented towards monolithic processes, where automation was complete, end-to-end covering the different branches and activities of the process [11]. However, it was found that this approach was excessively unrealistic, since the number of these ideal robotising processes was very low, and even required input data structuring that did not obey the reality of the processes. On the contrary, after the advance of the first years, it was detected that hybrid scenarios of robot-human collaboration were the most natural. In them, a part of activities was identified as convenient for execution by RPA, due to its high frequency and systematic nature [10]. The rest of the activities continue to be carried out with human participation, due to their low frequency, cognitive nature, or where there was no simple identification of performance criteria. This "blended" approach is the one that has had the most deployment in recent years. The challenge involved is tackled with different approaches [1,6]:

1. Segmentation of robot/human activities of the process, with the structuring of the robot - person contact points in the form of a "landing area" where the activity switch occurs. The key aspects of this "landing area" are the structuring of the data required for that activity switch completely, autonomously for both humans and robots, as well as control of the switch, avoiding the terrifying aspect of "cases in limbo" (cases of the process that neither robot nor human has clear or agile knowledge that they must treat).
2. Encapsulation of relatively short sequences of human activities of a systematic nature, theoretically of full application of RPA, where the immediacy factor of execution on demand is critical for the business, not being possible to "packet" or demand activity for the robot.

The first approach applies, for instance, to cases of information collection by robots from different information systems, so that once the required data set is available, the robot makes them available in a structured way for the human to execute cognitive action required or continue the process. The benefits obtained are multiple, not only the expected efficiency but others of greater significance that were not initially considered in a relevant way. In particular, the complete control of data involved in decision-making "within the process", as well as complete control of times and activities carried out by people with the data provided by robots. Therefore, an "mc-donalization" of the work of people in "stealth mode" is carried out. And at the same time the ways are laid so that once cognitive actions have been mc-donalized, they can be identified as efficient, either through deterministic rules or through machine learning algorithms. The second approach applies especially in call centres or back-office activities, applying "RPA steroids" to the traditional concept of "macros". Macros are not a new idea but were limited to mostly simple embedded spreadsheet actions or script execution on legacy systems. However, there were significant governance and maintenance problems, since most of these macros are based on "informal programming" carried out by the employees themselves. Even though activities were carried out in some cases of high critically, there were significant risks of operation (ignorance of the code, lack of maintenance capacity, high dependence on the person who carried it out). The application of RPA to these activities on demand of people allows solving these challenges, by providing a framework of governance and control, integrating interaction capabilities with any information system and execution of actions of any degree of complexity. However, the "reaction time" factor is critical, and that the human cannot remain "waiting" for the completion of the robot's activity since the efficiency would degrade and/or the process may lengthen its completion time. With this short introduction, we start from the hypothesis that Process Mining can be an extremely useful tool to facilitate this two-way RPA extension in human-robot collaboration [4]:

- In the case of a single process mining approach, it allows identifying both visually and quantitatively the elements of potential segmentation of robot vs. human activity. And equally important that the identification is the monitoring of the evolution of the process progressively since different segments of the "mc-donalization" are executed by robots instead of people. And equally important is identifying the "friction points" on the switch between robot and person due to incomplete data transfer and process control (what would be called a cold "weld" of the redesigned process).
- In the case of multiple process mining approach, it is possible to identify the "long tail" of systematic human actions in which attended robots allow the human being to have an "exoskeleton of administrative activity", along the lines in which mechanical exoskeletons are used on industrial production lines for heavy-duty. The identification of the long tail must allow identifying the aggregate volume as the prioritization of the candidates to robotize and its impact. There is a common benefit, and that is that the evaluation of processes to be robotized has generally required a high effort of analysis, generally starting from incomplete or even incorrect information (let's not forget that a process is analyzed to partially eliminate the human factor from the process, therefore that resistance to change is relevant). Process Mining contributes efficiency in this process of analysis and reduction of the "time-to-market" of obtaining results while incorporating a framework of continuous systematic evaluation.

With this initial context, in this paper, we analyse how the incorporation of human-robots and the users of process mining in RPA context, can offer a high positive impact, not only in large administrative and back-office processes of the medium-large company. They can also offer a suitable solution for SME (Small and Medium Enterprise). With this aim, this paper is structured as follow. In Sect. 2 a background description is presented. Section 3, presents a general view of our approach of human-robot interaction, which is illustrated with a real example in Sect. 4. We finalized the paper with related work (Sect. 5) and with conclusions and future works in Sect. 6.

2 Background

In the last 5 years, there has been a very high increase in the use of RPA (Robotic Process Automation) in medium-large organizations. Robotic Process Automation (RPA) is the automation of a wide set of administrative tasks using "Robotic FTE's" configured to have a "Virtual Backoffice" that perform manual activities without incorporating direct human participation with high efficiency and high speeds [15]. The application of RPA has been carried out mainly in the so-called "back-office" activities, mainly related to the areas of Administration and Finance, which includes financial analysis, financial reporting and planning, managerial accounting, treasury and cash management, payment and receipt of accounts, risk management and taxes. Another area of application in RPA has been carried out in customer service activities, in queries and claims for the services and/or products provided. These back-office activities are based on carrying out tasks, mainly administrative, systematic, of relevant volume, on already established information systems, where the required cognitive activity is limited [12]. The driver of the utilization of RPA has been fundamentally the generation of efficiency in these processes and cost savings in the main measure, and additionally the availability of flexibility of execution capacity to adapt to changes in the variable and fluctuating workload in the short term. Robotic Process Automation (RPA) is the automation of a wide set of administrative tasks using "Robotic FTE's" configured to have a "Virtual Backoffice" that perform manual activities without incorporating direct human participation with high efficiency and high speeds [8]. In the initial scope of RPA application back-office processes, it was later extended to activities called "front", in those where a human responds to a request for resolution of incidents, queries, claims, in usual environments of Customer Service Centers, mainly online both by phone and by other telematic channels. The main difference between "back" activities compared to "front" lies in that while "back" activities are usually complex, with relatively medium-high process time, highly systematized, generally requiring scaling between different levels of internal support, front activities tend to be more atomic, require immediate action (frequently the user or client is in interaction while the process is carried out), their process time is reduced and they involve a very high diversity of activities. It is for all these reasons that the initial application of RPA has been carried out strongly first in the areas of back-office where the return on investment materializes more quickly and then has been extended to the areas of front-office later. This application extension has also been favoured in that the separation between back-office and Frontoffice is often fuzzy and there is generally a union of back/front activities that separating them in a watertight way makes processes inefficient. Over the last few years, powerful manufacturers of RPA solutions have established themselves in the market, with the main UiPath, BluePrism and Automation Anyware, being the natural focus of RPA application the activities of Backoffice [14]. The focus of RPA application in Front activities carried out by the manufacturer PegaSystems is remarkable. These solution manufacturers have provided benefits in the maturation and extension of the application of RPA through:

- Availability of component framework and robot construction environment with a low-code approach that allows for the agility of construction, reuse of components and "developer independence" (increasingly relevant factor in the software industry) are significant tools for the control of deployment and governance of robot farms of dozens of robots that execute operations in real-time, where the identification of incidents in their execution is a critical factor
- Disseminate RPA knowledge and application methodologies, so that the generation of RPA-trained personnel has accelerated over time, reducing the barriers to entry of such knowledge through the availability of RPA MOOC environments, generating high liquidity of personnel qualified in RPA tools.
- Incorporate machine learning elements that allow the systematic actions to be extended to others where cognitive elements have intervened to date. These factors of market needs together with the availability of solutions have allowed the explosion of RPA application. There are numerous experiences with massive deployments of dozens of robots in financial companies and utilities, where the back-office and front-office processes are highly relevant.

These massive deployments initially tried to address a one hundred per cent RPA approach to processes, trying to incorporate all possible activities to be carried out in the process in robot execution, with very high expectations for savings and return on investment. However, as the deployment of RPA in these organizations has matured, it has been confirmed that this approach has been excessively optimistic, since it has the weakness of implying a monolithic application approach, trying to incorporate the end-to-end process into RPA. covering the different branches and activities of the process. In many, there are fractions of the process whose casuistry or complexity do not make the incorporation of RPA profitable to address them. In turn, the discovery effort of all the activities to be carried out in the processes has been identified as a relevant factor both in the investment required for the deployment of RPA and in the time involved from the identification of opportunity to the availability of RPA. running stably. That is why the RPA approach is considered a much more efficient and effective approach considering from the beginning the collaboration of robots and people in an integrated way in the process, which has been called "human in the loop". Therefore, hybrid scenarios for robot-human collaboration were established in the natural ones, where:

- A part of activities were identified as suitable for execution by RPA, due to their high frequency and systematic nature
- The rest of the activities were kept to be executed by the robots, due to their low frequency, cognitive nature, or where there was no simple identification of execution criteria.

Fig. 1. The defined process

3   Robot-Human Interaction and Process Mining

In this section, we are going to present a proposal that we have drawn mainly from research experience in the business environment and that is validated in Sect. 4 with a real example. This proposal starts with the hybridization scenario discussed in the previous section.

3.1   Applying Our Approach

Our approach is thinking about a very concrete set of stakeholders. It is oriented to help the development team who wants to create an RPA hybrid solution enriched with process mining. In this sense, the first part of our approach presents a set of steps that should be executed and consider the definition of the RPA hybrid solution. The factors identified to perform a successful hybridization are presented in Fig. 1 as a process composed of five steps that should be executed to rightly defined the hybrid process.

- **Step 1.- Identification of the activities carried out by both robots and people.** It is necessary to clearly and exclusively segment the activities carried out by each one, but at the same time, it is necessary to include in this identification of activities the design of mechanisms that prevent the human from bypassing the robot. This can be done either by designing execution methods for "poka-yoke" tasks or by preventing the human from accessing certain information or system required for the execution of the tasks that must be performed on the robot. Although this process design orientation may not seem necessary, the experience in the deployment of RPA indicates that to maximize the probability of success, it is necessary to include these elements that some might consider "anti-ludicrous" mechanisms, since on numerous occasions the people involved in the human-robot hybrid process they visualize the impact on jobs that the incorporation of RPA implies for them
- **Step 2.- Identification and design of how the transfer of information is carried out between robot-human and/or vice versa.** Although the clear and exclusive identification of human and robot activities has been carried out, there are always points where to achieve the overall flow of the process, it is necessary to transfer the "ownership" and execution of the process from one to another. They are the checkpoints of the Border Control. Their characteristics are that *they must be clearly and unambiguously defined*

where they are, with a unique sense of the human/robot or robot/human infor-
mation flow, and the transfer information must be complete and transferred
in one go. These conditions are important to ensure that the human being
can continue with the process without reprocessing or reworking what the
robot has already done, which would cause a loss of efficiency in the process.
At the same time that it would generate distrust in the human being of what
has been performed the robot, producing the effect *"I review what the*
robot has done because I do not trust." That is why in these checkpoints it
is critical to provide the human-robot with all the information required for
the continuity of the process, and if for any reason it has not been possible
to complete or generate any information, it must be identified and the process marked as "KO", i.e. failed, To avoid confusion. In the process, these
Checkpoint points must, therefore, guarantee the robustness of the hybrid
process, experience shows that if it does not have that robustness, although
the activities performed by robots and humans are perfect, there is a "cold
welding" effect that produces the process is split.

– **Step 3.- Generation of capacity and feeling that the human who
executes the human part of the process knows the global evolution
of the process in real-time.** This factor is critical both for the efficient
execution of the process and to ensure effective change management in the
adoption of the new way of working. The ultimate goal of achieving the feeling
that the human is *"man-behind-the-wheel"*, or as the French Luddite anarcho-
syndicalist activist Émile Pouget (1860–1931) indicated, *"The worker will*
only respect the machine the day it is become your friend, reducing your work,
and not like today, who is your enemy, takes jobs and kills workers". The
elements that are part of this knowledge of the situation of the process can
be synthesized in:

  • Indicators of the number of cases of the process in execution in its different
    states (pending to be treated by robot and human, in the process by each
    and completed)
  • State OK/KO, i.e. passed or failed, of each of these cases completed
  • States of operation of each of the robots that collaborate with humans
    and details of the activity carried out.

It is critical to generate the feeling that this information is there for the human
when s/he needs it, in an agile way, although most of the time s/he does not
need it. Experience shows us that most of the time the humans who execute
the process do not need this information, only when there are incidents in
the execution of the process is access to this information necessary, avoiding
the perception of *unknown operation black box.*

– **Step 4.- Deployment of tools for control and governance of the
whole process.** The integrated control of the process must be carried out
in such a way that the process supervisor has the information in real-time
of how the process is executed as a whole, in both the human and robot
parts, allowing to balance workload between humans and robots, managing
respective work queues, identify the degree of saturation of human and robot
capacity, the status of OK and process KOs globally, and even, if necessary

in exceptional circumstances, take cases in process or pending execution for manual execution. These elements of the process are part of the elements of command and control of the integrated process, but as important as they are they make a design of the government of the process itself that guides its automatic execution and with the least human decision-making intervention. Although as indicated in the previous point that the human who executes the manual or cognitive part of the process must have the perception that he knows and controls the process, the design of the process must be oriented so that the cadence of activities of the process itself is marked by the robot's actions, aiming for robots to generate human work queues. This automatic process pulse dialling will generate greater process efficiency while reducing process adoption times by forcing faster and more focused adoption.

- **Step 5.- Centralization of human process data - robot.** Having a centralized repository of executed cases, their trace of execution, human actors and robots that have participated throughout its execution is essential to allow the aforementioned elements of process control and governance and online visibility of the process situation. But even more, it is the essential tool to evaluate the real performance of a new process executed in a hybrid way, its evolution over time and the detection of possible hidden inefficiencies. In addition, it becomes the "post-mortem" identification tool for actions performed by humans and robots in the face of unforeseen KOs or performance values out of range.

3.2   Measuring the Process

The design of the hybrid human-robot process it is not a simple problem and it requires the development team to work a guide for a set of measures that guarantee that the development is being successfully applied. It requires takes into account the above steps and implements them effectively will generate the fluidity and robustness necessary in the new process. However, it is critical to define a set of key indicators that help the team to value the success of the new process that is established. In our approach, the next ones are considered:

- The captured data allow knowing the complete cycle of activity of robots and humans, having enough fine grain of associated information for the discovery of causes involved in the KOs of the process? Percentage of process OK considered as cases that are executed end to end in human-robot collaboration as designed.
- Percentage of cases that have remained at some point in the process without being automatically transferred between humans and robots, and have had to be manually rescued to be manually inserted back into the process or reprocessed in the process.
- OMT (Operation Medium Time) of human activities concerning the forecast before design. In this aspect, it is necessary to identify the "pure" time for the execution of human tasks, and also, but separately, the time "around" the execution of tasks, related to the management of work queues, monitoring of ongoing activities, time non-productive around the task.

– Time of execution of tasks by humans that should be performed by robots, due to their unavailability, required operation windows exceeded, the operation performed OK only partially by robots. This indicator shows the degree of underperformance of the process, and the expectation of its improvement.

The implementation of a continuous improvement cycle based on these indicators allows us to iterative go through the 5 identified phases (see Fig. 1), helping us to solve the following questions:

– What new activities can be done by robots instead of humans? Are there systematic failures in tasks performed by robots that impact humans? How can they be avoided and make the process more robust?
– A higher than expected human BMT may hide friction in the transfer of information. Is there partial information on robots made available to humans? Are there new manual human activities not initially contemplated?
– What information is mainly used by humans for the execution of their tasks? Is there other information required and not covered?
– Are the process queues generated by the robots sufficiently optimized or are there capacity bottlenecks? Is the information required at the time it is needed?
– Are the data collected from robots and humans sufficient for the complete and effective measurement of the efficiency generated? The captured data allow knowing the complete cycle of activity of robots and humans, having enough fine grain of associated information for the discovery of causes involved in the KOs of the process?

3.3   Enriching with Process Mining

How to market technology solutions have addressed this challenge today comes from two different poles: • **Centric BPM**: BPM (Business Process Management) solutions that have allowed the design, construction, deployment and operation of processes through workflows and their integration with information systems, to which RPA elements have been incorporated as yet another system to integrate. The most significant example of this orientation is Appian, a benchmark in the BPM sector, which has facilitated integration with market RPA tools, and even by acquiring the RPA company. The advantages of this approach are its maturity in the process vision, the availability of out-of-the-box integration elements and the focus on the end-user experience that an integrated process working environment has. The disadvantage is that its application focus is mainly heavy processes, extensive in human activities, of high complexity, as well as the cost of the technology involved, which sometimes prevents a return on investment based on the efficiency generated (cost of human FTE removed). • **RPA centric**: RPA solutions that integrate elements of robot-human interaction in the event of or in certain situations of the designed process. As the most significant example of this orientation is UiPath, which has incorporated the generation and management of data entry forms and/or validation of information by humans, as an extension of its robot control and governance tool (component called "orchestrator"). The advantages of this approach are that it allows complete control of human activities within the process of interaction with the robot, as well as guiding the cadence of the process of the robot towards the human. However, the main disadvantages of this approach are the limited benefits in sophisticated interaction of the human with the robot (complex data involved, integrated validations and logic, global process vision), as well as lack of exploitation, monitoring and process control benefits. integrated both humans and robots. Additionally, the centric RPA approach also incorporates the RDA vision of robotising (RDA: Robotic Desktop Automation), focused on under-command activities ("unattended robots") where a human on-demand makes specific requests to execute automatism. This automatism generally implies a reduced number of activities by the robots, reduced execution time of the robots, and the need for immediate feedback to the user who requested the OK/KO completion. In the case of UiPath, this approach to RDA is made using its UiPath Assistant tool, which is its end-user manager for the available unattended robots. Although its operation is simple for the user, it has very limited deficiencies regarding feedback and sophisticated interaction with the user, and in the case of KO of the robot, the user has reduced information and is not quick to know what has happened in the process.

As previously indicated, the deployment of RPA systems that allow human-robot collaboration is not a big bang process, on the contrary, its success is associated with a process of continuous improvement. Process Mining allows a successful initial design of collaboration and continuous monitoring of the process to progressively increase the results, based on new activities identified to be carried out by robots and a progressive decrease in KOs. In this robot-human hybridization scenario, the Process Mining of the process constitutes a facilitating tool for said hybridization. Thus, Process Mining allows activities to be carried out as they are currently carried out before the design of the new hybrid process. This survey of the process should aspire not only to the identification of the activities involved carried out by humans in the process but also and most importantly, the effort involved in each activity to evaluate the business case of the hybridized process and its return on investment against the applied change. The great challenge of applying Process Mining to this type of process of the potential application of human-robot hybridization is the difficulty of having traces of human activity of each one of the activities carried out by humans, with which we have a relatively The grossness of human activities, which implies a significant degree of uncertainty and/or inaccuracy of the AS-IS situation, can invalidate the starting premises in the business case to be carried out. Once the robot-human hybridization process has been designed, this design should allow traces and activity records of the robots and humans to be available, which in turn allows Process Mining to be continuously incorporated into this evaluation, as information is now available "finer grain" in the process. The segmentation itself, a structure that requires hybridization, forces the generation of this process execution data that was not previously available. That is why the application of Process Mining in an RPA-human hybridization scenario should not be considered with an application focus of eighty percent of the effort in the design of the AS-IS and TO-BE process and twenty percent in monitoring. But on the contrary, thirty percent of the effort in design and evaluation of hybrid-robot MVP (minimum viable product) focusing on the elements of the greatest contribution of the robot and identification of critical aspects of the initial deployment, and seventy percent of the effort in continuous improvement of the process and efficient process monitoring.

4   A Real Project. Learning from the Trenches

The proposal presented in this work has already been applied in a real project entitled RAIL. This project was developed in collaboration between Servinform Inc. and the University of Seville. The objective of RAIL is to propose an innovative solution and supported by computer tools to identify the business activities to be robotized without any intrusion or requirement with the existing information systems, capturing the data of execution of the tasks at the same time that they are carried out by back-office people and automatically identifying the robotization elements of processes to be implemented, including cognitive elements. Rail is made up of a series of modules that allow its correct definition:

– **Non-intrusive monitoring.** Software component that can be installed in the workplace that intelligently captures and completes the interaction data with transactional systems, in real-time and generates a structured dataset for the analysis of the process, without causing any type of degradation in the person's activity backoffice nor jeopardizes the security and confidentiality of process data.
– **Automatic process survey module.** The component allows automatic generation of the work process with all workflow variants from the logs and images resulting from the non-intrusive monitoring module. This automatic process generation is based on the application of image-hash, image-match and OCR algorithms on said dataset.
– **Qualitative evaluation module.** On the automatic survey of the process resulting from the previous module, iterative analysis and refinement of the resulting process are applied by modifying the configurations of the different algorithms to generate new refinement of the analysis and comparatively evaluate the results obtained. The integration of ProM makes it easier for the user to refine the processes resulting from the analysis, facilitating the use of process generation algorithms and identification of evaluation metrics. As a result, the representation of the faithful image of the executed process is obtained, and in particular of the branches of the process that constitute exceptions and/or infrequent activities. These activities constitute the elements of the process that are most difficult to identify and which in turn generate the critical points of robotization since their non-identification generates untreated exceptions to the process that cause the robot to stop or incorrect actions (Fig. 2).

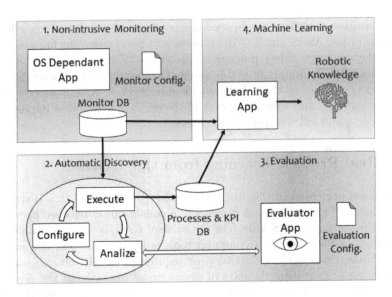

Fig. 2. A global view of RAIL project

– **Module for the identification and deployment of predictive algorithms.** It includes the learning components of the expert system (a neural network that will allow any type of action or actions as input, be it mouse clicks, keystrokes or any type of text and will transform all this type of input into a corpus) and the prediction component (Once the neural network has been trained, we are using the learning product to predict the behavior of the robot, so that it asks the RAIL system "what should it do" to continue with its functional process).

The Module 1 component aims to capture images and mouse and keyboard presses, to extract all the possible information from the process with which a person works on information systems, generating capture records that must allow the description of your full activity. Modules 2–3 are made up of three stages (Execute, Analyze and Configure) that can be cyclically executed as many times as desired. The component allows integration through the ProM framework, which allows the execution of an extensible set of algorithms for log management, process discovery and analysis. The Execute stage applies image analysis techniques using algorithms including image fingerprint, template matching and OCR. The Analyze stage includes various Group and Process refinement algorithms, to allow the discovery of groups of similar processes as well as exceptions to general threads. The Configuration stage allows modifying the configurations of the different algorithms to generate new refinement of the analysis and comparatively evaluate the results obtained. Module 4 includes the learning components of the expert system and the prediction component that allows integrating prediction algorithms in the identified processes. Additionally, Servinform has carried out the implementation for robot-human collaboration in the practical case of managing consumer claims for a Spanish national electricity company. The solution scheme deployed has been:

Farm of RPA robots made in UiPath that extract information from commercial information systems and CRM. They perform data extraction in the time window from 00:00 to 12:00. These robots extract the information, approximately 100 variables of various kinds, both text and numeric, which are all the data that may be required for a person to decide the resolution to apply to the claim.

– Solution prediction algorithms. Based on the dataset carried out during 6 months, 45 possible solutions to apply to a claim were identified, based on combinations of output variables from the cognitive resolution process. A model deployed in AWS Sagemaker was trained to predict these three priority solutions.
– Robot Control System, AWS prediction system and Human-Robot processes, which manages the queues of robot processes, the data collected by the robots, stores them in a database and generates queues of cases to be treated by humans. along with the predictions that have not exceeded the confidence threshold for human review, as well as the result of the resolution to the human claim.
– Human-Robot interface called "Dispenser", web front that makes available to the back-office team the data collected by the robots, the proposed solution, and allows the registration of the solution established by the human (which allows the refinement of algorithms)

The results obtained from the projected increase the efficiency of the process from ten percent of the start with the deployment of a collection robot farm until 10 months later, an efficiency of over sixty percent after including both optimization of the collection process, implementation of the three predictive solutions after ten iterations in predictive models and the implementation of deterministic solution rules identified with the dataset generated over time. The main conclusions of the project include:

– Criticality in maximizing the usability of the human-robot interface. Due to the high number of data to be displayed, the agility to display the data, ease of identification of the information provided and the management of the queue of cases to be treated are highly relevant due to their impact on efficiency.
– Easy and clear identification of incomplete information collected by robots. In the event of an incidence in the systems on which the collecting robots operate, it becomes very important so as not to degrade the efficiency generated, the immediate availability and at the human disposal of the trace of the actions of the robots on the systems on which they have worked, to unequivocally identify the existing and NOT existing information in the collection.
– Adaptation of the extraction rate by robots to ensure that humans always have a work queue available at the beginning of their time window. This

caused an increase in the number of robots to ensure the absence of bottle-necks.

- Results monitoring environment using KPIs that identify over time the evolution of the number of cases treated integrally by the human-robot collaboration system, cases treated from outside, the average BMT in each time window (time dedicated by humans in the collaboration process), the percentage of OK and collection KO, the percentage of prediction that exceed the thresholds established for each one and the segmentation of the efficiency provided.

5   Related Works

Definition of RPA is not new. As it was introduced in this paper, there is quite a literature in this environment. Some surveys or reviewers of the current situation of RPA have been found [3,5]. However, in this paper, we are trying to focus on a real view of the RPA technology. In this sense, our starting point is the recent paper [2]. In this paper, authors review 54 primary studies under the SMS (systematic mapping study) Kitchenham mechanism [7]. As the author introduced and demonstrate, the real application of the RPA that was published is still reduced. This could be motivated by industrial protection or patents on these functionalities or platforms. Nonetheless, it is not possible to confirm since no information has been found on related patents in the field of RPA. Authors add to the paper an industrial review in RPA where they identified some solutions and analyses different commercial tools.

6   Conclusions and Future Works

RPA has being a movement that is being applied in research and industry with successful results. However, after the first era of RPA, it is necessary to reconsider the situation to try to carry out its advantages to other environments, like SME. In this paper, we present a global discussion about how RPA can offer a suitable solution if we consider the human in the loop. Thus, the paper presents an approach to include the human effectively into hybrid RPA. This approach is enriched with a set of key indicators and with Process Mining principles. To illustrate our approach, we present experience from the trenches, RAIL Project. As future work, we want to continue working in our approach, both in the research and in the enterprise side. Our idea is to try to define a detailed process, based on the one presented in Fig. 1, with real mechanisms to measure its development in a very effective way. It is also very important to guarantee that the process mining principles are included in the right way, guarantee that the all approach can offer good results even for small and medium companies.

Acknowledgements. Research was partially supported by the POLOLAS project (TIN2016-76956-C3-2-R) of the Spanish Government's Ministry of Economy and Competitiveness, Trop@ project (CEI-12-TIC021) of the Junta de Andalucía and by RAIL project (Platform for the automatic and intelligence learning of Software Robots).

References

1. Chacón Montero, J., Jimenez Ramirez, A., Enríquez, J.G.: Towards a method for automated testing in robotic process automation projects. In: 2019 IEEE/ACM 14th International Workshop on Automation of Software Test (AST), pp. 42–47 (2019)
2. Enríquez, J.G., Jiménez-Ramírez, A., Domínguez-Mayo, F.J., García-García, J.A.: Robotic process automation: a scientific and industrial systematic mapping study. IEEE Access **8**, 39113–39129 (2020)
3. Gami, M., Jetly, P., Mehta, N., Patil, D., et al.: Robotic Process Automation-Future of Business Organizations: A Review, April 8, 2019
4. Geyer-klingeberg, J., Nakladal, J.: Process mining and robotic process automation: a perfect match. In: 16th International Conference on Business Process Management, Industry Track Session, number July, pp. 1–8 (2018)
5. Ivančić, L., Suša Vugec, D., Bosilj Vukšić, V.: Robotic process automation: systematic literature review. In: Di Ciccio, C., et al. (eds.) BPM 2019. LNBIP, vol. 361, pp. 280–295. Springer, Cham (2019). https://doi.org/10.1007/978-3-030-30429-4_19
6. Jiménez-Ramírez, A., Chacón-Montero, J., Wojdynsky, T., Enríquez, J.G.: Automated testing in robotic process automation projects. J. Softw. Evol. Process, e2259 (2020)
7. Kitchenham, B., Brereton, P.: A systematic review of systematic review process research in software engineering. Inf. Softw. Technol. (2013)
8. Leno, V., Dumas, M., Maggi, F.M., La Rosa, M.: Multi-perspective process model discovery for robotic process automation. In: CEUR Workshop Proceedings, vol. 2114, pp. 37–45 (2018)
9. Madakam, S., Holmukhe, R.M., Jaiswal, D.K.: The future digital work force: robotic process automation (RPA). JISTEM-J. Inf. Syst. Technol. Manage. **16** (2019)
10. Mendling, J., Decker, G., Hull, R., Reijers, H.A., Weber, I.: How do machine learning, robotic process automation, and blockchains affect the human factor in business process management? Commun. Assoc. Inf. Syst. **43**(Art. 19), 297–320 (2018)
11. Penttinen, E., Kasslin, H., Asatiani, A.: How to choose between robotic process automation and back-end system automation? In: 26th European Conference on Information Systems, ECIS 2018, pp. 1–14 (2018)
12. Penttinen, E., Kasslin, H., Asatiani, A.: How to choose between robotic process automation and back-end system automation? In: European Conference on Information Systems 2018 (2018)
13. Taulli, T.: Future of RPA. In: The Robotic Process Automation Handbook, pp. 293–316. Apress, Berkeley, CA (2020). https://doi.org/10.1007/978-1-4842-5729-6_13
14. UiPath. UiPath Enterprise RPA Platform, where the future of RPA arrives first (2019). www.uipath.com. Accessed September 2019
15. Willcocks, L., Lacity, M., Craig, A.: Robotic process automation: strategic transformation lever for global business services? J. Inf. Technol. Teach. Cases **7**(1), 17–28 (2017)

A Framework to Evaluate the Viability of Robotic Process Automation for Business Process Activities

Christian Wellmann, Matthias Stierle$^{(\boxtimes)}$, Sebastian Dunzer,
and Martin Matzner

Institute of Information Systems, Friedrich-Alexander-Universität
Erlangen-Nürnberg, Nürnberg, Germany
{christian.wellmann,matthias.stierle,sebastian.dunzer,
martin.matzner}@fau.de
http://is.rw.fau.eu

Abstract. Robotic process automation (RPA) is a technology for centralized automation of business processes. RPA automates user interaction with graphical user interfaces, whereby it promises efficiency gains and a reduction of human negligence during process execution. To harness these benefits, organizations face the challenge of classifying process activities as viable automation candidates for RPA. Therefore, this work aims to support practitioners in evaluating RPA automation candidates. We design a framework that consists of thirteen criteria grouped into five perspectives which offer different evaluation aspects. These criteria leverage a profound understanding of the process step. We demonstrate and evaluate the framework by applying it to a real-life data set.

Keywords: RPA support · Viability assessment · Process activity evaluation · Process characteristics

1 Introduction

The state of technology is continuously advancing, resulting in shorter intervals to scrutinize whether tasks can be automated or rely on human execution [1]. The recent rise of robotic process automation (RPA) challenges this status quo once more and further blurs the boundaries of human computer interaction [22]. RPA automates repetitive and monotonous tasks by configuring software robots to mimic the actions of the user on the presentation layer [2]. Organizations are hoping for RPA to lead to an increase in time for employees to focus on value-adding activities and to cut costs [18] through eliminating time spent interacting with information systems and data transfer [32]. Furthermore, companies expect RPA to improve the quality of their work, eliminate human negligence and increase reaction time around the clock [9]. Primarily driven by changing market dynamics and global competition, companies are forced to cut

© Springer Nature Switzerland AG 2020
A. Asatiani et al. (Eds.): BPM Blockchain and RPA Forum 2020, LNBIP 393, pp. 200–214, 2020.
https://doi.org/10.1007/978-3-030-58779-6_14

costs through the implementation of new technologies like RPA, especially when they promise a quick and high return on investment [1].

While the benefits for organizations in applying RPA seem evident, the question remains as to why there are currently only few success stories of RPA adoption. One of the biggest challenges identified for a successful RPA implementation is the selection of suitable processes or process activities for RPA [1,13,32]. The methods available to date mostly offer high-level decision-making support with the focus set on profitability rather than assessing the RPA viability of processes or tasks [5,22,33].

The objective of this work is to offer practitioners a process characteristic evaluation framework including a set of criteria and exemplary evaluation metrics. To understand the parameters of RPA, the following research question needs to be answered:

What are the characteristics of a process activity, or a set of process activities, that facilitate viable robotic process automation?

By answering the question, this work contributes to broadening the understanding in the selection of process activities for RPA. Furthermore, it serves as a basis for the creation of a framework that examines the process activity from different perspectives for its suitability for RPA. In addition, the application of the framework highlights challenges when assessing the criteria and opens up new research opportunities.

This study is structured as follows: In Sect. 2, the term robotic process automation is defined and the results of a literature review are presented as a concept matrix. Further, the existing methods for process or process activity selection are compared to derive the similarities and differences. In Sect. 3, the process characteristic evaluation framework is presented. Section 4 outlines the evaluation approach, the data set and the pre-processing of the process before the framework is applied and validated. The contributions, limitations and future research are summarized in Sect. 5.

2 Background

2.1 Robotic Process Automation (RPA)

While the interest in RPA is still steadily increasing [29], there is no well accepted definition found in literature. Despite the arguable lack of definition, certain characteristics describing the term Robotic Process Automation are found throughout the literature.

RPA incorporates different tools and methodologies [1,9,23,27] aiming to automate repetitive and structured service tasks that were previously performed by humans [1,2,21]. This is achieved by the application of software algorithms known as software robots or *bots*, which are imitating the execution flow of humans on the front-end [1,2,11,16,24,26]. Just as a human user, robots can interact with the user interface through mouse clicks, key board interactions and interpretation of text and graphics [26], as well as log into multiple applications to extract, process and enter structured or semi-structured data from different sources [33]. RPA usually does not require defined interfaces as the software sits on top of information systems and accesses applications only through the presentation layer [2,35], thus the back-end systems remain unchanged [1,20]. As a result the robots perform activities in a non-invasive manner [16] without the need of application programming interfaces (API) to transfer and process data [33].

Depending on the configuration approach for software robots, little to no programming knowledge is required to implement and manage the orchestration and execution of the robots often referred to as *low-code development* [13,16,20, 25,26]. Although RPA typically favors less complex and cognitive tasks, advances in machine learning can extend the range of RPA application in the future [3,33].

In this work, we define RPA as an automation technology which performs work on the presentation layer, can be set up by a business user, and is managed on a centralized platform.

2.2 Process Characteristics of Automatable Activities

In order to develop the framework, the question - *What are the characteristics of a process activity, or a set of process activities, that are suitable for robotic process automation?* - must first be answered. To obtain a comprehensive list of potential process characteristic evaluation criteria, a literature review following the guidelines proposed by [34] is conducted. For an exhaustive review, sources are searched for in the databases Scopus, Google Scholar, and IEEE Xplore Digital library. The identified criteria are then compiled, checked for redundancy and listed in a concept matrix (Table 1) that relates the criteria with the source articles and visualizes the acceptance and relevance through the number of mentions. In particular, we used the criteria presented by Wanner et al. [33] as a starting point and extended the list through several iterations.

Ideal candidate processes for automation must be standardized [2–5,7,9–17,19–22,24–26,28–33,36–38]. Therefore, the process or task needs to be strictly defined and structured [3,15,17,24,33,37]. A high degree of standardization before automation is necessary to result in a low amount of process variations and outcomes [33]. No or low subjective judgment or interpretation skills [7,17,32,37] are required for decision making as the process follows a rule-based flow [5,7,13,14,16,19,24,26,29,32,33,37,38]. Well-suited tasks for standardized processes are also mentioned to be mundane, simple and monotonous [7,9,31].

In combination with a high degree of standardization, the execution frequency of a process or task has a big impact on the automation potential. In favor of RPA suitability, tasks need to be performed repetitively and in high transaction volumes [7,9,10,13–17,19,22,24–26,29,31–33,37]. Besides the volume of transactions it is mentioned that the transaction of a substantial amount of data implies an aptitude for RPA [37].

Furthermore, the maturity of a process is an indicator as to whether it fulfills fundamental requirements for an automation effort. Maturity describes the frequency of changes to the logical execution flow of the process [5,32] and further, that the process and its tasks are specified, predictable, stable and measurable [13, 15, 22, 29, 32]. Contrary to standardization, the failure rate describes the amount of deviations from the defined process flow. Candidate processes suited for RPA show little or no amount of exceptions when tasks are being executed [5, 10, 17, 32, 33] and do not require human intervention. Additionally, the ratio of process tasks that undergo an unusual process flow or inhibit the structured flow to completion is limited or zero [5, 33].

Table 1. Concept matrix with dimensions [34]

Characteristics / Articles	Standardization	Frequency	Number of systems	Structuredness of data	Maturity	Proneness to human error	Failure rate	Stability	Value	Handover of work	Execution time
[10]		•	•				•	•	•		
[3]	•		•								
[9]	•	•	•			•					
[22]	•	•			•						
[24]	•	•		•	•						
[26]	•	•	•					•	•		
[5]	•			•	•		•				
[7]	•	•	•	•							
[14]	•	•	•								
[15]	•	•	•	•	•						
[16]	•	•	•			•					
[17]	•	•	•			•	•				
[19]	•	•	•	•						•	
[25]	•	•	•	•							
[29]	•	•	•	•	•	•		•			
[31]	•	•	•								
[33]	•	•	•	•	•	•	•	•		•	•
[37]	•	•	•			•			•		
[38]	•		•								
[13]	•	•			•	•					
[32]	•	•	•	•	•		•				
Total	20	18	17	9	8	7	5	4	3	2	1

With the objective to further minimize the exceptions, stability of the systems in use and the process outcome is crucial. For an execution following the predefined rules, the stability of user interfaces and the interaction between different systems is essential [26]. Ideal candidate tasks for RPA have as a result a limited number of exceptions and high predictability of their outcomes to avoid uncertainties and disruptions [10,33].

The speed of tasks that require access and interaction with multiple systems can be increased immensely (e.g. data entry between systems). In 17 out of 21 examined papers, tasks including the access to different systems are mentioned to be suitable for RPA (see Table 1). Whenever multiple systems need to be accessed by a user, the manual effort is high and also reflected by the time consumption for this task. A software robot can work within the different systems flawlessly and execute the tasks more rapidly, enabling not only the extraction of information but also the triggering of events, when a task is completed [3,9,16,17,25].

In order for process activities to be performed between multiple systems, the data needs to be in a structured and digital form. When data is structured [5,7,15,19,24,25,29,32,33,38], the software robot can then successfully interpret the given input and follow the execution flow of the process activities.

Apart from process and process activity characteristics, literature mentions that proneness to human errors is also an indicator for RPA potential. This assumption is based on the fact, that with increasing volume of tasks, humans will more likely cause exceptions by false entry or incorrect data manipulation than a program would [9,13,16,17,29,37].

Moreover, a process or task can be judged by its impact or value to the business. This is where literature does not provide a clear outline due to the small amount of mentions. While some argue that automation potential exists for processes with a low degree of business value [9], others state that processes with a low execution frequency but a high business value are suitable candidates for automation [10,37].

Focusing on the voluminous and repetitive processes, the number of users involved in the execution reflect another perspective on RPA suitability. Kokina and Blanchet [19] indicate potential benefits where several people are performing the same processes, when these are repetitive and require no or low subjective judgment. A different perspective highlights the handovers of work between different stakeholder across departments as a factor to consider [33].

Last, the execution time of a process is a criteria to assess the suitability of processes for RPA [33]. Decreasing the time spent with repetitive and highly transactional jobs, increases time for employees to focus on more value-adding tasks [3].

3   Process Characteristics Evaluation Framework

To support practitioners in evaluating the viability of RPA for process activities, we summarized the findings of our literature review in a framework.

Table 2 visualizes the process characteristics evaluation framework (PCEF). We present five perspectives – task, time, data, system, and human – that contain several characteristics that analysts can use to evaluate a process accordingly. We present examples for evaluation of the criteria but the list is certainly not exhaustive. We decided to exclude *value* as a criteria from the framework as it is implicitly covered by other criteria such as frequency and urgency.

Table 2. Process characteristics evaluation framework

Perspective	Criteria	Exemplary Evaluation
Task	Standardization	Number of different activities Number of variations to execution flow in business
	Maturity	Number of deviation cases over time Ratio of deviation cases over time
		Number of deviation cases over time Ratio of deviation cases over time
	Determinism	Number of manual interactions Time to solve manual interaction
	Failure rate	Number of unsuccessful terminations Number of manual interactions Number of rework loops
Time	Frequency	Number of executions
	Duration	Average time to task completion
	Urgency	Average reaction time
Data	Structuredness	Consistent use of data objects
System	Interfaces	Number of execution steps Time spent on application interface
	Stability	Number of exceptions
	Number of systems	Number of systems involved (e.g. CRM, ERP)
Human	Resources	Number of users performing same task Number of users involved in process
	Proneness to human error	Number of exceptions Time to solve exception

Task Perspective. The task perspective refers to the execution of process activities. Its criteria are standardization, maturity, determinism, and failure rate.

First, standardization refers to a process's degree of structure. In standardized processes, every process element is unambiguous, and the execution order remains the same in each process instance. As a result, stakeholders receive the same outcome from a standardized process [20, 22]. Thus, we examine the execution order and the number of process variants to measure a process's standardization. We can, for instance, analyze predecessors and successors of the process of interest. Ideally, the order of execution remains the same and equals to the desired process flow.

Maturity indicates that no frequent changes to the process flow are observable. Therefore, processes need to be specified and predictable over a period in time [5, 22]. Mature processes usually terminate successfully and show a comparably low number of variants [15, 32]. The evaluation focuses on the number of process variants and the difference between the ideal and variant process paths.

Determinism is one of the most distinctive criteria to assess the viability of RPA. Deterministic activities consist of logical execution steps without any form of cognitive assessment [7, 17, 32, 37]. This is a fundamental requirement for software robots since human judgment aggravates automation. To fulfill the criterion, logical and rule-based steps suffice to describe a process. Hence, the evaluation examines manual interactions and execution time.

Last, the failure rate relates to self loops to repair previous executions and a non-recoverable unsuccessful termination. A low failure rate leverages automation. The failure rate subsequently focuses on the amount of deviations from the ideal process flow caused by failures, and their respective causes [5, 10, 17, 32, 33]. A high failure rate might correspond to poor standardization, maturity or determinism as the causes for exceptions.

Time Perspective. The criteria listed under the time perspective focus on the duration and frequency of processes and process steps.

First of all, the frequency describes the absolute number a process step occurs over time. The execution frequency is high when tasks are repeated daily and in high transaction volumes [7, 9]. The criterion measures the number of an activity's occurrences in a certain period.

Additionally, the framework includes the duration which expresses the time required to execute a process or an activity. The duration needed to execute a process or an activity is a quantifiable indicator of the time-saving potential.

The final time-based criterion of the framework is urgency which describes how critical the immediate execution of a process step is. The delayed execution may cause an increasing overall duration, or may hinder progress. Software robots are working 24/7, unlike users with relatively short time frames. For this reason, the evaluation focuses on the time needed to react to execute such urgent tasks.

Data Perspective. In many processes, information is processed in multiple systems. Therefore, the data perspective resembles the structuredness of data. If a robot shall process data, the data source must be digital [25]. Moreover, the data must at least be semi-structured to enable automation [5]. When a process involves handling data, users may perform simple operations to extract it from the source and enter it into a system [15, 19, 24, 33, 38]. This is a crucial requirement for the successful interpretation and execution of process steps. To evaluate this criterion the data source is analyzed. Typically structured data is in semi-structured forms like spreadsheets, websites, or emails. Unstructured and hardly accessible data impedes RPA.

System Perspective. The fourth perspective in the framework is related to the underlying systems. The perspective poses the interaction with interfaces, and the stability of information systems.

Due to our preceding research we added the criterion interface to our framework. The criterion interface is evaluated by identifying whether the task could be solved using software robots. Here, the time spent in an application's interface and the number of required execution steps serve as indicators.

Another system-related criterion is the stability. Ideally, systems and applications involved in process automation are stable. During process execution, all operations on the user interface perform accordingly, and users only seldom experience interruptions [10,26,33]. A stable operating system also relates to this criterion. It guarantees the absence of system related exceptions during automation. For analyzing system stability, we propose the number of soft- and hardware exceptions. Important in practice is to distinguish between exceptions caused by the systems or applications themselves and external factors such as capacity errors or connection.

The last system-related criterion in the framework is the number of systems. It deals with process parts or activities that interact with multiple information systems. Consequently, the interaction between systems is necessary, but no value is added when performed by a person [16,17,25]. In fact, robots outperform humans in atomic operations, like copy and paste [3,9]. Thus, automation candidate tasks transfer information from one to other systems. The potential of more involved systems is higher, if these are running stably.

Human Perspective. The last perspective deals with humans computer interaction focusing on the human. The perspective comes with two peculiarities, resources and proneness to human error.

The framework includes resources as criterion to highlight the number of users involved in the process. Especially frequent activities require resources to deal with the volume of work. This criteria can be assessed from two view points. First, based on the number of users performing the same task. Second, multiple users contribute to an activity's instance. [19,33]. To assess the resource savings, we utilize the count of users performing the same task, and the number of users involved in one task instance.

The last aspect in the PCEF is the proneness to human errors as a criterion. Humans tend to erroneous behavior when executing monotonous and voluminous tasks which results in such errors that solely relate to human nature [9,13,16,17,29,37]. Eliminating such mistakes with business rules or robots yields to additional savings regarding costs and time. Measuring the error proneness relies on the number of human mistakes and the required time to fix those.

4   Evaluation

The evaluation focuses on event logs generated through PAIS. Event logs reveal insights about the business process and its execution. We aim at an objective evaluation by using a publicly available data-set to show the applicability of the PCEF [8]. We determine process characteristics with Process Mining Software[1]. Hence, we test the framework for its applicability in a practical environment.

The candidate process describes a P2P process of a multinational coatings and paints enterprise. Due to its administrative character, it is a suitable candidate for automation. In this case, RPA minimizes manual work and increases efficiency at the enterprise's bottom line. The candidate process covers the steps from creating a purchase order to the clearance of the invoice. A purchase order contains at least one purchase order item. An item stores attributes describing the resources involved, value of events and anonymized company information.

In total, the data set includes more than 1.5 million events, and 251,734 purchase order items (cases) in 76,349 purchase orders. To illustrate the structure of the event log, Table 3 visualizes an event log from the data set.

To analyse the framework, we focus on the paths related to *Item Category: 3-way match, invoice before GR*. We further drill down selecting the most common variants (90%) in 2018. These filters result in 197,010 cases with 136 process variants.

Examining the event log reveals that traces including the manual activity 'Change Quantity' take a month longer on average.

Thus, we select 'Change Quantity' as our process step of interest, and apply our framework to evaluate the activity. Note that we consider the deletion of a purchase order item and the reoccurrence of 'Change Quantity' as incompliant. *Standardization.* The criterion examines a process's degree of structure, and it relates to a low number of overall variants.

Our analysis of 'Change Quantity' reveals that it has five valid predecessors covering 95% of all incoming process paths, and two valid successors that cover 94% of all outgoing traces. Additionally, we examine the activity's process segment in different business units.

Every business unit conducts the activity in the same context. Consequently, we identify a logical and structured process flow. The assessment shows that the process is rather standardized, since 95% of all preceding and 93% of all following activities are compliant and follow a certain pattern.

Maturity. The maturity expresses the number of compliant process variants which establish over time. In total there are 25 variants containing the activity. Out of these 25 variants, 22 are following compliant pre- and sucessors while three are incompliant. There are 2 variants reworking the activity and one which causes the deletion of purchase order items.

---

[1] https://www.celonis.com.

Table 3. Exemplary event with contextual attributes from the event log

Attribute	Value
Case ID	2000000000_00001
Activity	Record Goods Receipt
Resource	user_000
Complete Timestamp	2018/03/06 07:44:00.000
Variant	Variant 65
Variant index	65
(case) Company	companyID_0000
(case) Document Type	EC Purchase order
(case) GR-Based Inv. Verif.	false
(case) Goods Receipt	true
(case) Item	1
(case) Item Category	3-way match, invoice before GR
(case) Item Type	Standard
(case) Name	vendor_0000
(case) Purch. Doc. Category name	Purchase order
(case) Purchasing Document	2000000000
(case) Source	sourceSystemID_0000
(case) Spend area text	CAPEX & SOCS
(case) Spend classification text	NPR
(case) Sub spend area text	Facility Management
(case) Vendor	vendorID_0000
Cumulative net worth (EUR)	298.0
User	user_000

Determinism. To assess the criterion, we must know the steps done on the user interface and the respective throughput time of steps need to be evaluated. The event log does not include information about the performance of the activity 'Change Quantity' on the presentation layer. Therefore, the criterion can not be evaluated for this data set.

Failure Rate. In this process, the execution fails when a self-loop occurs or the process ends with the activity 'Delete Purchase Order Item'. Reworking 'Change Quantity' occurs in 3,91%, and the process determination with order item deletion happens in 1,42%. Since we only consider the outcome of one activity, we ignore the full process context, since we cannot determine which cases actually terminated and which are still running.

The resulting failure rate of the process is 5,33%.

Frequency. The average number of 'Change Quantity' occurrences is 31 times a day. Although the execution of 'Change Quantity' varies month by month, it occurs at least 379 times a month. Regarding frequency, the activity is a valid automation candidate.

Duration. The duration expresses an activity's impact on the overall process throughput time and its own required time. Information about its own execution time to execute is missing. However, while processes without have an average throughput time of 64 days, processes including the activity take 93 days on average.

Urgency. The majority of the tasks are executed during the main business hours. But, 'Change Quantity' quite often occurs outside of these hours. This incidence might indicate, that certain purchase orders need fast reaction. Automation runs all the time and minimizes the delay caused by the working hours of a user.

Structuredness of Data. To perform the activity 'Change Quantity', workers modify the purchase order document. If the source data containing the new quantity and the purchase order document are structured data objects, a software robot could perform the transaction. However, as the event log does not contain related information, we cannot evaluate the criterion.

Interfaces. This aspect analyses the number of interfaces and the interactions with these interfaces. The event log does not contain such information. Thus, we cannot evaluate the criterion.

Stability. The stability corresponds to a low number of deviating paths and software exceptions. The event log does not include information about exceptions and their cause. Thus, the criterion can not be evaluated for the data set.

Number of Systems. Since the event log originates from an SAP ECC system, which is a roofing system, we cannot determine whether there are more systems involved in the process. Therefore, our evaluation of the number of systems is incomplete.

Resources. Analyzing the number of users that execute the 'Change Quantity' unveils that 138 different users execute the task. With the successful implementation of a robot, we can spare working time of these users.

Proneness to Human Error. Since the process step is exclusively executed by users, we assume that all related errors are of human origin. Since only about every twentieth case fails, we assume the process is rather stable, and software robots could not leverage better performance.

As we demonstrate, the RCEF aids in determining characteristics of processes or process steps which are automation candidates. Although we could not assess all criteria in our case, the evaluation provides important insights.

The process flow is quite standardized. On one hand the activity is in 22 different compliant process variants, on the other hand only three infrequent variants lead to non-compliance. In total, the overall failure rate is 5,33%, highlighting that 94,67% of all executions are fully compliant. The activity constantly occurs during the observation, 31 times per day on average. Since 'Change Quantity' occurs outside usual business hours, we assume the execution is urgent to a certain extent and is restrained by manual execution. Moreover, we can spare working hours of 138 users, if we can automate the activity successfully. Without being able to assess the determinism, we cannot assess the viability of RPA implementation for the activity. Still, without knowing anything about the process context, the framework enables wide assessment.

However, the application of the framework also revealed some deficits when validating the efficacy and validity through process mining software. First, missing attributes such as starting timestamps in the event log impede the possibility to assess typically easy to evaluate criteria like the execution time or execution urgency. Second, the possible lack of information about exceptions in the event log inhibits the ability to distinguish between a system-related stability or human error caused issue. Third, crucial information about the interaction on the user interface is missing and prevents the examination of the criteria determinism, structuredness of data, interfaces and number of systems. The missing information prevents the extraction of information such as the degree of deterministic behavior when executing a sequence of steps, the throughput time for individual steps or the number of applications and web-based systems used. To extend the detail of information, the use of an user interaction logger [6] can bridge the gap between front-end and back-end information gathering.

5   Conclusion

By conducting a literature review, this study identified process activity characteristics for RPA. These insights were used to develop a process characteristic evaluation framework that assesses the suitability of process activities for RPA. The framework includes a set of thirteen criteria grouped into five evaluation perspectives, enabling the examination of a process activity on different reference levels. This abstraction of a process step emphasizes its connections to preceding and succeeding steps and provides a concrete decision support considering the most important factors involved.

Therefore, this study offers practitioners a guideline to evaluate a process activity for an RPA implementation effort through the application of process mining. The analysis reveals the standardization of the activity, its maturity over time, the determinism of execution steps, the failure rate, the volume of executions with respect to completion and reaction times, the structuredness of data used, the interaction on the user interface, stability and number of systems, users involved and the cause of exceptions related to human error. This study proved the efficacy and validity of the framework by evaluating a process activity through event logs out of a real-life data set. Based on the universal perspectives within the framework, the applicability in different organizations and industries is seen as given.

Despite the demonstration and application of the framework, it is tested only with one data set and process. The evaluation has shown that not all criteria can be tested against this data set and to guarantee generalization, the framework must be validated through application to multiple and different kinds of processes. In particular, the framework contains qualitative criteria that could not be tested with the data set. Further evaluation of these criteria – e.g. through case studies – is necessary. Another important aspect is that the data set was anonymized and modified before publishing, limiting the accessible information stored in the event logs. Further, the assumptions made about the data set, including filters set for the focus on one execution flow, limit the significance of the evaluation results. Additionally, the criteria must be tested for redundancy and their respective evaluation examples need further validation and extension.

Although these factors impair the evaluation of the framework, they offer various opportunities for future research. First, the framework should be evaluated in different ways to ensure comprehensive validation. These can include the application of the framework to new data sets as well as the assessment of a process with a process owner. Conducting expert interviews to assess the usefulness of the framework is another option to account for the solution objective. Changing the evaluation approach and substituting process mining through robotic process mining [6] can also widen the scope of information extraction. Second, the increasing number of articles on this topic generates new insights that can derive additional perspectives and criteria. By conducting a case study research further evaluation examples could surface and help practitioners to examine their processes. Finally, possible advances also include the quantification [33] or the weighting of criteria to signal if the process activity is suitable for RPA or not.

Acknowledgments. This project is funded by the German Federal Ministry of Education and Research (BMBF) within the framework programme *Software Campus* (https://softwarecampus.de) under the number 01IS17045.

References

1. Hofmann, P., Samp, C., Urbach, N.: Robotic process automation. Electronic Markets **30**(1), 99–106 (2019). https://doi.org/10.1007/s12525-019-00365-8
2. Aguirre, S., Rodriguez, A.: Automation of a business process using robotic process automation (RPA): a case study. In: Figueroa-García, J.C., López-Santana, E.R., Villa-Ramírez, J.L., Ferro-Escobar, R. (eds.) WEA 2017. CCIS, vol. 742, pp. 65–71. Springer, Cham (2017). https://doi.org/10.1007/978-3-319-66963-2_7
3. Anagnoste, S.: Robotic automation process - the next major revolution in terms of back office operations improvement. In: Proceedings of the International Conference on Business Excellence, vol. 11(1), pp. 676–686 (2017)

4. Asatiani, A., Penttinen, E.: Turning robotic process automation into commercial success-case opuscapita. J. Inf. Technol. Teach. Cases **6**(2), 67–74 (2016)
5. Beetz, R., Riedl, Y.: Robotic process automation: developing a multi-criteria evaluation model for the selection of automatable business processes. In: AMCIS 2019. AIS Electronic Library (2019)
6. Bosco, A., Augusto, A., Dumas, M., La Rosa, M., Fortino, G.: Discovering automatable routines from user interaction logs. In: Hildebrandt, T., van Dongen, B.F., Röglinger, M., Mendling, J. (eds.) BPM 2019. LNBIP, vol. 360, pp. 144–162. Springer, Cham (2019). https://doi.org/10.1007/978-3-030-26643-1_9
7. Cooper, L.A., Holderness Jr., D.K., Sorensen, T.L., Wood, D.A.: Robotic process automation in public accounting. Acc. Horiz. **33**(4), 15–35 (2019)
8. van Dongen, B.: Dataset BPI Challenge 2019. 4TU. Centre for Research Data (2019). https://doi.org/10.4121/uuid:d06aff4b-79f0-45e6-8ec8-e19730c248f1
9. Fernandez, D., Aman, A.: Impacts of robotic process automation on global accounting services. Asian J. Acc. Gov. **9**, 123–132 (2018)
10. Fung, H.P.: Criteria, use cases and effects of information technology process automation (ITPA). Adv. Robot. Autom. **3** (2014)
11. Geyer-Klingeberg, J., et al.: Process mining and robotic process automation: a perfect match. In: BPM (Dissertation/Demos/Industry), pp. 124–131 (2018)
12. Hallikainen, P., Bekkhus, R., Pan, S.L.: How OpusCapita used internal RPA capabilities to offer services to clients. MIS Q. Execut. **17**, 41–52 (2018)
13. Hindel, J., Cabrera Pérez, L., Stierle, M.: Robotic process automation: hype or hope? In: Proceedings of the 15th International Conference on Wirtschaftsinformatik (2020). https://doi.org/10.30844/wi_2020_r6-hindel
14. Hofmann, P., Samp, C., Urbach, N.: Robotic process automation. Electronic Markets **30**(1), 99–106 (2019). https://doi.org/10.1007/s12525-019-00365-8
15. Huang, F., Vasarhelyi, M.A.: Applying robotic process automation (RPA) in auditing: a framework. Int. J. Acc. Inf. Syst. **35**, 100433 (2019)
16. Ivančić, L., Suša Vugec, D., Bosilj Vukšić, V.: Robotic process automation: systematic literature review. In: Di Ciccio, C. (ed.) BPM 2019. LNBIP, vol. 361, pp. 280–295. Springer, Cham (2019). https://doi.org/10.1007/978-3-030-30429-4_19
17. Jimenez-Ramirez, A., Reijers, H.A., Barba, I., Del Valle, C.: A method to improve the early stages of the robotic process automation lifecycle. In: Giorgini, P., Weber, B. (eds.) CAiSE 2019. LNCS, vol. 11483, pp. 446–461. Springer, Cham (2019). https://doi.org/10.1007/978-3-030-21290-2_28
18. Kaya, C.T., Turkyilmaz, M., Birol, B.: Impact of RPA technologies on accounting systems. J. Acc. Financ. **82**, 235–250 (2019)
19. Kokina, J., Blanchette, S.: Early evidence of digital labor in accounting: innovation with robotic process automation. Int. J. Acc. Inf. Syst. **35**, 100431 (2019)
20. Lacity, M.C., Willcocks, L.P.: Robotic process automation at telefónica o2. MIS Q. Execut. **15**(1), 21–35 (2016)
21. Lacity, M.C., Willcocks, L.P.: A new approach to automating services. MIT Sloan Manage. Rev. **58**, 141–149 (2017)
22. Leshob, A., Bourgouin, A., Renard, L.: Towards a process analysis approach to adopt robotic process automation. In: 2018 IEEE 15th International Conference on e-Business Engineering (ICEBE), pp. 46–53. IEEE (2018)
23. Mendling, J., Decker, G., Hull, R., Reijers, H.A., Weber, I.: How do machine learning, robotic process automation, and blockchains affect the human factor in business process management? Commun. Assoc. Inf. Syst. **43**(1), 19 (2018)
24. Moffitt, K.C., Rozario, A.M., Vasarhelyi, M.A.: Robotic process automation for auditing. J. Emerg. Technol. Acc. **15**(1), 1–10 (2018)

25. Osmundsen, K., Iden, J., Bygstad, B.: Organizing robotic process automation: balancing loose and tight coupling. In: Proceedings of the 52nd Hawaii International Conference on System Sciences (2019)

26. Penttinen, E., Kasslin, H., Asatiani, A.: How to choose between robotic process automation and back-end system automation? In: European Conference on Information Systems 2018 (2018)

27. Ratia, M., Myllärniemi, J., Helander, N.: Robotic process automation-creating value by digitalizing work in the private healthcare? In: Proceedings of the 22nd International Academic Mindtrek Conference, pp. 222–227 (2018)

28. Romao, M., Costa, J., Costa, C.J.: Robotic process automation: a case study in the banking industry. In: 2019 14th Iberian Conference on Information Systems and Technologies (CISTI), pp. 1–6. IEEE (2019)

29. Santos, F., Pereira, R., Vasconcelos, J.B.: Toward robotic process automation implementation: an end-to-end perspective. Bus. Process Manage. J. **26**(2), 405–420 (2019)

30. Seasongood, S.: Not just for the assembly line: a case for robotics in accounting and finance. Financ. Execut. **32**(1), 31–32 (2016)

31. Sönmez, Ö.E., Börekçi, D.Y.: A conceptual study on RPAs as of intelligent automation. In: Kahraman, C., Cebi, S., Cevik Onar, S., Oztaysi, B., Tolga, A.C., Sari, I.U. (eds.) INFUS 2019. AISC, vol. 1029, pp. 65–72. Springer, Cham (2020). https://doi.org/10.1007/978-3-030-23756-1_10

32. Syed, R., et al.: Robotic process automation: contemporary themes and challenges. Comput. Ind. **115**, 103162 (2020)

33. Wanner, J., Hofmann, A., Fischer, M., Imgrund, F., Janiesch, C., Geyer-Klingeberg, J.: Process selection in RPA projects-towards a quantifiable method of decision making. In: ICIS 2019 Proceedings (2019)

34. Webster, J., Watson, R.T.: Analyzing the past to prepare for the future: writing a literature review. MIS Q. **26**(2), xiii–xxiii (2002)

35. Willcocks, L.P., Lacity, M.: Service Automation Robots and the Future of Work. SB Publishing, Ashford (2016)

36. Willcocks, L.P., Lacity, M., Craig, A.: Robotic process automation at xchanging. The Outsourcing Unit Working Research Paper Series **15**(03) (2015)

37. Yatskiv, S., Voytyuk, I., Yatskiv, N., Kushnir, O., Trufanova, Y., Panasyuk, V.: Improved method of software automation testing based on the robotic process automation technology. In: 2019 9th International Conference on Advanced Computer Information Technologies (ACIT), pp. 293–296. IEEE (2019)

38. Zhang, C.: Intelligent process automation in audit. J. Emerg. Technol. Acc. **16**(2), 69–88 (2019)

From Robotic Process Automation to Intelligent Process Automation
– *Emerging Trends* –

Tathagata Chakraborti, Vatche Isahagian$^{(\boxtimes)}$, Rania Khalaf,
Yasaman Khazaeni, Vinod Muthusamy, Yara Rizk, and Merve Unuvar

IBM Research AI, Cambridge, MA, USA
`vatchei@ibm.com`

Abstract. In this survey, we study how recent advances in machine intelligence are disrupting the world of business processes. Over the last decade, there has been steady progress towards the automation of business processes under the umbrella of "robotic process automation" (RPA). However, we are currently at an inflection point in this evolution, as a new paradigm called "Intelligent Process Automation" (IPA) emerges, bringing machine learning (ML) and artificial intelligence (AI) technologies to bear in order to improve business process outcomes. The purpose of this paper is to provide a survey of this emerging theme and identify key open research challenges at the intersection of AI and business processes. We hope that this emerging theme will spark engaging conversations at the RPA Forum.

Keywords: Robotic Process Automation · Intelligent Process Automation · Artificial intelligence

1 Introduction

Business processes are an integral part of every industry, such as government, insurance, banking and healthcare. Examples of such processes include automobile insurance claims processing, handling prescription drug orders and patient case management. The business process management (BPM) industry is expected to approach $16 billion by 2023 [43]. With recent advances in machine learning and artificial intelligence (AI), the automation of steps in a business process – which came to be known as Robotic Process Automation (RPA) – is undergoing a radical transformation. The industries that are most eager to adopt automation are transportation, manufacturing, packaging and shipping, customer service, finance, and healthcare [18].

As noted in "The Transformation of RPA to IPA: Intelligent Process Automation" [63]: *The convergence of AI, automation and customer data has now seen the emergence of a new class of tools, known as intelligent process automation*

Authors are in alphabetical order.

© Springer Nature Switzerland AG 2020
A. Asatiani et al. (Eds.): BPM Blockchain and RPA Forum 2020, LNBIP 393, pp. 215–228, 2020.
https://doi.org/10.1007/978-3-030-58779-6_15

Fig. 1. Example of a mortgage loan application process.

(IPA). This view is also echoed in market outlook reports from industry leaders, including PwC's recent analysis of rising trends in RPA in the financial sector [31] and the 2020 AI predictions from IBM research [55] outlining the potential of AI-fueled automation to transform how people work. Recently AAAI, one of the leading AI conferences, also hosted the first workshop on Intelligent Process Automation [24]. In this survey, we explore this nascent field of inquiry at the intersection of AI and business process automation in greater detail. We begin first with some background on BPM and RPA.

2   Business Processes

A business process is a collection of connected tasks that once completely executed delivers a service or product to a client or accomplishes an organizational goal within an enterprise [65]. A mortgage loan application (shown in Fig. 1) is a common example of a business process where the process flow is the set of linked loan application tasks such as collecting client related data (e.g. verifying employment, requesting credit report), performing a title search, receiving the title report and so on. The goal of this process is to approve or reject a loan application once all the required tasks are fully executed. The process is expressed in the business process model and notation (BPMN) graphical notation [21]. Circles denote events, activities are denoted by rounded-corner rectangles and diamonds depict gateways that allow paths to conditionally merge or diverge.

2.1   Business Process Management

Business Process Management (BPM) is a multi-disciplinary field that supports the management of business processes with some combination of modeling, automation, execution, control, measurement and optimization. BPM involves business activity flows (workflows), systems, and people such as employees, customers and partners within and beyond the enterprise boundaries.

Business processes in reality have a wide scope from the traditional rigid processes (modeled and running under the supervision of a strict workflow management system) to completely ad-hoc unstructured flows driven by humans over e-mail, chat and phone. Traditional BPM systems, at one end of this spectrum, demand a process model that can be completely defined in advance and typically include restrictions such as rigid control flow and context tunneling [39].

Case management is closer to the other end of this spectrum: a case consists of people, documents, and tasks [64]. Flexible ordering of task execution is enabled through Event-Condition-Action rules as well as the ability for a user to add new (ad-hoc) tasks. A task itself may be defined as a fully structured workflow, making case management a hybrid model.

2.2   Business Process Automation

Businesses seek to support growth while maintaining low costs by automating repetitive and time consuming tasks, especially seeking to eliminate costly and error-prone manual steps. Business Process Automation (BPA) seeks to improve the efficiency of business processes in terms of cost, resources and investment through automating the management of relevant information and data, the time spent by team members, and the execution logic.

RPA is an emerging technology in BPA that creates software robots that perform tasks previously done by humans. RPAs are one form of BPA implementation that is specifically focused on repetitive workflows. The overall goal of RPA is to provide the shortest route to automation by introducing a user interface automation layer rather than interacting deeply with the application code, system or database that are behind those applications.

2.3   Performance Measures

Performance measurement in business processes is the first step for analyzing and monitoring the process health and progress for process automation. Identifying the right measures for process performance is extremely important. Performance of a process measures how well the process is doing with respect to chosen indicators. Examples of such performance indicators can be time to execute a task, cost per task in terms of employee head count or number of approved loans [46]. Numerous authors have proposed a fixed number of category classes for indicators in order to provide a structure. The majority of authors, including [58], proposed a process-oriented view of the indicators which resulted in four groups of performance indicators: quality, time, costs, and flexibility. As [1] indicates, better processes contribute to meeting the strategic objectives of an organization. Therefore, we specifically call out another association with respect to existing groups of indicators that focuses on the impact of all the indicators towards the business goals. Such indicators can be, for example, analyzing the process performance indicators with respect to profit and revenue of the organization.

In practice, most business process owners focus on productivity measures related to time and cost. The challenge with flexibility and quality measures is that they are difficult to standardize, optimize, implement and generalize. It is common to use indicators related to a process's utilization and assignment of resources, such as repeated tasks or time to execute a task. Resources are usually aligned with the length of the task to avoid bottlenecks in the process. However, shortening the time of task execution or lowering the cost of resources does not necessarily yield better business outcomes. Therefore, it is important to consider methods for measuring process performance that can assess the impact of indicators on business goals and outcomes.

Adopting the right measures is crucial to the success of BPA. They would then be used to evaluate the performance of RPAs and other automation solutions, allowing business users to assess the effectiveness and return on investment of these solutions. Furthermore, these measures can be used by the RPAs themselves to iteratively improve their performance using machine learning models.

2.4 Digital Transformation of Business Processes

While the use of automation has been gaining traction across many industries, its incorporation into business processes poses several challenges. Automation capabilities such as RPAs can provide transformational benefits, however, it is unclear where their use can provide the highest value. Tools and analytic approaches for identifying high value automation opportunities in a process are still nascent. As we discussed previously in Sect. 1, recent innovations in machine intelligence stand to disrupt this field through the digital transformation of business processes. Throughout the rest of this paper, we will take the reader along this journey, starting from the state of the art in RPAs, through the vision and promise of IPAs, to the major challenges to be overcome to reach this goal. Finally, we will conclude with a quick overview of a recently concluded workshop on this topic.

3   State of the Art: Robotic Process Automation

RPA operates on the user interface of software tools and automates mouse and keyboard interactions to remove repetitive, labor intensive tasks. This minimizes human error due to mental lapses resulting from boredom or exhaustion. RPA's outside-in approach avoided the overhead of changing the internals of legacy software and as a result, its adoption rate has been increasing, leading to its multi-billion dollar valuation. Among academic contributions to the field, we distinguish between three approaches to building RPAs.

The first approach learns to automate tasks by example or demonstration. RPAs either observe humans perform the tasks or process the behavior logs of the software. One example of this approach is if-then-else rule deduction from behavior logs; the form-to-rule approach consisted of identifying the tasks in the logs as humans perform actions on forms and then deduced the rules from the IO data [17]. Another example is [34] which provided the input-output examples from which the RPA can extract the underlying rule or program based on the inductive program synthesis paradigm. Miltner et al. [47] detected repetitive edits to text documents by keeping track of a graph of edits and suggested automation rules by adopting a greedy algorithm that finds short explanations of users' edits. All these algorithms rely on humans in the loop. This is one of the more popular approaches to RPAs. However, it does not generalize well to new applications due to the highly specific design of logs and user interfaces.

The second approach learns tasks from step-by-step natural language text descriptions of the process. Leopold et al. [38] learned process activities from text documents using supervised machine learning, namely feature extraction using WordNet and support vector machine training (a quadratic optimization approach that finds the optimal separator of activities). Han et al. [23] adopted a deep learning approach, long short-term memory recurrent neural networks specifically, to learn the relationship between activities in a business process from text documents describing business processes. This approach also relied on humans in the loop, although in an indirect fashion, since the text documents that describe the processes were written by humans. Since it does not require the existence of an embodied business process (i.e. through a UI), it can be more difficult to learn the rules that should be automated.

The third approach learns from the task as defined by an environment with its reward function or some input/output examples. Often referred to as RPA 2.0, this approach seeks to eliminate human-dependent training. It relies on adopting reinforcement learning algorithms on the rewards to RPAs and train them to achieve better performance. This approach is the least mature to date but will lead to generalizable RPAs that approach intelligent automation.

A critical component to the success of RPAs is identifying the opportunities for automation to add RPAs in the right place and maximize their potential. Bosco et al. [8] presented a method to analyze user interaction logs in order to discover routines that are fully deterministic and therefore amenable to automate via RPAs. Klingeberg et al. [19] used process mining to assess the automation opportunities for RPAs with a requirement for processes to be standardized, repeatable and scaleable. Leno et al. [36] proposed a vision for robotic process mining, an approach to achieve end-to-end automation of mining RPA-amenable tasks from logs and generate RPA scripts from these logs to perform the tasks. In practice, these automation opportunities are usually identified manually by subject matter experts comparing potential automation rates. Even though the research in RPA shows promising methods and guidance for assessing automation opportunities, there is still minimal insights on how this could be efficiently automated and implemented in practice at scale.

4   The Vision: Intelligent Process Automation

RPA has enabled integration of systems that otherwise would not have been integrated and eased the workload of business process workers automating repetitive and routine tasks (e.g., copying data from one system to another). Beyond automating simple repetitive tasks, IPA achieves more complex automation by using AI to minimize human-dependent training and automating more complex tasks that entail decision making. The IPA vision builds on traditional RPA technologies, while going a step further to automate complex tasks which require decision making, insights and analysis or the composition, coordination, and collaboration of multiple IPA solutions (outside the scope of RPAs as shown in Fig. 2). While current efforts are a step in the right directions, IPA still falls short of achieving that promise because of the reasons discussed in this section.

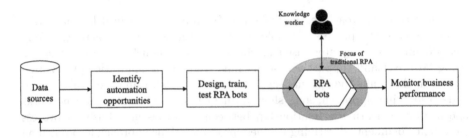

Fig. 2. Traditional RPA is focused on building individual bots that automate a repetitive human task. The scope of IPA is broader addressing the coordination between humans and multiple bots, and encompassing the entire lifecycle of the process including identifying automation opportunities and continuously retraining the bots based on monitored performance.

4.1   Automation Opportunities

Implementing an RPA requires a costly manual analysis of the tasks performed by the users either by observing their behavior, which does not scale when there are hundreds of processes, or through careful analysis of process-related documentation, which can be outdated. Finding opportunities to automate tasks that are more complex than routine repeatable tasks requires the use of structured and unstructured data from process logs. There have been several research efforts to identify candidate tasks for automation [29,38] from textual descriptions, but they focus on particular business domains (e.g generating utility bills) and are still not implemented at scale. Identifying automatable tasks only solves part of the problem. The results should also be augmented with a recommendation of possible IPA templates or AI models that are suitable to automate these tasks, as in [35].

4.2   High Cost to Build and Maintain

Unlike RPAs whose overall potential results in a significant increase in turnaround time and cost savings of up to 30% [32], there is a higher cost associated with developing IPAs. To build the next generation of IPAs requires data preparation (identifying relevant data, and cleaning and transforming it) and feature engineering (extracting appropriate features), before building and validating the AI capabilities. Similarly, there is a higher cost associated with maintaining IPAs in comparison with RPAs. In addition to the deployed code, the AI capabilities within have a lifecycle of their own.

The AI models must be retrained in response to changes in the business process (control flow drifts) or changes in the data (data drifts). These higher costs require larger return on investment for IPAs to be suitable. Some ways to mitigate the cost required to build and maintain IPAs include decreasing the effort to develop them, enabling them to be reused for different types of processes, or using them to replace/augment different customer tasks.

4.3   Low Adoption

Adopting IPAs comes with an added risk of monetary or reputation loss. For example, data used for training may be manipulated or contain implicit racial, gender, or ideological biases [67]. In addition, business users are risk-averse and do not implicitly trust AI models. Mitigating the risk of deploying the AI models requires staged deployment techniques such as canary deployments, bandit services, and A/B testing [49]. Increasing business users' trust will require a variety of solutions including maintaining action provenance for audits and providing explanations for any automated IPA decisions.

4.4   Beyond a Single IPA

IPA research currently focuses on non-routine tasks. Handling more complex tasks will require the composition of multiple IPAs, as well as the collaboration and coordination of these IPAs. To achieve this, new frameworks need to be developed that enable IPA cooperation. Previous research efforts to use multi-agent systems in BPM [12,52] need to be adjusted and revised for IPAs. Frameworks must now take into account the diversity of automation tasks and domains, and the fact that RPAs can be created by different developers without shared development guidelines. Maintaining compatibility between RPA and business process versions as each co-evolves is also crucial. Finally, a unified interface such as a conversational system may also be required to facilitate the interaction among IPAs and end users [57].

5   Research Opportunities

This section highlights research from the BPM and AI literature to achieve the IPA vision in Sect. 4, and outlines opportunities for future research.

5.1   Business Process Automation

The BPM literature offers a variety of AI solutions to cluster process traces [50, 51] for better process discovery, predict business outcomes [9,33], and provide decision support [42]. Deep learning models, including those in the NLP domain have also been applied [15,62]. Recent efforts attempt to discover automatable routines from user interaction logs [8]. Unfortunately, due to the reasons mentioned above, very little of these innovations have been applied and adopted by enterprises [13], and those adopted are limited to narrow domains such as customer service, enterprise risk, and compliance [66]. Solutions need to take into account the structure of these highly regulated domains that require paper trails of all transactions and must adhere to privacy and security laws.

5.2 Composition and Synthesis

An area of AI that is readily applicable to business processes is automated planning, which concerns itself with generating sequential courses of actions or plans from its declarative components and thus provides a powerful framework for sequential decision making in a BPM system. [44] provides an overview of existing work and challenges at the intersection of planning and BPM. Perhaps the most important (and natural) among them is the specification and synthesis of business processes in the form of planning problems [54]: the planner composes workflows on demand automatically based on the components specified by the process author or workflow designer.

A particular area of interest here is that of the composition of automated services for the optimization of a business process [5,10,14]. This work is motivated by research on "web service composition" [53]. We refer to [56] for a comprehensive summary of work in this area, while [60,61] provides an overview of many of the challenges involved.

5.3 Risk Management

Another key application of planning to business process management is in the prediction of how different process components will evolve over time, thereby anticipating possible risks. Generative model-based approaches such as planning are uniquely situated to do this, finding applications in the robustification and adaptation of processes to failures [27], validation, verification, and monitoring of processes [37], and so on. A particular useful tool towards achieving this is referred to as top-k and diverse planning [30] where a set of solutions are computed instead of a single one thereby allowing one to anticipate likely ways a process may evolve. Such approaches have found many applications[1] in enterprise risk management and scenario planning recently.

5.4 Chatbots

Reducing the need for direct human involvement with the business process is one of the main goals of automation. There is a very strong trend of automating people-driven processes to chatbot interactions throughout the industry [22]. According to Gartner[2], by 2020 customers will manage 85% of their relationship with the enterprise without interacting with humans. Conversational interfaces apply not only to customer facing businesses but also to employee services such as help-desk and support bots which have been deployed within almost all enterprises. The focus has also expanded to carrying out a business process with a conversational agent [41], or automating tasks such as placing orders, paying and following up invoices, repetitive data base queries, external service inquiries and automatic analytics and reporting.

---

[1] http://ibm.biz/ai-scenario-planning.

[2] https://www.gartner.com/imagesrv/summits/docs/na/customer-360/C360_2011_brochure_FINAL.pdf.

Chatbots bring ease of access to all these applications in one interactive mode. The natural language interaction helps democratize access to data, automation, and analytics for a broader range of business users enabling faster adaptation by users and greater personalization [69]. Chat interactions also serve as a rich source of data to mine for additional automation candidates, closing the loop on bringing intelligence into process automation.

5.5 Explainability

Introducing AI into mission-critical business applications can be a risky endeavor. The software engineering community has developed formal methods to verify the correctness of programs in critical systems [68], but these techniques are not applicable to learned AI models. Approaches to improve the interpretability and explainability of AI models are a more promising avenue [2]. For example, knowing why a model recommended denying a loan to an applicant is important to ensure adherence to anti-discrimination regulations [20]. These approaches, however, need to be expanded along at least two dimensions. First, existing interpretability techniques such as perturbation-based methods or interpretable proxy models [2] need to be augmented with domain knowledge of the business process, including the control flow semantics, decision rules, and business objects, thereby leading to more complete and accurate explanations [26]. Second, the explanations need to be targeted at non-technical subject matter experts. Statistical measures of feature importance or Shapley values are useful to data scientists but do not give actionable insights to a loan officer or process owner. The explanations need to be tailored to the business user, including using the business domain vocabulary and concepts as well as taking into account the context of the user's needs and preexisting knowledge.

5.6 Modalities

We posit that business process data should be considered a new modality in machine learning, similar to image, text, audio, or video. At the very least, it should be treated as a multi-modal domain [7]. A non-exhaustive list of the different types of data embodied in a business process includes the control flow (graph structure), the execution of a process trace (sequence of events), the metadata associated with an event (multi-dimension set of attributes), references to unstructured documents (images or text), interactions between participants (both graph and time series representations), and the social networks (also graphs).

Many existing techniques exploit one or more of these data structures to extract insights or build predictive models [15,42,50,51,62]. We believe that a more principled approach to unify these different sub-modalities of business processes will accelerate research in this area. Reifying business process data as a distinct modality opens up a number of research questions for the machine learning community including developing novel techniques for representation learning, explainability, and transfer learning for this new modality.

Table 1. A summary of the 1st International Workshop on Intelligent Process Automation (IPA) at AAAI 2020 (NYC, Feb 2020).

Paper	Topics from the survey	Comments
[16]	Performance Measures, Synthesis	This paper attempts to provide a formal framework to facilitate end user programming of IPAs so that they can be synthesized and evaluated in a principled manner
[4]	RPA –> IPA transformation	The authors here echo the message of this survey in terms of the transformation of RPAs into IPAs, and provide a classification of existing RPA tools towards this end
[23]	Process Mining	This paper focuses on automated discovery of process components from textual descriptions. The authors use ordered neurons LSTMs with special process-level language models to capture process information
[45]	Process Automation	Authors here focus on automation of the procure to pay process (P2P) by means of similarity measures learned from recordings of a case worker's manual workflow
[28]	Modalities	The authors here explore a stochastic model of spatial demand in a commercial store in order to optimize produce placement. Approaches based on deep q-learning techniques provided promising results
[59]	Modalities	This paper utilizes an R-NET with modified attention to translate instructions in English to navigational plans, providing useful insights on the representation of graphs with known landmarks and natural language annotations
[6]	Process Mining, Modalities	This paper explores how an agent can be taught the rules of a game (process) interactively using a combination of demonstration, active learning, and game theory
[11]	Process Mining, Synthesis	Authors here attempt to learn data analysis widgets from SQL query logs and optimize the resultant interface using Monte Carlo tree search methods
[57]	Chatbots, BPA, Modalities	As discussed in the survey, this paper explores a multi-agent framework that allows the integration of conversation components in a single interface for the end user
[25]	Modalities, RPA –> IPA transformation	This paper explores a natural language interface to IPAs to bring down the expertise level required to manage IPAs using semantic parsing techniques
[10]	Chatbots, Explainability Composition/Synthesis	This work also focuses on the end user programming in how complex business processes with conversational components can be specified declaratively for automated synthesis and easy debugging
[40]	Modalities, Process Mining	Authors here again highlight the use of natural language as a means of training IPAs but specifically highlight the effectiveness of a multi-model approach using natural language and GUIs
[35]	Process Mining	This paper revisits the process mining theme and attempts to learn routines where a user transforms data from one form (spreadsheet or web) to another, by using logs of interactions on a GUI
[48]	Chatbots, BPA	Authors here re-emphasize the usefulness of a conversation interface for business process automation, this time using the assistant to augment unstructured resources with additional training data in order to aid in transfer learning

6   Closing Remarks: State of the Art in IPA

So far, we have discussed the promise of IPAs and AI challenges towards realizing that promise. We will now conclude with a brief summary of the recently concluded (inaugural) international workshop on Intelligent Process Automation (IPA-20) [24] at AAAI 2020. To the best of our knowledge, this is the first workshop of its kind at one of the major AI conferences, and it perfectly reflects the current excitement around business process automation and artificial intelligence. Thus, it is worthwhile to explore the proceedings of the workshop for the latest areas of interest in this field.

Table 1 summarizes the papers presented at IPA-20. It is particularly interesting to observe recurring themes in the papers from topics discussed so far in this survey. Popular topics revolve around process mining and automation (particularly from natural language), automated synthesis and composition of processes for end user programming, conversational interfaces to business processes, and the need to deal with multi-modal inputs. Multiple keynote speakers also touched on the importance of synthesis from examples and natural language understanding in business process automation.

While these topics covered in the proceedings of IPA-20 largely validate the research agenda laid out in the survey so far, it also reveals how much exciting work still needs to be done for the digital transformation of RPAs to IPAs. Most importantly, this transformation cannot be successful without the effective synergy across the BPM community [3] and the AI crowd at conferences like AAAI [24], which has largely remained separate in spite of the growing overlap in their interests. We hope that this survey can act as a springboard for the exchange of ideas across the two communities and motivates exciting research opportunities going forward, combining the power of AI and the real-world complexities, challenges, and scale of business process automation problems.

References

1. Aalst, W., La Rosa, M., Santoro, F.: Business process management - don't forget to improve the process! Bus. Inf. Syst. Eng. **58**, October 2015. https://doi.org/10.1007/s12599-015-0409-x
2. Adadi, A., Berrada, M.: Peeking inside the black-box: a survey on explainable artificial intelligence (XAI). IEEE Access (2018)
3. Agostinelli, S., Marrella, A., Mecella, M.: Research challenges for intelligent robotic process automation. In: Di Francescomarino, C., Dijkman, R., Zdun, U. (eds.) BPM 2019. LNBIP, vol. 362, pp. 12–18. Springer, Cham (2019). https://doi.org/10.1007/978-3-030-37453-2_2
4. Agostinelli, S., Marrella, A., Mecella, M.: Towards intelligent robotic process automation for BPMers. In: AAAI IPA (2020)
5. Araghi, S.S.: Customizing the Composition of Web Services and Beyond. Ph.D. thesis, U. Toronto (2012)
6. Ayub, A., Wagner, A.: A robot that learns connect four using game theory and demonstrations. In: AAAI IPA (2020)

7. Baltrusaitis, T., Ahuja, C., Morency, L.P.: Multimodal machine learning: a survey and taxonomy. IEEE Trans. Pattern Anal. Mach. Intell., February 2019. https://doi.org/10.1109/TPAMI.2018.2798607

8. Bosco, A., Augusto, A., Dumas, M., La Rosa, M., Fortino, G.: Discovering automatable routines from user interaction logs. In: Hildebrandt, T., van Dongen, B.F., Röglinger, M., Mendling, J. (eds.) BPM 2019. LNBIP, vol. 360, pp. 144–162. Springer, Cham (2019). https://doi.org/10.1007/978-3-030-26643-1_9

9. Breuker, D., Matzner, M., Delfmann, P., Becker, J.: Comprehensible predictive models for business processes. MIS Q. (2016)

10. Chakraborti, T., Khazaeni, Y.: D3ba: a tool for optimizing business processes using non-deterministic planning. In: AAAI IPA (2020)

11. Chen, Y., Wu, E.: Monte carlo tree search for generating interactive data analysis interfaces. In: AAAI IPA (2020)

12. Coria, J.A.G., Castellanos-Garzón, J.A., Corchado, J.M.: Intelligent business processes composition based on multi-agent systems. Expert Syst. Appl. 41(4), 1189–1205 (2014)

13. Daugherty, P.R., Wilson, H.J.: Human+ Machine: Reimagining Work in the Age of AI. Harvard Business Press, Boston (2018)

14. Dong, X., Halevy, A., Madhavan, J., Nemes, E., Zhang, J.: Similarity search for web services. In: VLDB (2004)

15. Evermann, J., Rehse, J.R., Fettke, P.: Predicting process behaviour using deep learning. Decis. Support Syst. (2017)

16. Ferreira, D., Rozanova, J., Dubba, K., Zhang, D., Freitas, A.: On the evaluation of intelligence process automation. In: AAAI IPA (2020)

17. Gao, J., van Zelst, S.J., Lu, X., van der Aalst, W.M.: Automated robotic process automation: a self-learning approach. In: OTM Confederated International Conferences (2019)

18. Gartner: A Future that Works: Automation, Employment, Productivity (2017)

19. Geyer-Klingeberg, J., Nakladal, J., Baldauf, F., Veit, F.: Process mining and robotic process automation: a perfect match. In: BPM (2018)

20. Goodman, B., Flaxman, S.: EU regulations on algorithmic decision-making and a "right to explanation". In: ICML Workshop on Human Interpretability in Machine Learning (2016)

21. Grosskopf, A., Decker, G., Weske, M.: The Process: Business Process Modeling Using BPMN. Meghan Kiffer Press, Tampa (2009)

22. Han, S.: Business process automation through chatbots implementation: a case study of an it service process at philips. Thesis, TU Delft (2019)

23. Han, X., et al.: Automatic business process structure discovery using ordered neurons LSTM: a preliminary study. In: AAAI IPA (2020)

24. IPA: Proceedings of the AAAI-2020 Workshop on Intelligent Process Automation (2020)

25. Ito, N., Suzuki, Y., Aizawa, A.: From natural language instructions to complex processes: issues in chaining trigger action rules. In: AAAI IPA (2020)

26. Jan, S.T., Ishakian, V., Muthusamy, V.: AI trust in business processes: the need for process-aware explanations. In: IAAI Conference (2020)

27. Jarvis, P., Moore, J., Stader, J., Macintosh, A., Casson-du Mont, A., Chung, P.: Exploiting AI technologies to realise adaptive workflow systems. In: AAAI Workshop on Agent-Based Systems in the Business Context (1999)

28. Jenkins, P., Wei, H., Jenkins, J.S., Li, Z.: A probabilistic simulator of spatial demand for product allocation. In: AAAI IPA (2020)

29. Jimenez-Ramirez, A., Reijers, H.A., Barba, I., Del Valle, C.: A method to improve the early stages of the Robotic Process Automation lifecycle. In: Giorgini, P., Weber, B. (eds.) CAiSE 2019. LNCS, vol. 11483, pp. 446–461. Springer, Cham (2019). https://doi.org/10.1007/978-3-030-21290-2_28
30. Katz, M., Sohrabi, S., Udrea, O.: Top-quality planning: finding practically useful sets of best plans. In: AAAI (2020)
31. Kavas, I.: RPA vs IPA: Intelligent Process Automation is the Next Frontier (2018)
32. Lacity, M.C., Willcocks, L.P.: A new approach to automating services. MIT Sloan Manage. Rev. **58**, 141–149 (2017)
33. Lakshmanan, G., Shamsi, D., Doganata, Y., Unuvar, M., Khalaf, R.: A Markov Prediction Model for Data-Driven Semi-Structured Business Processes. Springer London Publishing (2015)
34. Le, V., Gulwani, S.: Flashextract: a framework for data extraction by examples. In: Proceedings of the 35th ACM SIGPLAN PLDI (2014)
35. Leno, V., Dumas, M., La Rosa, M., Maggi, F.M., Polyvyanyy, A.: Automated discovery of data transformations for robotic process automation. In: AAAI IPA (2020)
36. Leno, V., Polyvyanyy, A., Dumas, M., La Rosa, M., Maggi, F.M.: Robotic process mining: vision and challenges. Bus. Inf. Syst. Eng., 1–14 (2020)
37. de Leoni, M., Lanciano, G., Marrella, A.: Aligning partially-ordered process-execution traces and models using automated planning. In: ICAPS (2018)
38. Leopold, H., van der Aa, H., Reijers, H.A.: Identifying candidate tasks for robotic process automation in textual process descriptions. In: Gulden, J., Reinhartz-Berger, I., Schmidt, R., Guerreiro, S., Guédria, W., Bera, P. (eds.) BPMDS/EMMSAD -2018. LNBIP, vol. 318, pp. 67–81. Springer, Cham (2018). https://doi.org/10.1007/978-3-319-91704-7_5
39. Leymann, F., Roller, D.: Production Workflow: Concepts and Techniques. Prentice Hall PTR, USA (1999)
40. Li, T.J.J., Radensky, M., Jia, J., Singarajah, K., Mitchell, T., Myers, B.: Interactive task and concept learning from natural language instructions and GUI demonstrations. In: AAAI IPA (2020)
41. López, A., Sànchez-Ferreres, J., Carmona, J., Padró, L.: From process models to chatbots. In: Giorgini, P., Weber, B. (eds.) CAiSE 2019. LNCS, vol. 11483, pp. 383–398. Springer, Cham (2019). https://doi.org/10.1007/978-3-030-21290-2_24
42. Mannhardt, F., de Leoni, M., Reijers, H.A., van der Aalst, W.M.P.: Decision mining revisited - discovering overlapping rules. In: Nurcan, S., Soffer, P., Bajec, M., Eder, J. (eds.) CAiSE 2016. LNCS, vol. 9694, pp. 377–392. Springer, Cham (2016). https://doi.org/10.1007/978-3-319-39696-5_23
43. Marketwatch: Business Process Management (BPM) Market 2019: Key Findings, Regional Study, Size, Growth and Global Trends by Forecast to 2023 (2019)
44. Marrella, A.: Automated planning for business process management. J. Data Semant. **8**, 79–98 (2017)
45. Maurya, C.K., Gantayat, N., Dechu, S., Horvath, T.: Online similarity learning with feedback for invoice line item matching. In: AAAI IPA (2020)
46. Leyer, M., Heckl, D., Moormann, J.: Process performance measurement. In: vom Brocke, J., Rosemann, M. (eds.) Handbook on Business Process Management 2. IHIS, pp. 227–241. Springer, Heidelberg (2015). https://doi.org/10.1007/978-3-642-45103-4_9. Please check and confirm the edit made in Ref. [46].
47. Miltner, A., et al.: On the fly synthesis of edit suggestions. In: OOPSLA (2019)
48. Moiseeva, A., Trautmann, D., Schütze, H.: Multipurpose intelligent process automation via conversational assistant. In: AAAI IPA (2020)

49. Muthusamy, V., Slominski, A., Isahakian, V.: Towards enterprise-ready AI deployments: minimizing the risk of consuming AI models in business applications. In: AI4I (2018)
50. Nguyen, P., et. al: Process trace clustering: a heterogeneous information network approach. In: SIAM SDM (2016)
51. Nguyen, P., et al.: Summarized: efficient framework for analyzing multidimensional process traces under edit-distance constraint. arXiv preprint (2019)
52. Norman, T.J., Jennings, N.R., Faratin, P., Mamdani, E.: Designing and implementing a multi-agent architecture for business process management. In: International Workshop on Agent Theories, Architectures, and Languages (1996)
53. Papazoglou, M.P., Georgakopoulos, D.: Service-oriented computing. Commun. ACM (2003)
54. R-moreno, M.D., Borrajo, D., Cesta, A., Oddi, A.: Integrating planning and scheduling in workflow domains. Expert Syst. Appl. (2007)
55. Raghavan, S.: 2020 AI Predictions from IBM Research (2019)
56. Rao, J., Su, X.: A survey of automated web service composition methods. In: Workshop on Semantic Web Services and Web Process Composition (2004)
57. Rizk, Y., et al.: A unified conversational assistant framework for business process automation. In: AAAI IPA (2020)
58. Sarin, S.C., Varadarajan, A., Wang, L.: A survey of dispatching rules for operational control in wafer fabrication. Prod. Plan. Control **22**(1), 4–24 (2011). https://doi.org/10.1080/09537287.2010.490014
59. Shrestha, A., Pugdeethosapol, K., Fang, H., Qiu, Q.: High-level plan for behavioral robot navigation with natural language directions and r-net. In: AAAI IPA (2020)
60. Sohrabi, S.: Customizing the composition of actions, programs, and web services with user preferences. In: ISWC (2010)
61. Srivastava, B., Koehler, J.: Web service composition - current solutions and open problems. In: ICAPS Workshop on Planning for Web Services (2003)
62. Tax, N., Verenich, I., La Rosa, M., Dumas, M.: Predictive business process monitoring with LSTM neural networks. In: Dubois, E., Pohl, K. (eds.) CAiSE 2017. LNCS, vol. 10253, pp. 477–492. Springer, Cham (2017). https://doi.org/10.1007/978-3-319-59536-8_30
63. Tuttle, D.: The Transformation of RPA to IPA: Intelligent Process Automation (2019)
64. Weske, M.: Business process management architectures. In: Business Process Management, pp. 333–371. Springer, Heidelberg (2012). https://doi.org/10.1007/978-3-642-28616-2_7
65. Weske, M.: Business Process Management (2012)
66. Wilson, H., Alter, A., Shukla, P.: Companies are reimagining business processes with algorithms. Harvard Bus. Rev. (2016)
67. Wolf, M.J., Miller, K., Grodzinsky, F.S.: Why we should have seen that coming: comments on microsoft's tay "experiment," and wider implications. ACM SIGCAS Comput. Soc. (2017)
68. Woodcock, J., Larsen, P.G., Bicarregui, J., Fitzgerald, J.: Formal methods: practice and experience. ACM Comput. Surv. (2009). https://doi.org/10.1145/1592434.1592436
69. Zumstein, D., Hundertmark, S.: Chatbots-an interactive technology for personalized communication, transactions and services. IADIS Int. J. WWW/Internet **15**(1) (2017)

Author Index

Printed in the United States
By Bookmasters